"He ain't heavy, Father... he's m' brother"

Mr. Walter J. Whitney
425 West St.
Winchendon, MA 01475

GHOSTLY AMERICAN PLACES

A Ghostly Guide to America's Most Fascinating Haunted Landmarks

by ARTHUR MYERS

WINGS BOOKS

New York • Avenel, New Jersey

This book is dedicated to
Charlotte Clarke,
the first psychic I met,
who showed me there is more to the world
than meets the eye

Copyright © 1990 by Arthur Myers
Originally titled "The Ghostly Gazetteer"

This 1995 edition is published by Wings Books, distributed by
Random House Value Publishing, Inc., 40 Engelhard Avenue, Avenel,
New Jersey 07001, by arrangement with Contemporary Books, Inc.

Random House
New York • Toronto • London • Sydney • Auckland

Printed and bound in the United States of America

Library of Congress Cataloging–In–Publication Data

Myers, Arthur.
    [Ghostly gazetteer]
    Ghostly American places / by Arthur Myers.
        p.   cm.
    Originally published: The ghostly gazetteer. Chicago :
Contemporary Books, © 1990.
    Includes index.
    ISBN 0-517-12391-6 (hard-cover)
    1. Ghosts—United States.   2. Haunted houses—United States.
I. Title.
BF 1472.U6M93   1995
133. 1 ' 0973—dc20   94-44788
                                                            CIP

8   7   6   5   4   3   2   1

Contents

Introduction

Welcome to *The Ghostly Gazetteer*.

It's pleasant to know that my previous efforts at chasing phantoms, rappings, the odd mysterious odor, and disembodied voices that resulted in *The Ghostly Register* have made enough impact that the publisher has asked me for a sequel.

Being somewhat of a movie buff, I was torn between two good sequel titles—*Son of the Ghostly Register* and *The Ghostly Register Meets Abbott and Costello*— but cooler heads prevailed.

In any case, I am more certain than I was four years ago, when I first began seriously investigating disembodied spirits, that there are such things. In the course of researching *The Ghostly Register* and *Ghosts of the Rich and Famous*, as well as *The Ghostly Gazetteer*, I have interviewed some five hundred people who testify to having had experiences that don't fit into our familiar physical dimension, and none of them seemed crazy or even flaky.

Somewhere along the line, I decided that we definitely are surrounded by other worlds and their inhabitants, that there is an afterlife—and also probably a beforelife and perhaps various simultaneous lives— and that at times these lives can impinge noticeably on this life of which we are currently aware.

I know exactly, in fact, when I decided there are ghosts. It was on January 2, 1987. I've done a couple of hundred radio and TV interviews—ghosts are popular—and Larry King had me on his show twice, first on his radio show and later on his TV show. On the radio show, he had asked me the obligatory question "Do you believe in ghosts?" and I had gone into my usual cautious circumlocution to the effect that I really didn't know for sure but I believed in keeping an open mind and perhaps checking things out.

Two months later, on his TV show, he asked the same question. I was about to give him the same answer when I thought, "Wait a minute. I've talked with a few hundred people who say they have had these experiences, and by now I'd have to be crazy not to believe it—or at least very strongly suspect it."

The day before, I had gone to a New Year's Day party in Boston. Most of the people there knew I had written a book on ghosts. An elderly, conservative-appearing lady said to me, "I believe the veil between the living and the dead is about to dissolve."

I suspect so too, at least to some extent. I suspect we are moving into a new era of earthly consciousness. I see it all around me, the interest people are taking in where they came from and where they are going—and not according to rigid theological dogmas but through personal investigation and experience, by checking things out.

I have a suspicion that we are moving into a much deeper, more sophisticated knowledge of what life and death are all about, and I hope that books such as mine—reportorial, narrative, and objective though they may be—will open new avenues of awareness to many people.

But believe me, some folks just haven't caught up yet to this new way of thinking. I recently bought an electronic thesaurus and one of the first words I tried out was *ghost.* This is what it showed me: delusion, illusion, aberration, fantasy, figment, hallucination, mirage.

I decided to try *haunt,* and this is what I got: bar, tavern, barroom, cocktail lounge, den, dive, dump, gin mill, hangout, joint, lounge, saloon, watering hole.

These electronic thesauruses are obviously put together by drunken computer jocks.

They've got a much more civilized attitude over in Europe. I was reading in the paper that in Norway some highway workers believed a certain road was haunted, so the government put up a sign: GHOST CROSSING.

I like this practical approach. I know a bricklayer named Bob Nation who came to Boston because there is very little work in his native Nebraska. I sometimes have trouble scaring up good ghost stories in the Midwest, so I asked him if he knew of any ghosts in Nebraska.

"Ghosts in Nebraska," he snorted, "they'd starve to death!"

Speaking of foreign shores, here's an intriguing ghost story from the Far East. I teach in a correspondence school for people who aspire to writing careers, and occasionally I get a foreign student. The best foreign student I have ever had is Vincent Foo, a civil servant in Malaysia. Vincent read some of my stories in *The Ghostly Register* and came up with one of his own.

His small daughter had been frightened by the apparition of a woman. Vincent—although he could not see it—asked the apparition to stop appearing to the little girl, and after several appeals it apparently did. However, after that he became aware that his house, which was government quarters, was known to be haunted.

Vincent Foo.

There were reportedly two women ghosts in the place. In fact, when he was transferred, the wife of his successor refused to move in.

"Years later," Vincent wrote me, "I learned the story behind the two female ghosts. The house was built by the Lutong Shell Company for its expatriate staff. In the early 1930s it was occupied by an Englishman. As was the prevalent custom then, he had a mistress, a beautiful local girl. When his wife joined him a couple of years later, he stopped the relationship.

"The girl was madly in love with him. She felt cheated and considered herself to be his lawful wife and the English woman as the interloper. One day when the Englishman was working, this girl went to the house. Nobody knew what actually happened but the English woman was found dead inside the house of stab wounds. She clutched a 'kris,' a Malay dagger, in her hand. The other girl was found dead in the compound, also of stab wounds.

"The poor fellow was sent back to England not knowing he had left behind the spirits of two women who had, in their own way, loved him and who still resent the presence of strangers in the house, for I've learned that other government officers who stayed there also had ghostly experiences."

Somerset Maugham couldn't have told it better.

While I'm at it, let me quote a letter of my own to my literary agent, Bert Holtje.

"Whenever I write these books," I wrote him during the middle of this one, "psychic things start happening around me. My notes disappear and then reappear, a film roll disappears from plain sight never to appear again, strange things happen to tape recordings while I'm interviewing people. Sometimes their voices don't appear on the tapes, or mine doesn't, or the talk is all backwards.

"Now I'm having problems with photos. I took photos of the house in Templeton, Massachusetts, and the old couple standing in front of the house. On the same roll, down on the Cape, I took photos of the Dillingham House, and an hour later went to the home of the pretty ex-cop and took photos of her and her little son.

"I gave the roll to a drug store, and when I got the negatives and prints back neither of the houses had come out. They were black on the negatives, and the developers had not printed them. But the ex-cop and her little boy had come out fine.

"Now why should this happen? I had not touched the camera's adjustments. All the photos on the roll were taken under the same conditions, outside in bright sunlight. I think the spooks were gumming up the works."

I took the black negatives to a place that provides special service, and they were able to get dim prints of both the houses, for use in this book. I had the same thing happen with a Florida restaurant while doing *The Ghostly Register*, and people praised me for the "spooky look" of the place and asked me how I'd done it. The same thing happened when I took a photo of the restaurant in Nashua, New Hampshire.

There is a plus and a minus to these incidents. They can inconvenience me, yes; but on the other hand, they are indications of real paranormal activity. And for a writer about ghosts who has never actually seen a ghost, this can be comforting.

One noticeable aspect of these events is that they never seem to be fatal; they never trash the project. If the prints are missing, I can always find the negatives and get more prints. If an interview didn't record, well, maybe it wasn't that good in the first place, or I can do it over, or I can remember what was said. If a film roll disappears, as it did in the case of a photo of a psychic I took to accompany an article I was doing for a group of newspapers, I can call the editor and tell her to send her own photographer. No real harm done, just a delay.

It's as though the spirits are intrigued that I'm writing about the unseen world and want to show me they are real. They get playful—they say, "See, we're here." If they get too playful and start leading to serious author nerve wrack, I yell at them, and they seem to let up for a while.

Oddly enough, when I finish a book on the parapsychological and start working on more mundane projects, these things seem to quiet down.

This book is filled with references to photographic glitches in haunted places. Similar things happen on TV. I was on a show called "People Are Talking," on WBZ in Boston. There was a medium on the show, and the host asked her to try to bring in a spirit. She gave it a try, and I think succeeded, apparently contacting a young man who had died in an automobile accident and was wandering confusedly in the astral plane. Suddenly the show's staff noticed that the image on one of the cameras was rolling back and forth, something that had never happened before.

It reminded me of an incident of which I was told while researching *The Ghostly Register*. I was doing a chapter on a notably haunted restaurant in Merion, Pennsylvania, called the General Wayne Inn. A Philadelphia TV station had done a segment on the place's ghosts, and on the evening of the showing many staff and patrons gathered in the bar to watch the TV there. The moment the ten-minute part about the Wayne's ghost began, the TV picture started rolling. It stopped as soon as that section of the show was over. The TV set, I was told, had never done that before and never has since.

If you're reading this book, you probably find spooks fun. If they began to play around, you probably wouldn't want them to go away. In her book *Channeling*, Kathryn Ridall tells of a man who came to her complaining that spirits were smashing crockery in his house. When she tried to work with him to eliminate them, she felt that he wasn't really cooperating. Finally, she decided he really didn't want to get rid of them—they livened up his life.

Let's face it: life on this earthly, physical plane can sometimes be depressing, boring, lonely, uncomfortable, and just not a continuous wild blast of joy. It's nice to know that there is something else around—an adventure, something new—that quite a number of people are tuning in to the next dimension without the inconvenience of actually going there. And you don't need passports, visas, credit cards, or hard cash to make the trips.

So happy journeys. And in the meantime, enjoy this travel book.

**1
The Banker Who
Was Killed
Escaping from Jail**

His Ghost Reportedly
Haunts His Selma,
Alabama, Mansion

Location: Selma is situated on U.S. 80 in south central Alabama. The supposedly haunted Sturtivant Hall is in the center of town, at 713 Mabry Street.

Description of place: Selma, with a population of about twenty-eight thousand, is touted by its residents as a center of culture and antebellum architecture, of which Sturtivant Hall is perhaps its prime example. However, in the world beyond Alabama, Selma is most familiar as the place where in 1965 blacks organized by Martin Luther King, Jr., tried to register to vote and were confronted by police. When they tried to march to Montgomery, the state capital, they were driven by police back into the town. A short time later, under a federal court ruling, the protesters did march on Montgomery, protected by National Guardsmen.

Sturtivant Hall, built in 1853 by a plantation owner, is an impressive, columned, neoclassic mansion of two stories. It has been filled with antique furnishings and is a key stop on the Selma tourism circuit.

Behind the main building is a small house with a

1

Sturtivant Hall.

kitchen downstairs, customary in the last century to preclude a kitchen fire burning down the big house. The upper floor, once quarters for slaves who maintained the house and grounds, is now an apartment.

Ghostly manifestations: Legend has it that soon after the death of the unfortunate banker, John Parkman, in 1867, servants began to see his apparition, particularly in the area of the back house but also in the orchard and in the big house.

Parkman, an ambitious young man who had become a bank president, died at the age of twenty-nine. He had illegally used bank funds in cotton speculation and had been clapped into prison by the Yankee general who commanded the federal troops occupying Selma at the time. Accounts as to how Parkman died differ. Some say he was shot by guards while his cronies were aiding his escape. It's also speculated that the cronies shot him to prevent him from implicating them in the bank irregularities. Others say he drowned in the Alabama River during his lunge for freedom.

Parkman was married and had two small girls. Shortly after his death his widow was forced to sell the mansion, which he had bought six years before for

$65,000, for the sum of $12,500. This might be considered enough to make the shade of any banker restless.

My preliminary research on the validity of Sturtivant Hall hauntings was frustrating; my interviewees either seemed *too* eager to get the place into this book or they seemed reluctant to testify to anything remotely unusual. But eventually it seemed obvious that *something* parapsychological is going on there.

The president of the Sturtivant Museum Association, Betty Calloway, was gung ho for the ghosts, throwing in an experience of her own. At one time she lived across from the mansion, and she reported she once saw the faces of two small girls, presumably the Parkman children, peering out an upstairs window.

Another time, she said, "We called the fire department because there was smoke coming out the window of that room, but the window was closed and they found no evidence of anything."

An anecdote I heard repeatedly is that when the commandant of an air force base near Selma was visiting the place he saw the little girls at the window.

Among guides and former guides, I continually heard such remarks as, "I don't believe in ghosts" and "I think these Southern places exaggerate all these things; they're stories that have been passed down for generations." But in a situation of this sort, I cling firmly to the adage "Where there's smoke there's fire"—or maybe could be.

Azile Ellis, a guide, said "One time I was in the house alone downstairs in what they call the warming room. All of a sudden I could hear someone walking upstairs. It sounded like he had stopped at the head of the stairs, so I went to the stairs and looked up. There was no one there. Then the walking noise turned and went into another room. The footsteps went on for about twenty-five minutes. I'm not one who goes bananas over ghosts, but there wasn't enough money to make me go up there and look."

The present cocurators are Marie Barker and Pat Tate. "We do hear walking upstairs," Pat said, "and doors open and close for no reason." She and Marie have had identical experiences. There is a back door on the second floor that opens onto a porch. Both have gone out on the porch and had the door close behind them, without any wind. They had to walk down the outside steps.

"I don't want to believe in ghosts being there," Pat told me. "We don't want to admit there might be a possibility."

I was repeatedly referred to Anne Davidson, who had retired as a guide two years before at the age of ninety. She led off by saying she is the widow of a Baptist minister and doesn't believe in ghosts. But she did describe what she says is her one odd experience in the big house.

"One day a man came in to go through the house spraying for pests. He went upstairs, but in a few minutes he came hurriedly down. He was a newcomer in Selma, and he hadn't heard any of the stories. He said to me, 'Has anybody had any unpleasant experiences in that room at the head of the stairs?' He said someone or something had almost pushed him to the floor."

Bessie Ratcliffe, a former curator who expressed skepticism about Dixie ghost stories, on further interrogation mentioned that one day while alone in the house she heard the sound of shutters being shut, and they can be shut only from the inside. This brings me to my star witnesses, people who have lived in the little house in back. Roy Nix, a Selma police sergeant, lived there for five years. "It was weird," he said. "I made rounds every night. It would be warm in a room, but suddenly it would go cold. Others have had this experience."

Encouraged by this report of possible psychic cold, I interviewed the young couple who now live in the little house, Troy and Camille Hughes.

Camille is familiar with the phenomenon of the second-story back door. She has seen it open and called police, only to find it had been closed by the time of their arrival. The alarm system in the big house goes off continually, she said, but nothing is found there and there is no sign of a malfunction. (See chapter 18 for another example of ghosts possibly tripping alarm systems.)

Troy Hughes, a medical supplies salesperson, is charged with keeping an eye on the big house. "The shutters keep opening and closing," he told me. "The only way you could open them would be from the inside of the house, and then you'd have to open the windows to get at the shutter latches. When you close the shutters a hatch will catch and there is no way they can be opened from the outside. It's my responsibility to make sure that the shutters are closed each night. But the shutters will be open in the morning."

Strange doings are prevalent in the small house too, he says. "Below us is the old kitchen, and at night you'll hear things down there rumbling around."

Sometimes things happen in their apartment, he said. "One time when we were out of town we came home and all the pictures on the wall were turned crooked. A lot of things were moved around. The windows were sealed; there is no way anyone could have gotten in. There's a bolt lock down below us which leads to a stairway up to our door, which is also bolt locked. We considered calling the police, but since nothing was missing we didn't do it."

History: The house has had only three private tenants. It was built in 1853 by a plantation owner. In 1864 it was purchased by John Parkman, and in 1870 it was sold by Parkman's estate to a family that retained possession until 1957. It was then turned into a museum.

Identities of ghosts: The traditional local nominees are John Parkman and his two small daughters.

Personalities of ghosts: Seemingly harmless.

Witnesses: Anne Davidson, Marie Barker, Azile Ellis, Betty Calloway, Bessie Ratcliffe, Pat Tate, Roy Nix, Troy and Camille Hughes.

Best time to witness: Day or night, it would seem.

Still haunted?: Apparently.

Investigations: No formal psychic inquiries reported.

Data submitted by: The above-named witnesses. Also, Edie Morthland Jones, tourism director of Dallas County, and Carlton Speight, hostess. Material from book *Thirteen Alabama Ghosts and Jeffrey*, by Kathryn Tucker Windham and Margaret Gillis Figh.

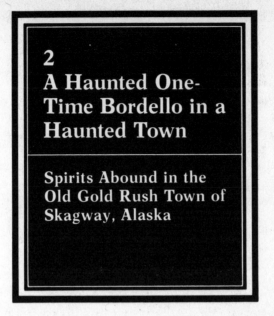

2
A Haunted One-Time Bordello in a Haunted Town

Spirits Abound in the Old Gold Rush Town of Skagway, Alaska

Location: Skagway lies about one hundred miles north of Juneau, the capital of Alaska. The town is situated, as one resident describes it, "in the northernmost part of southeast Alaska." It's reachable by ship—cruise ships dock there all summer—or by plane. It can be reached by road by going up through British Columbia to Whitehorse in the Yukon and coming down Route 2.

Description of place: Skagway is a town of some seven hundred permanent residents, although it swells to several thousand with the summer influx of tourists. A port town, it's overshadowed by rugged, snow-capped mountains. However, it doesn't have the weather that lower forty-eighters associate with Alaska. The latitude isn't all that northerly, and also the Japanese Current keeps things reasonably benign. The winds are very high and whistle through the old buildings, making it difficult to tell whether you're hearing a ghost or just weather. But the winters aren't bad.

Skagway's main street. PHOTO BY DEDMAN'S PHOTO SHOP

"This is a real banana belt," one resident says, "a northern rain forest. We had a very unusual spring this year; we had temperatures in the seventies all through April."

For many years, Skagway has called itself the Garden City of Alaska.

The town looks pretty much as it did when it first sprang up, during the Klondike gold rush just prior to the turn of the century. The people who live there now work at keeping it historical in appearance; some of them even wear period costume. "We're not play acting," says Sharon Garland, who owns a gift shop. "It's like you put on those clothes and you go out in the street and it's like you're there during the old days. I live in a gold rush house, late Victorian, built in 1899."

Gary Danielson is director of tourism for the town and provides the following rundown on the place: "The Klondike was the largest gold rush in the history of the world. Skagway was the dropping-off point when they steamed up from Seattle. They went through Skagway on their way to the Klondike. The first wave started in 1897; by September there were over nine thousand people in town. By 1898 the town had swelled to about twenty thousand. It was the largest city in the North. By 1899 we were back with a population of seven hundred again.

"Now the number one industry is tourism. We're part of the Klondike Gold Rush National Historical Park. The rest of the industry is transportation. We're the farthest north port on the Inside Passage. Most of the goods shipped through here are going to Canada, to the Yukon. We have a large ore facility here that brings in lead, zinc, and silver from Canada and ships it out to worldwide destinations.

"The only thing we have changed is that we have paved our streets. But we still have board sidewalks and false-fronted buildings. The reason it's a national park is that it's the only gold rush city in Alaska that never had a fire or wasn't completely abandoned and just fell apart."

The name *Skagway* is of Tinglit Indian origin and according to local tourism literature has been defined as everything from "cruel wind" to "lady relieving herself on a rock." There seems to be some suspicion that the Tinglit leader who offered the latter definition may have been kidding.

Ghostly manifestations: In both *The Ghostly Register* and in this book, I have ordinarily limited chapters to one building or site. With this chapter, I started out to do a study of spooky happenings at the Red Onion Saloon, built as a bordello in 1897 and now a popular local watering hole. But about every second interviewee had a ghost story about some other place in town. At first I felt it a distraction, but about halfway through my research I switched channels and decided to write up the whole town, since ghosts seemed to be a sizeable proportion of the population. So this is an outsize chapter.

Why is the town seemingly so haunted? Possibly because so many people came to bad, often sudden, ends

in and around Skagway. Parapsychological wisdom
has it that unexpected, unhappy deaths tend to be
ghost-making. One ghost fancier, writer Shirley Jonas,
puts it this way: "What happened here was just horrendous. The corruption, the evil, all that sort of stuff.
There were terrible crimes committed here—people
being taken for all their money, people starving. There
was a diphtheria epidemic that killed a lot of small
children. It was a really terrible, terrible town in 1898
and 1899. I think most of the ghosts here date back to
that time."

Another local writer, Diane Brady, says, "Thousands
and thousands of people came here with hopes and
dreams and lost their lives and were taken for their last
penny. You have to look at the frenzy of the gold rush,
people struggling up the Chilkoot Trail into the Yukon
to Dawson. I've heard that you can hear moaning in
those places. So many people lost their lives unexpect-
edly and with hardships and dreams. A lot of them may
be hanging out, not ready to realize that their dreams
didn't work out."

The Red Onion building was built in 1898 and was
moved to its present location in 1914. For some reason,
the movers got it backward; the rear end faces Broadway, the main street. The building has had various
incarnations since its glory days as a sporting house;
it's been a warehouse, a curio shop, and since 1980 a
saloon owned by Jan Wrentmore. In the winter Jan
goes south to Juneau and works as a lobbyist for the
brewing industry. Her duties? "I try to get legislators
not to tax beer," she says.

The downstairs of the two-story building is now a
saloon. The upstairs is more intriguing, as in the days
of the building's youth, although for a different reason.
The upstairs is composed of ten small rooms—sometimes called *cribs*—where the working girls used to
work. Now Jan has her office up there. The bartenders
are decked out in turn-of-the-century dress, and they

use some of the rooms for dressing. Occasionally an employee will sleep upstairs. Jan has fixed up one room in old-time decor, which she calls the Madame's Room and herself the Madame. The ghostly vibrations seem to happen upstairs.

"I haven't had any ghostly experiences," Jan says, "it's always been people reporting to me. My bartender went in one day and she heard footsteps upstairs, and then the handyman came in and she said, 'I thought you were upstairs.' So they called the police. When the policeman came they heard running upstairs; they could hear this pounding. He called his backup and the two cops went upstairs, but they never could find a thing. One cop said he thought he saw a shadow go down the hall and into the Madame's Room, but they went in there and there was nothing. It was in the local paper, in the police blotter." (Jeff Brady, editor of the *Skagway News*, corroborates that the item appeared.)

Other employees have reported manifestations such as cold patches of air or a strong smell of perfume. Plants are sometimes reported to be watered when no live person can be found who admits watering them. "Another time," Jan says, "they called me in Juneau and asked why I had locked my office door. I said my office door doesn't have a lock on it. They said they had had three or four guys up there trying to get that door open and they couldn't. Then they went back and it was wide open."

Paul Lucas, a musician who has performed at the Red Onion and who once lived upstairs, says, "The second floor certainly had a strange air to it, and I thought I saw something there one night. I'm not susceptible to seeing things that are beyond normal ken, but I woke up and thought I saw a kind of shimmer. This combined with a very strange sensation. Of course, I'd heard the place might be haunted, so it might have been suggestion, but there does seem to be a lot of activity upstairs."

Buckwheat Donahue, an active citizen of Skagway—

he's president of the Eagles Club among his other attainments—says he's felt presences upstairs at the Red Onion. "I've never seen an apparition there, but sometimes you just know that somebody's there with you. I've felt that twice upstairs in the hallway." Buckwheat was more interested in telling me about presences at the Eagles Clubhouse: "That place *really* scares people to death," he said. More on the Eagles later.

John Wilson, another musician who worked at the Red Onion—he now lives in Juneau—isn't so sure the place was haunted. He is more interested in talking about a building called the White House. Wilson is also something of a carpenter and offered this opinion: "That's the original wood in the Red Onion, and when the wind blows there's no insulation. The building creaks, and it shifts. Drafts run through it and push curtains around. Anybody with any imagination at all could certainly put together a story that would make some sense. In Skagway the wind blows at incredible speeds. There certainly were a lot of howls running through that old building."

Jack Brown currently owns a resort in Missouri, but a few years ago he and his wife, Marjorie, lived in Skagway, where they owned a curio shop in the building now occupied by the Red Onion Saloon. He also owned the cable TV system. They suspect the Red Onion rumors are mostly results of the wind punishing the creaky old building. Jack has some intriguing comments on Skagway.

"It's a great little town," he says. "During the sixties a lot of people came up from California and Oregon. It was like a last frontier. They were like hippies, kind of a free bunch. That was when a lot of this ghost talk began. The locals had just taken all this for granted.

"In Alaska the booze flows pretty free," says Jack, "and some of the tales get pretty outrageous. I used to be able to spin a number of them myself."

Everybody in town agrees that the Golden North

Hotel is haunted, but there seems to be some difference of opinion as to what sort of spirit is haunting the place. Diane Whitehead, co-owner of the hotel, opts for a romantic, harmless ghost—a young woman who died in her room of pneumonia and general privation while hiding away from the ruffians of early Skagway, waiting in vain for the return of her fiancé from the gold fields. Diane has even given the pretty lady ghost a name, Mary. And this version of the Golden North parapsychological goings-on does have its partisans.

Other witnesses report a less appealing, rather frightening spook. Let's first take a look at Mary.

A strong witness for Mary is Doug Hulk, now a warehouse foreman, who has worked in the hotel at various times in his life. He was a bellhop there as a teenager and later had offices in the hotel as manager of an airline.

Doug's elderly mother, Kay Keith, was one of three women who once did a séance at the hotel. One of the women was very much against their findings being revealed. Doug does say, however, "They were trying to make contact with the purported ghost, and they did and found out some information about her and dispatched her, supposedly."

Doug is quite forthcoming about his own experiences. He felt things, he said, in one particular room, room 23. (Diane Whitehead also mentions several rooms where Mary is rumored to range.) Doug zeroed in on 23 and said that while he and three other people were investigating there he felt that he was being choked. Other people who have been in the room have had the same sensation, he says. "The lady who the ghost is supposed to be had died of pneumonia, so that would restrict breathing, which may have some correlation to what I felt. Chambermaids have reported happenings in that room. A maintenance man refused to go up there unless somebody was with him. I believe they experienced the image of a ghost. Two construction workers were in that room one night, and they got up in the middle of the night and walked."

Concerning his own ghost-hunting expedition, Doug says, "We also experienced a bathtub ring the night I was there. Like somebody had taken a bath during the night. The tub was clean when we started, and it was none of us who took a bath. The hotel was locked; it was a controlled situation. The four of us spent the night in the room. We slept to some extent, but nobody could have taken a bath."

He also had a curious encounter with a light bulb. "When we first got up to the floor," he says, "I went to turn a light bulb on in the hallway and it blew—kapow! It exploded when I turned on the switch."

Diane Whitehead says that she and a maid actually saw Mary at a hotel window while returning from grocery shopping one day. And, she adds, "We had a singer named Whitewater Willie who came in from Juneau. He was staying on the third floor. His girl-friend took some pictures of him, and when he had them developed there was a perfect image of a woman standing beside him."

The experience of Sharon Garland, now a permanent resident of Skagway, was not so agreeable. This was a few years ago, when the Garlands lived in Juneau and were having an excursion with their children to Skag-way.

"It was the middle of winter," she says, "and we were the only guests. My husband, John, and I stayed in room 14. The ghost had been seen in that room be-fore."

The second night they stayed there, Sharon says, she began to feel ill, to such an extent that they were think-ing of chartering a plane out. "I kept coming to and fainting," she says. "At one point I woke up, and John was awake. He is very skeptical, never believed in ghosts. I was facing the door and saw a light form. John said, 'What are you looking at?' I said, 'I don't know.' He said, 'I don't know, either.' He had been watching it for two hours. It was a light form that we could see through, grayish, about six feet from us. We couldn't tell if it was in the form of a person; we agreed that 'light form' was the best we could do to describe it. We watched it for another hour, and then it gradually faded out. Then I wasn't sick anymore.

"I was a hairdresser at that time, and two young men came in. We got to talking, and they had also stayed in Skagway at the Golden Northern. I told about my experience, and they had had the same experience. The fellow whose hair I was cutting said he too had gotten sick."

The Garlands moved to Skagway, where Sharon now runs a gift shop. "Once in my shop," she says, "I heard a customer talking about staying at the hotel and that she and her boyfriend had seen a 'light form.' She put the same term to it as we had."

Sharon says she is a "church person," conventionally religious, but has had experiences with ghosts. "I don't think they're of God," she says. "I think this darn town during the gold rush was so full of greed and violence, people so intent on becoming rich and doing for themselves, that there was an atmosphere here. I just think these things are of no good, whatever they are, although they don't seem to be doing anyone any harm."

Another landmark for ghostly tales is the Mulvihill House, described in Skagway walking tour literature as "a graceful Victorian residence." The house, built in 1904, was lived in from 1914 to 1949 by the family of "Mul" Mulvihill, chief dispatcher for the White Pass & Yukon Railroad. Doug Hulk says he has known people who lived in the house and had intriguing tales to tell.

"They talked about doors opening and closing," Doug says, "about the sound of somebody walking up and down the stairs, and the sound of a telegraph key clicking away. Mulvihill had a telegraph key in his house so he could keep in touch. Tenants said they kept hearing this click, click, click, click."

Present tenants are Jeff and Diane Brady, who run

the *Skagway News*. Diane is not only a published author of short stories and a bush pilot, she is also psychic. Unfortunately, she hasn't felt anything in the Mulvihill House.

"I'm pretty perceptive at picking up on ghosts," she says, and she feels there are many private and public buildings in the area that are haunted. But she says that if ghosts were now active at Mulvihill House she would not be living there.

"I'm the type of person who has had ghosts come up and put their hands on my shoulders and do weird things," she says. Apparently this doesn't make her happy. "My theory," she says, "is that as long as this is a family home it's not going to be bothered. The house is happy about who is now living here. I think the time when people would have heard something was when it was like a hippie pad, a place of transients." (See chapter 16 for a possible similar situation.)

Let's touch just a few more ghostly Skagway bases.

The White House has been a private residence, a World War II army hospital, and a small hotel, among other things. It is now fire damaged and empty. John Wilson, who expresses skepticism about the Red Onion, says the White House stories are the most credible he's heard in Skagway. He tells of a friend of a friend, a commercial fisherman and very down-to-earth fellow, who stayed there with his family. He and his wife reportedly saw the apparition of a woman standing at the foot of their bed one night. Later they became aware of their three-year-old daughter having conversations while alone in the kitchen. The little girl said she was talking with a lady and described the woman they had seen in their bedroom. According to Wilson's account, they did some research and found their ghost's appearance tallied with descriptions of a woman who had once used the building as a day-care center.

The city hall is the only stone building in Skagway. It

dates back to 1899, and it's rumored to be haunted. Tourism director Gary Danielson, who has offices in the building, declines to go out on a limb aside from saying, "People say there are strange noises upstairs every so often." The second floor is now a museum but once housed the first territorial court in Alaska, so maybe it's an outraged defendant still clanking around.

Skagway's municipal building.

The Eagles hall was "stitched together," as Eagles president Buckwheat Donahue puts it, from two old gold rush hotels. Buckwheat says he was scared out of his wits one winter's day when he was alone in the building and felt a presence on the second floor. He ran outside and stood in the street staring at the building, debating whether he had the nerve to go back in and retrieve some keys he had left on his desk, when along came Nola Hanson, assistant club manager. He told her his problem. He relates: "'Buckwheat,' she goes, 'I swear to God I have had some of the strangest feelings up there too.'" And Buckwheat says that Jeff Brady, the *News* editor who was secretary of the Eagles for a long time, "used to feel them up there too, although he thinks they're friendly ghosts."

During the summer a stage production, *The Days of*

'98 Show, is put on for the tourists in the Eagles building. The dressing rooms for the performers are upstairs. Debbie Ackerman says, "At a fire meeting recently we got off on a ghost story kick, and someone told about a couple of actresses who felt a coldness upstairs and who were terrified to go up there by themselves."

"This thing that happened to me at the Eagles plays with me all the time," says Buckwheat.

History: Originally a rough gold rush town, then a transportation center, now something of a tourist attraction. The town was given a shot in the arm by an influx of 1960s types seeking to get away from it all, and the place still seems to reflect their liveliness.

Identities of ghosts: Many seem to date from the rampaging gold rush days, when large numbers of people met untimely ends.

The Red Onion Saloon manifestations seem to have a feminine feeling about them, according to Jan Wrentmore, reflecting the building's bordello days. "A lot of the men," Jan says, "feel there is a hostile female presence watching them. It could be their guilty consciences."

Personalities of ghosts: Quite a variation. The Red Onion's spirit seems to be restless, and male frequenters of the saloon suspect she is hostile. The spirit at the Golden North Hotel could be the gentle, frightened Mary, or it could be the vaguely menacing "light form" experienced by the Garlands and others. Or it could be both. The White House spirit that talked with the fisherman's child seems a gentle woman. And if that's Mul Mulvihill still clicking his telegraph key, he must be setting some sort of record for job conscientiousness.

Witnesses: Sharon and John Garland, Jan Wrentmore, Paul Lucas, John Wilson, Gary Danielson, Kim Matthews, Jack and Marjorie Brown, Bob Rapuzzie, Buckwheat Donahue, Shirley Jonas, Diane and Jeff Brady, Bruce Weber, Diane Whitehead, Clay Anderson,

Carl Gurkee, Doug Hulk, Kay Keith, Jack Jackson, Debbie Ackerman, Nola Hanson, the two Skagway policemen who checked out the upstairs at the Red Onion.

Best time to witness: Manifestations seem to take place around the clock.

Still haunted?: No diminution seems to have been noted.

Investigations: Doug Hulk and his mother, Kay Keith, have participated in formal psychic investigations at the Golden North Hotel. Diane Brady, a sensitive, says she has felt psychic energy at the hotel. Shirley Jonas, a town resident and a writer, is preparing a book about ghosts of the North, including Skagway. And as for informal attention paid to hauntings and rumors of hauntings in Skagway, the ghosts seem to be as much a subject of conversation there as the Celtics and Red Sox are in Boston.

Data submitted by: Sharon and John Garland, Skagway residents; Jan Wrentmore, owner of the Red Onion Saloon; Paul Lucas, who has played the guitar downstairs at the Red Onion and slept upstairs; Eileen Hart, a friend of Lucas; John Wilson, who has played the piano at the Red Onion; Gary Danielson, Skagway tourism director; Kim Matthews, manager of the Red Onion; Jack and Marjorie Brown, who owned the Red Onion building before Wrentmore; Bob Rapuzzie, a retired railroad man and native of Skagway, whose family settled there during the gold rush days; Buckwheat Donahue, president of the Eagles and member of the board of directors of the local radio station; Shirley Jonas, writer; Jeff and Diane Brady, editor and writer, respectively, of the *Skagway News*; Bruce Weber, former bartender at the Red Onion, now a bartender at the Eagles club; Diane Whitehead, co-owner of the Golden North Hotel; Clay Anderson, superintendent of the Klondike Gold Rush National Historical Park; Carl Gurkee, resource management specialist for the park; Doug Hulk, longtime Skagway resident with an interest in the psychic; Kay Keith, Mr. Hulk's mother, also with an interest in the psychic; John Jackson, bartender at the Eagles club; Debbie Ackerman, Skagway resident; Nola Hanson, manager of the Eagles club; Eric Sauer, a current Skagway police officer; Rand Snure, a current Juneau resident with a knowledge of the history of Skagway.

3
The Old Bellhop Whose Ghost Still Hops Bells

Or So They Say at the Banff Springs Hotel Up in Alberta

Location: The Banff Springs Hotel is in the center of Banff National Park, just outside the town of Banff, about sixty miles west of Calgary, Alberta. Banff is a few miles from the border of British Columbia.

Description of place: This is a famous old luxury resort hotel that celebrated its one-hundredth anniversary in 1988. It was built to accommodate the new western Canadian tourism of a century ago, many of the tourists being rich Europeans seeing Canada via the Canadian Pacific Railway. Over the years the hotel has been expanded, renovated, and completely rebuilt, helped along in at least one instance by fire.

"It's a baronial castle," says Caroline Wilson, the social director. "The outside is Scottish baronial with a hint of French chateau." An architect described the place as Romanesque style with a chateau roof and Gothic and Moorish aspects.

The hotel is a landmark of the Canadian Rockies, with 829 rooms and a capacity of some seventeen hundred guests. Its central portion rises to eleven stories.

Banff Springs Hotel.

Summer and winter delights of the mountains are readily available—golf, tennis, riding, rafting, skiing.

Many films have been shot in the area. Some of the celebrity guests have been Brooke Shields, Marilyn Monroe, Queen Elizabeth II, Prince Philip, Teddy Roosevelt, Indira Gandhi, Robert Kennedy, Randolph Scott, Alan Ladd, and Shelley Winters.

Ghostly manifestations: Everyone at the hotel seems to talk about ghosts. Bob Warwick, editor of the local paper, *Crag and Canyon,* is new to Banff and may not yet be into the spirit of the thing, but he says, "It's my impression that some of it is the vivid imagination of the tour guides who are trying to liven up their tours." But even this skeptical immigrant from Ontario speculates that some of the reports might have factual bases.

The only person who says he was actually there when something ghostly happened is Louie Trono. Louie is now eighty; he started at the hotel as a busboy in 1923. Later he became a professional musician, and he has headed the band in the Rob Roy Room, a café and dining room, for many years.

"This was about fifteen years ago," he says. "We

played till about one in the morning. Then I went home. I was already in bed when I remembered I had left my microphone on the bandstand. That's an expensive item, not something to leave lying around. So I put on my clothes and drove back up to the hotel. I came in a back way; no one was around. It was fall and the hotel wasn't busy; just the night lights were on.

"I got my microphone and put it in my pocket. Then I noticed a drink on top of the piano. It was my drink that I had left there. In those days I was quite a drinker. I picked it up and was just about to drink it, and it was knocked right out of my hand. It landed on the carpeted floor. I didn't know what to think. I hadn't heard anything. I started to walk out—fast.

"That year our theme song was 'Canadian Sunset,' sort of a haunting, beautiful melody. It was written by an American guy. I had only taken a couple of steps when I heard this melody being played on the piano, like someone playing with one finger. I looked back, but the piano was an upright, and the back was toward me. From where I was I couldn't see the keys or whoever was playing. I didn't go back to find out, I just kept on going. Before I had left the room the melody faded away.

"On the way back I was stopped by the RCMP [the Royal Canadian Mounted Police]. They used to stop everybody in the early hours and check for drinking. They asked me to take a breathalyzer test, and I did. It registered .08, which is just on the borderline of impaired driving. Now if I had taken that drink I'd have been over .08 and I'd have been charged with impaired driving. Is there such thing as a friendly ghost, like a fairy godmother?"

Being musically oriented, Louie also mentions a manifestation no one else did. "They feature bagpipes around here all the time," he says, "and you hear about people hearing pipes and even encountering a piper in the hallways."

Dave Mobert, superintendent of services, tells about Sam McCauley, the ghostly bellman; Dave knew the old Scotsman well. McCauley was a bellman for many years at the hotel. Before he died, he told people he would come back and haunt the place.

"The best-known story about Sam," Dave says, "is when a couple of old ladies locked themselves out of their room and sent down to the desk for someone to come up and let them in. So they sent a young bellman up, but when he got there he found the ladies were already in their room. They said an elderly bellman with white hair had come along and opened the door. The young bellman told them that we didn't have anybody elderly on our staff. The old bellman was wearing a double-breasted plaid jacket that we hadn't used for many years.

"I used to work for Sam when he was head bellman. When he retired he worked for me part-time. We've had appearances of Sam at other times. Other guests have had contact with an elderly bellman. We had a businesswoman who checked into one of our suites. She came downstairs in the middle of the night and demanded a change of rooms. She said she had woken and seen a ghostly appearance in the corner, a sort of foggy type thing. Sam's office was in that space before there was some remodeling."

Dave also gives his version of the widely prevalent French maid story. "This was in the late seventies," he says, "and it happened in the Rob Roy Room. It was late at night, and this maid went in the men's room to clean it up. All of a sudden, all the toilets flushed at the same time. She got a little nervous.

"She went back out into the main room, and a big table in the middle of the room and the chairs started to move. She dropped her cleaning supplies and ran. The next morning she took a Greyhound bus back to Quebec."

Other staffers at the hotel tell of a female ghost who

is reputed to sing in one of the ladies' rooms from time to time. She seems to be primarily an auditory phenomenon, although legend has it that one woman, sitting in front of a mirror in this room, was so frightened by something she saw in the glass that they had to carry her out on the chair and calm her down before she could get to her feet.

Another ghost, according to legend, is that of a bride who came to a sudden end at her wedding. Some say she was burned to death when she got too close to a candle. Others say she fell down a staircase. This story seems to go back quite a way and no one is sure of the details, but no recital of Banff Springs ghosts and rumored ghosts would be complete without it.

History: Built in 1888, the hotel immediately became the chief ornament of tourism in western Canada. Odd miscalculations abound in its history. For example, it was put up backward, facing 180 degrees in the wrong direction. Someone misread the blueprints. One of the walls of the main tower is conspicuously out of plumb. The tower is faced with beautiful Mount Rundle limestone, which is blue when first quarried. Unfortunately, it turns brown in the sun, something no one mentioned to the hotel owners. At one time employees of the opposite sex were not allowed to speak to each other in the hallways.

Identities of ghosts: Most are unidentified, such as Louie Trono's unseen benefactor who kept him from being busted for impaired driving. Perhaps it was this spirit who scared the French maid by shaking the furniture in the Rob Roy Room. Then there is Sam McCauley, plus whoever is hanging out in the ladies' room and the unfortunate bride whose wedding turned into a shambles.

Personalities of ghosts: None seem particularly alarming, although the French maid might have something to say about that. Sam McCauley is actually quite helpful. And Louie Trono's friend seems a really nice guy, with something of a gift for prophecy.

Witnesses: Louie Trono, the locked-out elderly ladies, the lady in the lavatory, the frightened French maid.

Best time to witness: The spirits seem to walk by day and by night, with night predominating.

Still haunted?: Probably.

Investigations: No formal psychic inquiries were reported.

Data submitted by: Caroline Wilson, Louie Trono, Frank Bergdoll, Dave Moberg, Bob Warwick. Articles from *Canadian Geographic*, November 28, 1988, and *Ski* magazine, November 1987. Tip from Josie Helder of Barrhead, Alberta.

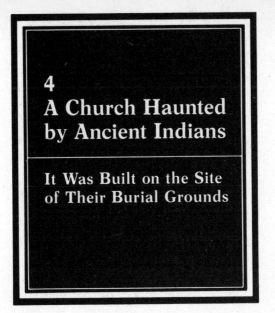

4

A Church Haunted by Ancient Indians

It Was Built on the Site of Their Burial Grounds

Location: St. Andrew's Episcopal Church is situated at 201 Country Club Road, on the northern edge of Nogales, Arizona.

Description of place: Nogales is a city of about twenty thousand on the Mexican border. It is adjacent to Nogales, Sonora, the Mexican city, which is considerably larger. The area is heavily Hispanic and is a crossroads for the shipping of produce.

The church is built on a hill, with a swampy area below. Built in 1969, it is a tall, modern structure, a sprawling building with the church and rectory under one roof.

Ghostly manifestations: Apparitions and other phenomena have reportedly been experienced by a number of parishioners and at least two pastors. A key witness, the Reverend Doug Lorig, declined to be interviewed. In the time since his experiences, he has become a Roman Catholic priest, and I was told that his archdiocese takes a dim view of the occult. Lorig re-

27

fused to come to the phone when I called, apparently taking no chances.

About a dozen years ago, however, he was quite public about his experiences. He described them on television and gave an interview that was published in a Tucson newspaper. He also spoke of his experiences with Frank Baranowski, who has conducted talk shows about the mystic over Phoenix radio, and he also discussed the phenomena with his predecessor in the St. Andrew's pulpit, the Reverend Leonard Evans.

According to Baranowski, "Lorig said he woke up in the middle of the night and saw a ghost standing at the foot of his bed, an old Indian. He said it didn't look ghostlike; the old man had substance. He wore a shawl or a blanket. He hung around for a few minutes and then vanished. Lorig said he grabbed his prayerbook and did prayers, because he didn't want to see that Indian again, but he could still sense that someone was in the room.

"Not long after, he had a visit from Leonard Evans, the former pastor, and Evans asked him if he had seen anything unusual. Lorig said, 'How about a ghost?' And Evans said, 'Oh, you mean the old Indian? He's harmless. He shows up around the building all the time.'"

St. Andrew's Episcopal Church.

Evans, now an Episcopal priest in Kansas, told me that he and his wife, Anne Louise, while in bed at night heard voices in the next bedroom on many occasions. "They sounded like a bull session. The first time it happened, in the morning I said to my wife, 'Did you hear that last night?' She said, 'I'm so glad you said that. I was afraid I was the only one.'"

Evans mentioned that there was an area in the church where mailboxes were posted. There were benches in the area, and he said that this sort of place is usually frequented by the people who attend a church. However, nobody seemed to congregate there. There seemed no reason, he said; people just kept away from that area. Later he found out that there had been an ancient grave discovered underneath that spot when the building was being put up, although he doubted that the parishioners had been aware of that.

Another former pastor, the Reverend Rex Broyles, mentioned that there had been a display case of Indian artifacts there when he was pastor but that most have been turned over on permanent loan to the University of Arizona. "Very obviously," he said, "this was a burial ground."

The wife of a former minister at the church—she asked to remain anonymous—gave me this account: "We met a policeman who came in to borrow some chairs for a service club function, and he told us that some years ago the church did not have a rector. The policeman felt he would check the church occasionally, since no one was living there. He told us this before Father Lorig had made a bit of a to-do over television about having seen this ghost, long before any of this had been made public.

"He said that as he was driving slowly around the building, he heard voices. Nobody was supposed to be there, so he drew his gun and started to follow the voices. He followed them into a corner outside the church, where they were strongest. It was the sound of men's voices in some kind of deep, earnest discussion. There was absolutely no one in that corner. The policeman was of Hispanic background, and he knew they were not speaking in either English or Spanish. He knew he was not in the presence of flesh and blood, and he got out of there in a hurry."

Leonard Evans said that a former organist at the church spoke of often seeing apparitions and that other people connected with the church also had. This aspect of the hauntings expanded considerably when I spoke with parishioner Jean Bache-Wiig.

The organist saw not only one Indian, she said, he saw a considerable part of an Indian tribe. He said that when he came in late at night to practice, they would drift in and sit down in the front pews and listen to him play.

Bache-Wiig said her daughter, Carol, had a psychic gift and often saw the Indians when she came in to do cleaning work. Jean mentioned various standard manifestations: "The place would be locked up tight, and you'd hear things slamming around in the kitchen, and there'd be nobody there."

She also mentioned one occasion of apparent music criticism. "One time," she said, "two hard-headed gals—I was one of them—who don't believe in any nonsense, came in to practice singing. We went up into the choir loft and began. Suddenly there was all this pounding on the roof over our heads. Finally, one of the lights broke, and we left. There was nobody around, and there was no way to get up on the roof without ladders, and there were no ladders.

"I guess that was it," she replied. "Maybe they didn't like your singing," I suggested. "It was real strange. The roof over the choir loft leaked after that."

Bache-Wiig added another new dimension to the hauntings. "People would be knocked down on different occasions," she said. "But I don't think it was the

Indians who were doing that." She felt it was being done by some sort of negative spirits.

"I was on the scene almost immediately after one lady was pushed over," she said. "These people were reliable, solid citizens who wouldn't go around making up stories just to get attention."

History: Digging on the grounds of the church, as a result of sewer problems, turned up a variety of pottery identified by archaeologists as cremation urns used by Indians between eight hundred and one thousand years ago. They contained ashes and remnants of human bones.

Leonard Evans told me, "This was very much a campground and burial site for the ancient people, who probably were nomadic and came through here on their north-south route. Quite often after a rain, we would go out there and be able to pick up pot shards and arrowheads and things like that."

Identities of ghosts: Apparently the ancient Indians who inhabited the space, although Jean Bache-Wiig's negative spirits must also be considered.

Personalities of ghosts: The Indians seem harmless and possibly something of music connoisseurs. "They were not frightening," says Jean Bache-Wiig. However, whoever is pushing people over is impolite, to say the least.

Witnesses: The Reverends Doug Lorig and Leonard Evans; Anne Louise Evans; Jean Bache-Wiig, her choir companion, and her daugher, Jean; the former organist; a number of parishioners.

Best time to witness: Most of the incidents seemed to take place after dark.

Still haunted?: Lorig felt that he had eliminated the hauntings, according to Evans. Bache-Wiig told me, "Father Lorig had a reparation service, along with some of the vestry people and the real prayers in the church. They said, 'We're sorry,' and laid them to rest.

We haven't had any trouble since."

Investigations: No outside psychic inquiries were reported.

Data submitted by: Frank Baranowski; the Reverends Leonard Evans, Rex Broyles, and Ed Gustafson; a pastor's wife; Jean Bache-Wiig.

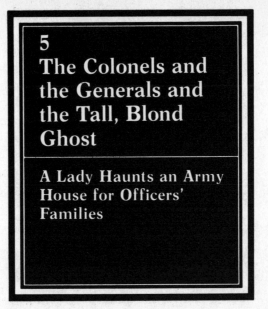

5
The Colonels and the Generals and the Tall, Blond Ghost

A Lady Haunts an Army House for Officers' Families

Location: Carleton House is part of officers' family row at Fort Huachuca, an Army post in the town of Sierra Vista, in southeastern Arizona about fifteen miles from the Mexican border.

Description of place: Fort Huachuca (pronounced WAH-*CHU*-KAH) is one of the oldest active posts in the U.S. Army. Spreading over 77,000 acres, some 10,500 Army personnel and civilians work there. It houses the U.S. Army's Information Systems Command and also the Army Intelligence Center and School.

The fort was founded in 1877 during the Indian wars, and Carleton House, built in 1880, was the first permanent building. For its first year, it was a six-bed hospital; since then it has served for a variety of uses, including a schoolhouse, an officers' mess, and currently as officer family quarters. At one time it was the summer quarters for the governor of Arizona.

A two-story building, Carleton House is constructed of sand-colored adobe brick. A ground-floor room at the right side of the house was originally the morgue of the old hospital.

Ghostly manifestations: Brigadier General Roy ("Bud") Strom, who was deputy commandant of the U.S. Army Intelligence Center and School, moved into Carleton House with his family in July 1980.

"It was beautiful quarters," he says. But he and his wife—the children arrived later—had a busy first day.

"The first thing that seemed odd," he says, "was that one of the moving men wouldn't go in the house. The Mayflower driver was from somewhere else and had hired this local man, and when the guy found out what house it was, he wouldn't enter it."

Carleton House. PHOTO BY TIM ELLIS

Within a couple of hours, more fun ensued. Strom and his wife, Joan, began to hear doorbells ringing all over the house. They would go to the doors and there would be no one there. Finally, he says, he detached all the door chimes.

Their next surprise was when they went down to the room that had been the old morgue to find that the linens and blankets that had been carefully stacked there a few hours before were scattered all over the room.

There was an attractive living room, but one corner was very cold.

"After we'd been there a few hours," Strom says, "the next-door neighbor, Mary Walker, the wife of a general, sent her ten-year-old son over with some cookies. He had a story he hastened to tell us. He said that he had once come over on some errand and thought he saw the lady of the house through the front door, which was glass. He saw the tall figure of a woman, with white or blond hair. He went home and told his mother that she wouldn't answer the door. His mother called up to see if there was any problem. The woman who lived there said no, that they had just come home, that the phone was ringing as they walked in. The boy probably had seen the ghost."

A few days later, Strom went about hanging pictures and trivets. "It was all up, and then in the middle of the night all of it came crashing down, on one wall of the living room. The nails were pulled out. Nothing was severely damaged. I kept trying to explain away everything. I wondered if we had had a tremor or something. But I doubted it."

Joan Strom became one of the few people to actually see Charlotte, the name the Stroms gave the spirit. It was about eleven in the morning, and she was alone in the house with their youngest daughter, Amy, who was eighteen.

"I was sitting in the kitchen," Joan says, "writing a letter to my mother, when I thought I saw Amy go by in the hall. I just saw her out of the corner of my eye. She was tall and seemed all white, like Amy does when she gets up in the morning—white skin, white hair, white legs, white T-shirt. I thought, it's about time that kid got up."

She went into the hall to see where Amy had gone to, couldn't see her, and then found her asleep in bed. It wasn't Amy she had seen.

"I only saw Charlotte once," Joan says, "but one afternoon I was taking some towels into the bathroom and I realized there was this swirling miasma of cloudlike stuff—like you see in the movies before a ghost appears or something. I kept going right on through it without any sensation at all, and when I turned around it was gone. My mother was visiting and I ran out to get her so she could see it too, but when we got back to the bathroom of course it had disappeared. It was so depressing not to be able to share that."

The next occupant of the house was Colonel Robert Bishop, a graduate of West Point. Although I wasn't able to catch up with Bishop, Frank Baranowski, who hosts radio shows in Tucson, relates the Bishops' experiences.

"Bishop said that he had gotten up at 4:30 A.M. to study for a class he was taking at the University of Arizona. He was sitting in the kitchen having a cup of coffee when he heard a small child's voice say, 'Daddy, Daddy, Daddy.' He had a six-year-old son, but it didn't sound like him. He opened the door to the dining room but there was no one there. A few minutes later, he heard the voice again calling, 'Daddy,' and again opened the dining room door, but there was still nothing there. He ran to his son's bedroom, but the child was asleep."

Baranowsky tells of odd behavior of lights in a long hallway in the house. It normally takes three switches to turn on all the lights, but sometimes the lights would go on simultaneously. Bishop is an electrical engineer and he called an electrician, but between them they could not figure out how this could happen.

Bishop's wife, Connie, several times heard footsteps, but the high point of the Bishops' tenure has to be the time when Bishop opened a closet door and came face-to-face with a tall, blond woman. Then, says Baranowsky, Bishop "closed the door and walked away fast."

Carleton House's next occupants were the family of Colonel Warren Todd, head of the post hospital. He is now stationed in Washington, D.C., as chief of assignments of the army medical corps. He makes the assignments for all the doctors in the army.

"I'm a doctor," he says, "and we're the most doubting people, but to tell you the truth I was kind of frightened when the Bishops told us about the house—the closet door and this, that, and the other thing. Bishop opened the closet door and there she was. He closed the door and said not a word. I was waiting for it to happen to me and I had my speech all prepared, but it never happened."

But Charlotte et al. did not disappoint the Todds. Early one morning, Todd's wife, Nancy, heard a voice speak to her from the living room that said, "I'm tired, I'm sleepy." Todd told me he heard a voice call, "Father, Father." "My sons have never called me Father," he says.

One of the Todd sons said he saw a lady in a dress in the living room about three in the morning. "Our youngest son," Todd says, "never said anything, but for the three years we were there he refused to sleep in his bedroom. He slept in a room off our bedroom." One can hardly fault the kid.

The Todds experienced the simultaneous goings on and off of lights. Todd mentions a light show that he and a son saw one night from the kitchen. "To do it would be like a five-switch job," he says, "all the lights going on and off at once."

"When we were moving in," Nancy Todd says, "the post electrician came by and said, 'Don't call me. You will have problems, but there's nothing wrong with the electricity.'"

History: Exactly when the spirit manifestations began in Carleton House is vague. These are not the sort of records the army keeps, and military personnel move so often that oral history goes back only a short time. The earliest accounts I was able to turn up concerned the Koenigs, occupants of the house before the Stroms arrived in 1980; one of the Koenig daughters is reported to have seen the ghost, Joan Strom says.

Identities of ghosts: Brigadier General Strom says that he feels that the ghost would probably be a woman who had died in the building, probably when it was a hospital. "There were very few women here in the early days," he says. "My wife went to the graveyard looking for the grave of a woman, one who might have died in childbirth, but didn't find anything that fit. We named her Charlotte, which seems a good nineteenth-century name. The figure was a woman. Why would she be in the oldest house on the post? Why would she be walking the halls? Maybe she had something to do with the hospital. There were no nurses, no female attendants, so maybe it was related to something that happened to her in the hospital, and with childbirth as dangerous as it was then, maybe she was a woman looking for the benefit of her child. Our thought is that she was unhappy with the way her child died or was treated or disposed of, or whatever."

The childish voice that has repeatedly been reported might well fit in with the Charlotte surmise, given the theory that sometimes infants continue to mature in the next world. (See the account of the twin girls, chapter 7.)

Personalities of ghosts: Like many earthbound spirits—lost, confused, seeking contact with the physical world and its inhabitants.

Witnesses: Brigadier General Roy Strom and his wife, Joan; Colonel Warren Todd and his wife, Nancy; Colonel Robert Bishop and his wife, Connie; the Walker boy; children who lived in the house.

Best time to witness: Apparently around the clock.

Still haunted?: Margaret Liebchen, of the post public affairs office, checked with the current residents, and she says a boy now living there told her, "We've been looking all over the house for this ghost, and we haven't found it yet."

Investigations: No one seems aware of specific inquiries, but Colonel Todd says that he has heard that parapsychologists say the baby is buried somewhere and the spirit of the woman is looking for her baby.

Data submitted by: Roy and Joan Strom, Warren and Nancy Todd, Frank Baranowski, Major Dennis Seely and Margaret Liebchen of the post public affairs office. Articles from area newspapers, such as the *Huachuca Scout,* the *Arizona Republic,* the *Sierra Vista Herald,* and the *Arizona Daily Star.* Tip from Gabriel Hoyos.

6
A Ghost Town That Is *Really* a Ghost Town

The Old Gold Town of Bodie, California, Seems Full of Haunts

Location: "Out in the middle of nowhere," as one Bodie State Park aide puts it. More specifically, the park is located about 225 miles east of San Francisco, almost on the Nevada border. The nearest live town is Bridgeport, about twenty miles away. If you go south from Reno, Nevada, on Route 395 to the California state line, you'll be practically there.

Description of place: "Middle of nowhere" or not, the park gets upward of 170,000 visitors a year. No overnight camping is allowed, but people like to go up to this high, dry, five-hundred-acre park on a spur range of the Sierra Nevada and look around. There are motels and campgrounds on Route 395, about thirteen miles away. There are 168 buildings left in the town, which in 1932 was ravaged by a fire that leveled 95 percent of it. Up until then it was a working gold mining town.

Bill Lindemann, museums coordinator for the State Park and Recreation Department, Tahoe-Sierra District, told me that people can look at the houses and that there is a museum with artifacts and display cases. One of the pine-slat houses is open to the public, as is a quartz mill that was used for processing gold from ore.

"It's a ghost town," Lindemann said. "Most of the possessions of the people who lived in the houses still remain in them—furniture, personal mementoes, paintings by the residents, photographs of the residents."

A corps of park rangers and park aides—paid and volunteer—are on hand to conduct the functions of the park. Some of them live there year-round. The park is open all year but in the winter is accessible only by skis or snowmobile. Some twelve feet of snow can fall at that altitude.

"Bodie has about an eight-thousand-feet elevation," Lindemann said. "It's a dry area, with a sandy ground cover—sagebrush and antelope brush. Last year there were only seventeen days when the thermometer did not fall below thirty-two degrees. There are no trees at all; it's too high and dry for trees."

Ghostly manifestations: The first person I encountered at Bodie was Walter Stone, a park aide who was on the gate that day. He gave me a rundown of some of the standard Bodie ghost stories, plus one experience he had himself. He and two other park aides, Slim Osborn of Sacramento and Leslie Smith of Bishop, had gone to an old gold mine shaft to throw rocks down it. Smith, a minister, told it this way: "The Lent Shaft goes straight down about twelve hundred feet. We were tossing rocks down it, and just as clear as a bell we heard a voice come up out of there, a nice easy voice, and it said, 'Hey, you.' It was so clear you would think you could look over the edge of the shaft and see the person. The impression we got was that someone was annoyed at our throwing rocks down the shaft. This was in the late evening. We had hiked up there just for the purpose of throwing rocks down the Lent Shaft. It's a great recreation up there. Old Bob Bell, who was born there and lived there until five years ago, we talked to him the next evening and he said that shaft has been collapsed for years. He mined in all those shafts."

I traced Bob Bell to his present home in a tiny Nevada settlement. He said, "There's no way anyone could get down that shaft. It's all caved."

Bill Lindemann had a heart-warming response when I asked him if he knew any Bodie ghost stories. "I can give you an earful," he said. And he told me a couple of stories I was to hear from several sources. One involves the J. S. Cain House. Cain was a businessman who seems to have more or less got the town off the ground, many years ago. The basic outline of this story is as follows: At one time a maid—some versions have her a very attractive Chinese woman—worked for the Cain family. Mrs. Cain became jealous and fired her. The maid took this as a disgrace; there is speculation that

The J. S. Cain House.
PHOTO BY MARCIA DIDTLER

she committed suicide. The story goes that children sometimes see a friendly Oriental lady in the bedroom upstairs.

Other people have had more frightening experiences in the Cain House. Elizabeth Fetherston lived there about two years with her ranger husband, Ken. She said, "I was lying in bed with my husband in the lower bedroom and I felt a pressure on me, as though someone was on top of me. I began fighting. I fought so hard I ended up on the floor. It really frightened me. Another ranger who had lived there, Gary Walters, had the same experience in the same room, except that he also saw the door open and felt a presence and a kind of suffocation."

This heavy spirit seems to get around. Midge Reddon, administrative officer of the Sierra District, told me of spending a night at Bodie with her husband, Bob, at a different house. It's really Bob's experience, so let him tell it: "I was lying on my stomach, asleep, and

The J. S. Cain House and woodshed.
PHOTO BY MARCIA DIDTLER

all of a sudden I woke up and felt something pushing me down in the bed. My legs were pinned; I couldn't move them. I couldn't move my arms. I couldn't even turn my head to see what was happening. I could feel the bed giving. It went on for a few seconds. Finally, I could speak—or rather, squawk—and it stopped."

Getting back to the Cain House, Brad Sturtivant, the supervising ranger, told me one that reminded me of the Dillingham House in Sandwich, Massachusetts (see chapter 17). The fifteen-year-old daughter of a ranger went to bed in her upstairs bedroom. She turned out the light and lay down to sleep. Suddenly the light went back on. She got up and turned it off. It went back on again. She got up and turned it off again. It went on again. Sturtivant wasn't sure how long this game went on, but he said, "Finally, when it turned on she yelled, 'Turn that light off!' At that point she got up and ran downstairs."

It was first told to me by Bill Lindemann. A little girl, he said, had taken a shine to a miner and constantly followed him around. They became close friends. One day she stood too closely behind him as he threw his rock pick over his shoulder. It accidentally hit her in the head and killed her. She is buried in the Bodie Cemetery. There are a number of stories about this little girl, who is sometimes called "The Angel of Bodie."

Lindemann also told me of a little girl who was visiting Bodie with her father. They stopped by the cemetery, and while walking around the father noticed his daughter, at a distance, giggling. Later, she asked him who the little girl was with whom she had been playing. The father had not seen anyone.

Marcia Didtler, a high school art teacher who has worked several summers as an aide at Bodie, told me of an incident that happened one day when she was on the gate. "A guy came along and I got to talking to him. He said he had once worked at Bodie, when he was in the CCC. He and another guy had been sitting on the bench in front of the Miners Union Hall, which is now the museum. All of a sudden they heard a voice that said, 'Daddy.' It was a little girl's voice. Then they heard it again. I collect ghost stories about Bodie, so I got his name and was able to verify that he had really worked there in the CCC."

These stories have special significance for me, and I have an odd experience of my own to relate here. In the Introduction to this book I mentioned that when I work on these books about spirits strange things happen in my workroom. Research disappears, then reappears. My tape recorders sometimes don't record. Photographs turn up missing, although I know exactly where I had put them. I take most of this reasonably calmly; it can be irksome, but it does in a way encourage me, for it indicates there really is a paranormal, that I may have spirit companions when I do these books.

But one evening after I had been working all day on this chapter, I decided to arrange the chapters of the manuscript in alphabetical order by state, as they would appear in the final book. With some consternation, I discovered that one chapter was missing. It was the chapter about Wesleyan University.

I went through the manuscript over and over but could not find this chapter. Although I had taken the spirits' other shenanigans in stride, this really upset me. They were fooling around with the finished product. This was going too far! I dreamed about it all night.

First thing the next morning, I did two things. I ran off another copy of the missing chapter on my computer and carefully tucked it into its proper place in the manuscript. This made me feel slightly better. Then I phoned a psychic I had recently met and with whom I had been impressed. Her name is Nancy Regalmuto, and she lives in Bellport, New York. I told her what had happened and asked her what might be going on.

She went into a short trance and then asked me if I had been working on material involving California. I had said nothing about this, and I was again impressed. Then she said the chapter had been purloined by a little girl who had been egged on by a man spirit. They didn't want publicity on what had happened to them, Nancy said.

Well, I've made it clear that the girl's death was an accident, so I have decided to let it stand.

Bill Lindemann told me of two personal experiences he had had the previous fall. "I was staying at the Mendocini House. It was built about a hundred years ago and is now used by park personnel. The first night I was there I was making lasagna, but I didn't have any garlic, and I like seasoning. I began to eat the lasagna and read when I had this intense burning sensation in my nose, causing my eyes to water, and I sneezed quite hard. I went outside to get some fresh air, and when I came back in the whole place smelled strongly of garlic. It was as though someone was cutting garlic or crushing a clove of it right under my nose. I was told by Walt Stone, who has lived there, of his opening the house after no one has been in it all winter and smelling fresh-cooked Italian food.

The Mendocini House. PHOTO BY MARCIA DIDTLER

"The second night, I was sitting reading when I heard the kind of sound you hear when two radio stations are crossed. It sounds like a party or a number of people all talking at once. I went looking to see if Walt, the previous occupant, had left a radio going, but I couldn't find any. I tried to listen to the sound but I couldn't distinguish anything, and I couldn't tell where it was coming from. It just seemed to be an ambient sound. I checked with nearby residences and nobody was awake. I went back to my own place and heard it again, even a more gregarious sound. I finally said, 'Thank you for inviting me to the party, Mrs. Mendocini, but I really have a lot of reading to do.' And the sound went away."

Marcia Didtler gave me a number of stories she had collected, such as:

- The maintenance man who lived in the Seiler House sometimes would hear voices outside, as though people were talking under the street lamp, although no one was in sight.
- The sound of a piano playing in the museum would be heard when no piano player was around. This report is attributed to Bob Bell.
- The friend of a park aide reported that while staying overnight at the Gregory House he saw an elderly woman sitting in a rocking chair working on an afghan.
- The sound of children's laughter has been heard outside the Mendocini House.
- The sound of a music box can be heard upstairs in the Cain House.
- There have been occasional sightings of a woman peering from an upstairs window in the Dechambeau House.

History: The following rundown of the town's history is from Bill Lindemann. "In 1849 a man named W. S. Bodie and his partner, Black Taylor, discovered placer gold deposits near the Bodie town site area. They and others mined the area till the 1870s. Then the town began to grow, with the influx of money from New York through San Francisco. They began to build shaft and tunnel mine systems. By 1881 about ten thousand people lived there. There were five breweries, something like seventy saloons, a number of houses of ill repute, a school, churches, stores, banks. In 1893 a fire damaged quite a bit of the business section. In 1932 fire destroyed 95 percent of the town. Only the 168 buildings and structures remain."

Identities of ghosts: Apparently onetime residents of the town. There is a similarity between this town and the old gold rush town of Skagway, Alaska (see chapter 2), with both places' abundance of restless spirits. In the early days of Bodie, it was replete with the violence, greed, and intense emotion of a gold rush town. Liz Fetherston says, "They used to say, 'Good-bye God, I'm going to Bodie.'"

Personalities of ghosts: Seemingly harmless, except possibly for the spirit that presses down on sleeping people and possibly the ones who may be fooling around with my manuscript.

Witnesses: Marcia Didtler, Walter Stone, Leslie Smith, Slim Osborn, Bill Lindemann, Bob and Midge Reddon, Elizabeth and Ken Fetherston, Gary Walters, Bob Bell.

Best time to witness: Seemingly around the clock.

Still haunted?: Seems to be.

Investigations: Watching for spirit manifestations and talking about them seems to be the favorite indoor and outdoor sport at Bodie. No one seemed to be aware of any formal parapsychological inquiries.

Data submitted by: Marcia Didtler (in addition to interviews, she furnished an article on Bodie's ghosts she had published in the October 16, 1987, issue of the *Inyo Register*), Walter Stone, Leslie Smith, Bill Lindemann, Bob and Midge Reddon, Liz Fetherston, Bob Bell.

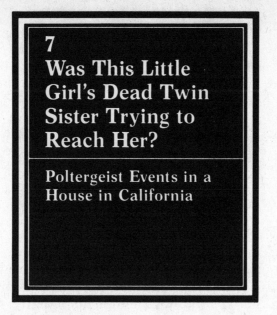

7

Was This Little Girl's Dead Twin Sister Trying to Reach Her?

Poltergeist Events in a House in California

Location: The house is situated at 2020 Tomah Avenue, in Porterville, California.

Description of place: Porterville is a town of about twenty-three thousand, some 140 miles north of Los Angeles. The house was built by Barry Johnson in 1979 as a retirement home. It is a one-story, rambling, frame house of eight rooms, with a brick and stucco exterior.

Ghostly manifestations: (At the request of the family, the names in the following story have been changed.) In 1984 eight-year-old Claire Johnson, who lived with her parents in Miami, Florida, was visiting her grandparents, Barry and Juune Johnson, in Porterville. After a camping trip of a few days, they returned to the Porterville home. A few days later, Claire noticed that her perfume bottle had disappeared. The next day she told her grandfather, "I found my perfume in the bookcase. Now my comb is missing." A day later she told her grandfather that her wallet had somehow gotten from her purse to a dresser drawer, without her being aware how it had happened. Johnson told her that perhaps a poltergeist was at work.

The Johnson home.

This frightened the little girl, since she had seen the scary movie *Poltergeist*. He tried to reassure her that such things were not real. However, she was disturbed enough that she did not mention such matters to him again. But soon after, she did go to Juune, who told Barry, "Claire says that more things have disappeared or been moved. She is really scared." She wanted to leave, and a few days later they took her to the airport for the flight to her home in Miami.

Two nights after she had left, the Johnsons heard a single sharp rap on their bedroom ceiling. Juune told Barry she had heard several knocks since Claire had left, and Barry replied that he had been aware of the same thing. The rappings continued for three or four weeks. Barry recalls: "One afternoon as I sat in my study my playful guest rapped five times—twice in the hallways, twice in a closet attached to the room I was in, and once from the next room. They came so close together a human could not possibly have moved fast enough to do it. I felt 'it' laughing.

"Several times it greeted me as I stepped into the kitchen in the morning. One day I answered by rapping on the wall. Every time it 'spoke' in the next three days I responded, in the study, the bathroom, and elsewhere."

One morning as the sun was rising, Barry entered the kitchen, and instead of what seemed a cheerful, playful rap, he heard what he describes as a "soft, mournful rap." He replied but never heard from whatever it was again.

History: Johnson is a psychologist who entered industry and became executive vice president of a company in Los Angeles that specializes in research of environmental problems. His wife died in 1988, and he now lives alone in the house.

His son is Dr. Joseph Johnson, a professor of linguistics on the faculty of a Florida university. Claire, now thirteen, lives with her mother and father in Miami.

Barry Johnson.

Identity of ghost: I read of the Johnsons' experience in a short article written by Barry that appeared in *Fate* magazine. I called him and he outlined the above facts, adding little to those in the article.

I mentioned that the poltergeist activity seemed to be something that Claire had brought. This had not occurred to Barry. I also suggested that the raps had a childish character about them, mentioning a house I had researched in Sandwich, Massachusetts, that seems to be haunted by an entire family of children, who rap about the house with abandon and seem especially pleased when people rap back (see chapter 17).

Barry then said thoughtfully: "Here's something that might possibly be of interest. Claire had a twin sister named Deborah who died at the age of five months of a form of cancer."

I asked if he sensed a childlike quality to the rapping, and he replied, "Well, I felt a time or two it was just kind of playing a trick on me. Those five raps in a hurry from different parts of the house. I felt I was being kind of teased."

I asked Barry if he had any psychic abilities, and he replied that he did, that he sometimes had ESP experiences. He said he had an unusual card sense that bordered on the parapsychological and often had very specific prophetic dreams, which came true.

Soon afterward, I talked with Claire, who denied remembering what had happened five years before at her grandparents' home. She said she did not have any contacts with spirits, her dead sister or any other spirit. But she did volunteer that she had recently become very psychic with her best friend. "We're really close," she said. "Lots of times when we're talking with each other we say the same thing at the same time. We started practicing, and we could call each other with our minds, and it worked. We could give each other messages, real short ones. She'll sit across the room in class, and I'll call her with my mind, and she'll look."

I told Barry that I had heard that sometimes children who die continue to develop in the spirit world and contact people they had known in this one. Anne Gehman, an excellent psychic and medium, offered this opinion of what had been happening. "Children do continue to grow up in the spirit world and especially someone as close as a twin. It would sort of grow up with her."

I mentioned that both the grandfather and granddaughter seemed to have psychic proclivities, and I wondered if together they were able to get something going? "Yes," Anne replied, "it just happened to be that there were the right conditions. It just can't happen any time; there has to be the right chemistry and the right energy for the spirits to work through the veil. With the grandfather drawing on that, plus the child, this could happen."

About Claire's psychic abilities, Anne said, "Probably this sense will stay with her for some time, and then she'll have a time when she can choose whether she wants to further develop it or let it fall away."

Personality of ghost: Seemingly playful, wistful, reaching out.

Witnesses: Barry, Juune, and Claire Johnson.

Best time to witness: Poltergeist activities happened both day and night.

Still haunted?: The events seemed to happen only over a few weeks, during Claire's visit and shortly afterward.

Investigations: None, except my own, with the aid of Anne Gehman.

Data submitted by: Interviews with Barry, Claire, and Joseph Johnson and Anne Gehman. Article by Barry Johnson in the June 1989 issue of *Fate* magazine.

8
The Gambler Who Was Shot in the Armoire

An Old-Time Fracas and a New Hotel in San Diego

Location: The Horton Grand Hotel is at 311 Island Street, in an area that has been called San Diego's "reawakened" downtown. Dan Pearson, the developer and chief owner of the hotel, describes the location as "the heart of Old Chinatown, three blocks from the waterfront."

Description of place: The hotel is an impressive if unusual looking four-story building. Viewed head-on, the right wing is stately Victorian, with squared cornices and huge windows from a hundred years ago; the left wing is a fabulation of gingerbread and gives a more elegant impression than the right wing. The two wings are connected at street level by an ultramodern glassy atrium, which encloses the lobby. This is a luxury hotel, "elegantly recreated," as one travel writer puts it. It was put up in 1986 from a couple of other hotels built a few blocks away in 1886. The new hotel has 110 rooms with fireplaces, furnished with antiques. The external brickwork dates from 1886, as do the bay windows, door frames, and the main stairway. The ghosts also probably date from the 1800s.

The Horton Grand Hotel. PHOTO BY HORTON GRAND HOTEL

Ghostly manifestations: The focal point of the Horton Grand hauntings seems to be room 309. Owner Dan Pearson says "We had been open tén days when one of the maids, Martha Mayes, came to my office and said she was afraid to go into the room, that strange things were going on in there. As time went on, it got to where two or three people would insist on going in at the same time to clean the room; no one would go in there alone. They said lights were going on and off, pictures would be moved around."

Martha, now a bookkeeper at the hotel, says, "It was going on for about a year before anyone would take us seriously. One of the beds would shake. Lights would come on. I've seen both those things. What really got me one day was when a closet door flew open. I never saw a ghost, but some people say they did. I heard one lady guest say she was walking down the hall looking for the ice machine and she stopped to ask a man where it was, and he faded away."

An unusual feature of the hotel is that diaries are placed in each room, and guests are encouraged to write in them. Most of the entries have to do with how nice it is to get away from the kids or some such mundane observation, but in Room 309 and some other rooms some of the jottings concern odd happenings. Of course, the news of the hauntings has leaked—a better word might be gushed—to the media, so no one seeing a ghost at the Horton Grand should be surprised. As Pearson puts it, "You don't know whether to believe the entries in room 309's diaries or not." In fact, management seems to walk a nervous tightrope concerning the hauntings. "I have been accused of a PR scam," Pearson says. "Actually, I almost never go into that room. I want to have deniability. I want to be able to say, 'Here's what the guests said, here's what the employees have said.' I don't want to have any experiences myself, so I won't go in there."

Billy Riley, managing director of the hotel and somewhat the grande dame of the San Diego business world, talks about the haunts in a voice that has quotation marks around every word. For example, the Horton Grand may be the only hotel in America, or anywhere else, that has a resident psychic. Billy will refer to her but is careful not to go overboard.

"We have a woman," Billy says, "who—I guess she's in dead earnestness, but we are not sure—she's sort of the in-house psychic; she's not above giving a little reading or something. So we have a little fun going with it. It has been kind of incredible."

Pearson says, "We didn't know what to do with it. If you made a publicity stunt out of this, it might backfire. We didn't know; people might react negatively and it would hurt our business. But before we knew it, it was in the newspapers, and next thing the TV stations were here doing shows."

There seems little doubt that the hauntings are something of a bonanza; people are lined up for months for

room 309. And guests also tend to wander the corridors
of the third floor, looking for the tall, thin man in old-
time clothing who fades away.

The "in-house psychic" is Shelly Deegan, a local
young woman. Accounts of how she arrived at the hotel
differ, but she spends a lot of time psyching out the
place and giving readings for guests. She spent her first
night in room 309 in November 1987, and she recalls it
this way: "The spirit was very active. I asked him to
give me a sign that he was in the room. Then I went
down to dinner. When I came back up, a picture on the
wall was off balance quite a bit; one end was about
four inches higher than the other. It was a picture of a
woman of the last century. He also turned the lights on
and off about 2 A.M., and I knew that was my signal to
go to sleep."

Psychic Shelly Deegan.

It is Shelly Deegan who has "identified" the chief
ghost. She says he is named Roger Whittaker, that he
was a gambler, that he was shot in an armoire—where
he had hidden—in 1843 by the father of his fiancée.
The father disapproved of Roger. (Shelly has also been
known to surmise that Roger was plugged by a gam-

bling associate and that Roger was on occasion a pimp. He refers to himself as a "dude," she says.)

Shelly says there are two other ghosts in the room or at least on the general premises. Their names are Henry and Gus, and they are juveniles. Henry was in his late teens when he died, and Gus was twelve. The two boys have no connection with Whittaker, she says, but were friends of each other. They worked in a hotel—it doesn't seem to be clear what hotel—during their lives, she says.

"The entire hotel is haunted," Shelly says. "A guest will be checking out and will go back to the room for something, and she'll find hangers scattered all over the floor. I had a lady guest tell me that. I've had reports of people hearing glasses clinking over their heads. You should see the eyeballs of the guests when they tell me these things. And they tell the front desk people. The front desk people salivate until they can tell me these stories; they even call me to tell me."

Pearson mentions a woman guest who stayed in room 309 with a small child. She wrote in the diary that her daughter was playing on the floor and talking to someone, that the little girl was having a conversation with a child ghost.

Pearson also mentions a reporter from the sensational tabloid press who stayed two nights and who told him of lights going out, of coins he had placed under doilies being switched around, and of a picture on the wall turning upside down while he was asleep in the night, with the door latched.

"He said he was used to writing about ghosts," Pearson says, "but he said, 'This happened to *me!*' He went on and on about that. He had friends with him who saw the same things."

And then, Pearson relates, there was the radio reporter who visited the room with a tape recorder. He said he could hear laughing, but when he later played back his tape, there was nothing on it.

Dick Nelson, sales manager of the hotel, told me that he knows of two occasions when a maid could not get into room 309 with her own key. She had gone down to the desk to see if anyone had checked in, and no one had. But the room was locked from the inside. Nelson said he went up with a master key and was able to let himself and the maid into the room, to find the lights on and the ceiling fan going around but no one there.

As I interviewed person after person about the hotel I felt I was getting somewhere, chapter-wise, but there was an underlying unease. At a certain point, I realized that everyone I had interviewed worked for the hotel. Was this a conspiracy? I wondered. Yet they seemed so sincere. P. T. Barnum once said, "There's a sucker born every minute." But he also said, "More people are humbugged by not believing than by believing." I decided to go with the second quote. Nevertheless, it was a relief when I ran across Chris McGuire.

Chris is an effervescent young woman who not only doesn't work for the Horton Grand but works on the front desk of one of its competitors, the local Marriott. She is the only female member of her Kiwanis Club and is its vice president. She is scheduled to become president in 1990. Now, someone like that, you've gotta believe!

Chris had heard about the ghosts, and she was interested in the psychic. She knew Dick Nelson from the Kiwanis Club and asked him if she could stay in the famous room on her birthday, December 14, 1987. He fixed it up.

"There were six of us," Chris relates. "We were up in the room for a while and then we went out for the evening. When we were trying to leave, the door stuck at the top. It was fine when we came in, but when we went to leave we had to pull very hard to get out.

"We came back to the room and we were sitting on the two beds and the chairs and one of my friends looked over by the armoire and there were three pictures there, and the top picture was upside down. It had not been upside down when we went out. The picture was flat against the wall, as though someone were holding it there. You couldn't put it back that way, because we tried. It was a picture of a man and a woman, in nineteenth-century dress.

"My girlfriend Helen Martinez and I brought along a Ouija board, and we started playing. Her hands were on the board, and they started shaking. She said, 'Chris, I can't control myself. I am not doing this.' And I had to push her to get her off the board. That happened twice.

"Later on, when we were sleeping, I woke up in the middle of the night and I felt like someone was pressing on my chest. I couldn't get up. So I just stayed there. I was held like that for about ten minutes. I didn't want to try to get up again. My friend was asleep the whole time. I couldn't talk. I wanted to say something and nothing would come out because it was so frightening.

"There is always a diary in the room, on the mantel. Dick called me a couple of days later and asked why I hadn't written in the diary. But it was missing the whole time we were there. He said he had gone back to the room the afternoon after we left, and it was sitting on the mantelpiece."

I interviewed Chris in March 1989, and she told me that she was going to stay at the Horton Grand again the following week. An aunt and uncle were visiting her, and she had made reservations for them in the hotel; while she was at it she had decided to stay another night in room 309, along with Helen Martinez. She suggested I give her a phone call at 9 A.M. the next morning, which I did. Her response when she answered the phone was encouraging: "Well, it was a real interesting night!"

Twice in the night, she said, she felt like someone was touching her on the upper arm. Each time she called her friend, who was sleeping in the other bed, and woke her up.

"The third time," she said, "I was lying there asleep, and I felt someone pulling my arm. I opened my eyes, and there was like a mist right beside me. I was pulling my arm back, and something was pulling it toward itself. I started to yell to my friend and she woke up.

"It was like he was trying to take me. It was just mist, hanging there beside me, but I felt it was a man. My arm was really being pulled. I looked at the clock and it was 2:30, and I thought, oh, it's only 2:30, I have the rest of the night yet! I could feel the bed vibrating, but nothing happened the rest of the night. It was the same bed I had slept in the first time I stayed in the room, and it vibrated that time too. I feel that Roger is still here, still in this room.

History: The new hotel was constructed of parts of two hotels that were built in 1886, which was a boom time in San Diego's history. "In 1881 there were five thousand people in San Diego," Dan Pearson told me. "In 1888 there were forty thousand." During that period, the city got its first transcontinental railroad, and a number of hotels were put up. One was called the Grand Horton, after the founder of San Diego, Alonzo Horton. (Pearson has reversed the name of the present-day hotel.) The other hotel was called the Brooklyn. The Grand Horton was the luxury hotel; the Brooklyn, which later came to be called the Kahle-Saddlery, was more working class. The Brooklyn's main claim to historical fame might be that Wyatt Earp, the noted gunslinger, lived there for a couple of years. On the other hand, the bar of the Grand Horton used to play host to such celebrities as Jack Dempsey, George Raft, Babe Ruth, and George Jessel. Then again, the first floor of the Brooklyn was for many years a saddle shop where Tom Mix and Roy Rogers had their saddles crafted. Perhaps the only way to resolve this celebrity competition between the two old hostelries might be to point out that Tim Earp, a direct descendant of Wyatt Earp, works at the new hotel. He's a bellhop.

Pearson got the idea of dismantling the Grand Horton and putting it back up in luxurious style. In 1981 he stored ten thousand pieces of the hotel in a warehouse until he could find a likely site. In 1982 the other hotel, owned by the Salvation Army, was about to be torn down for a parking lot, and it too got a new lease on life from Pearson.

Identities of ghosts: Psychic Shelly Deegan claims to have identified three spirits—Roger Whittaker, Henry, and Gus. But the whole place is haunted, she says. Rumors of spooks dogged both the hotels in their former incarnations.

"There are four or five hotels in San Diego that are supposed to be haunted," said Dr. Roy Brandes, professor of history at the University of San Diego. Brandes did research on the hotels' histories for Pearson. He's done studies of 252 buildings in San Diego for the federal government.

"I don't mind the haunting stories," he said. "I think they're pleasurable, and they help business."

Shelly Deegan dated Roger Whittaker's demise to a ballpark figure of 1843. The hitch is neither of the old hotels was built till 1886. Well, he was probably killed in that space, she told me, perhaps in another hotel that might have been there at the time. But Brandes said that all there was in that area in the 1840s was water. "He'd have had to been shot in a rowboat," Brandes said. How about the area where the old Grand Horton had stood, I asked desperately. Nothing but sagebrush, he replied. How about the Brooklyn Hotel? Nothing but sagebrush.

Well, another of Deegan's theories is that Whittaker was shot in an armoire in a hotel *somewhere* in San Diego, and haunting a gorgeous new hotel like the Horton Grand just struck his spirit's fancy, so he moved in.

Personalities of ghosts: Gus and Henry seem harmless. Roger also seems an easygoing sort, although trying to pull young women out of bed at night might not be considered constructive.

Witnesses: Martha Mayes, Shelly Deegan, Dick Nelson, Chris McGuire, Maria Mazzi and Jacqueline Williams (psychics who accompanied Deegan at various times), a number of hotel employees and guests.

Best time to witness: People report experiences both day and night.

Still haunted?: Seems to be.

Investigations: Shelly Deegan has spent a lot of time in the hotel, often visiting room 309 with other psychics. There seems to be no set management policy. Billy Riley says, "We've had calls from people who wanted to exorcise the ghost, and I've said absolutely not. If he's for real, we want him here. People rent that room hoping Roger will show up. It's a very, very popular room."

On the other hand, Dan Pearson said, "Several psychics want to exorcise the ghosts. My view had been, well, it's $109 a night, if you want to stay there, go ahead." But he doesn't think any professional psychics aside from Deegan and her assistants have stayed there.

Data submitted by: Dan Pearson, Billy Riley, Martha Mayes, Dick Nelson, Shelly Deegan, Maria Mazzi, Chris McGuire, Roy Brandes. Articles in the *San Diego Union* and *San Francisco Examiner*.

9

"Thomas Whaley Is Still Very Much in Possession of His Own Home"

The Whaley House, an Early Residence, Now a Museum in San Diego, California

Location: The Whaley House is situated at 2482 San Diego Avenue, San Diego, California. It is open to the public Wednesday through Sunday from 10 A.M. to 4:30 P.M. Admission fees are nominal.

Description of place: The two-story house is described in publicity material as a Victorian mansion, but it is not particularly impressive by modern standards or even the East Coast standards of its day, the mid-nineteenth century. It is, however, said to be the oldest brick structure in southern California and was quite a spectacular edifice for its time, as well as its place, the raw, pioneer West Coast. It was built by Thomas Whaley, a successful businessman, primarily as a home for his family. He also leased part of the building for a time to San Diego County as a courtroom and meeting room for the board of supervisors, and this aspect of the house has also been preserved.

Ghostly manifestations: The Whaley House administration is proud of its resident ghosts and lists four of them. They are Thomas Whaley; his wife, Anna; a little

The Whaley House.

girl named Annabelle Washburn, a friend of one of the Whaley children who ran into a clothesline in back of the house with fatal results; and Yankee Jim, a drifter who was hanged on the property before the house was built for the seemingly picayune offense of attempting to steal a boat.

According to June Reading, director of the museum, people not only often see ghosts but sometimes take photographs of them. "We have several pictures," she says. "Visitors come in and give us a copy." She says she has been aware of many ghostly manifestations over the years. "One I saw was Thomas Whaley, standing on the landing on a Sunday afternoon. Another guide called my attention to this figure standing upstairs. I saw a man wearing a black frock coat and a pair of pantaloons, with a broad-brim black felt hat. His face wasn't turned toward the staircase and he faded away, but I know it was Whaley. I have his passport with his physical description, and I know all about him. I was upstairs once with another guide and we heard a man's laughter, a baritone laugh, and I think it was Thomas Whaley.

"We have music boxes in the house, in the music room, and we've had the sound of music boxes playing. Not ours, but something from a long time ago. We've had organ music from the courtroom. We have an old-fashioned organ in there.

"One August we had a great deal of static electricity. One of the visitors called me upstairs, and in the girls' room we had something that looked like fireflies moving around in the room. I'd never seen anything like that. I called the Parapsychology Foundation and described it, and a woman said they sounded like ectoplasmic tubes. She said this is what a figure forms from, if there are enough present. She said to keep watching, and finally we saw what looked like half of a figure of someone, standing at the end of the bed, apparently folding clothes or doing something.

"We have anywhere from seventy-five hundred to ten thousand schoolchildren come through the house in a year. One time I was ushering seventy-five high school kids, three teachers, and a bus driver. At one point the room got very quiet, I noticed. We have a railing in the courtroom and an open area, with chains to keep people out of the front part of the courtroom. I was standing behind the railing, talking. When I finished I walked directly out of the room and waited for them in the hall to take them on a tour of the rest of the house. I waited and waited. I thought that was funny, because kids are usually very anxious to get up and leave when they've been listening to a talk. I turned, and here was the bus driver and the three teachers coming out. The kids were still sitting in the room. The driver said to me, 'Well, I've heard a lot of stories about your house but after what I saw this morning I really think the place is haunted.' And the teachers nodded. The driver said, 'I know you weren't aware of it, but at one point in your talk those chains on either side of the railing started to move. They weren't just swinging, they were moving in an undulating fashion, like waves.' Of course, the kids saw all this.

"We had a fellow in from New Jersey one day, and he had a Polaroid camera. We walked into the courtroom, and he started taking pictures while we were talking. He peeled off the picture and handed it to me, and across the top of the judge's bench was an energy form. It was cloudy and white, about eight inches across the length of the bench. It looked like a big, heavy piece of yarn. We get a lot of that. Sometimes you can see it. We had one energy form that developed in the study that was there off and on for a long time. It was filmy, and it would move. It would expand and contract, but it never developed into anything, and I used to watch it an awful lot. It seemed to be hanging right around Mr. Whaley's desk."

The spirit of Thomas Whaley seems to get out for a walk occasionally, according to testimony of Anita Kirwin, who has been a guide at the house. She says, "I started working there about seven years ago. Prior to that I had worked on the grounds in a small shop, a spice and tea shop. I knew nothing of the Whaley House at that time. When June called me to see if I would work there part-time, I went in without any preconceived notions about the house.

"But let me go back to when I worked at the spice shop, on the grounds. It was called the Spice of Life. The building itself was an old gunsmith shop from around 1838. In the afternoon I would hear a heavy man's footsteps on the porch in front. I would walk out to the door, and no one would be there. I dismissed it.

"After a number of years of working there, I also would see across the yard a gentlemen who would stand there near the ferns on a walkway. He would stand back of the ferns and stare into the shop. This is a beautiful place, it's a tourist attraction, and I thought, anyone is likely to just stand there and stare into this little shop—it's a very quaint shop. This man wore a black coat, which I later learned was a frock coat, and a black top hat. We have a small theater down the way from the Whaley House, and I thought he probably was from this theater. And then he'd be gone, as though he had just evaporated. I never saw him walking; he'd just be gone. Again, I dismissed it.

"When I went to work at the Whaley House, I had to learn the history of Old Town and of the house. Old Town is the oldest part of San Diego. Mrs. Reading told me nothing of the ghost stories. My job was to take groups around the house. The first time, several of the people in the group were smiling at me, which really unnerved me. I wondered if I were doing something wrong. Later, a woman went to June and told her she saw this man standing next to me. She described him and the description fitted Yankee Jim. Several people saw him."

Does she think this was the man with the top hat?

She replies: "That, they said, was Mr. Whaley. My debut as a guide wasn't the only time things happened. After that I would give talks in the courtroom and many times people would come up to me or go to Mrs. Reading and describe a man standing next to me, and it was always Yankee Jim they described.

"One time I was talking to a young girl I was working with. She said her hobby was collecting cigar box labels. As she told me this, we began to get the drift of a cigar odor. It became very, very strong. Now there's no smoking in there. Neither of us smoked. There was no one around who could have carried it in on their clothes. We searched all around. As we continued to talk, a door slammed. It sounded like it might be a door that would lead off the main corridor, somewhere between the front door and the back door. But there is no such door. We told Mrs. Reading, and we looked through the old records and found an old diagram of the house that Lillian, a daughter of the Whaley's, had kept, and it showed that there had been a door there at one time.

"The burglar alarm will go off without any provocation, but it's hard to get police officers to go into the house. One night I was called by the county security office and asked if I could meet a police officer at the Whaley House, that an alarm had gone off. I went in and looked around, but it didn't look like there was anyone there. But I had to wait and meet with the police officer to OK it with security. I waited for the police officer for an hour. I kept calling 911. The operator kept saying, 'He's there.' I finally looked around outside and found him sitting in his patrol car. He did not want to get out. He finally came to the door, but he would not come up the steps. I insisted he come in, because I had to check it out with security. He finally came in, but I could not get him to walk around the house. He finally did, but he drew his gun, and he wouldn't walk into the rooms, he'd just look in them with me. He'd say, 'You go in and check.' "

Another guide, Millicent Brabant, has worked in the house for nine years. She tells of a variety of experiences. "I've heard footsteps upstairs that I've been told are Yankee Jim," she says. "They're very heavy footfalls. I've heard what seems like a large meeting of men in the courtroom. There are chairs moving and feet shuffling. The chairs aren't actually moving, but there is that sound. There is like a cackle of voices. You also hear voices in the study, Mr. Whaley's office, in the back of the house, voices, and like moving of furniture, as if people are congregating, starting a meeting.

"I've opened the front door to come in in the morning and heard mandolins playing. I'd turn around to shut the door and the mandolins stop. And I've heard the music box and other instruments, including the piano. And nothing's moving."

History: Thomas Whaley was born in New York, went to San Francisco in 1849 during the gold rush days, and arrived in San Diego two years later, establishing a business in Old Town. He brought his new wife, Anna, from New York in 1853 and built the house in 1856 and 1857, in an effort to simulate her New York living. It was the first really fine home to be built in

San Diego and quickly became the social center of the town. Two presidents, Ulysses S. Grant and Benjamin Harrison, stayed with the Whaleys when they visited San Diego. Five generations of Whaleys lived in the house. The last to live there, Corrine Lillian Whaley, a daughter of Thomas and Anna and a teacher and San Diego's first librarian, died at the age of ninety in 1953.

In 1871 there was agitation to remove the county court and the board of supervisors meeting room from Whaley's house and move it to New Town, near the waterfront. One night when Whaley was out of town, agitators broke in and removed the county records. Anna Whaley confronted the intruders and was threatened at gunpoint. Aside from the historical interest of this violent contretemps, some observers suspect it might be a reason why the spirits of Thomas and Anna are still hanging around. Whaley was understandably outraged but never received any satisfaction from the board of supervisors. June Reading says, "The result is that Thomas Whaley is still very much in possession of his own home. He's very much the man of the house."

In the 1950s, Reading was part of a nonprofit group that prevented the house from being torn down. The restoration took four years, and the museum was opened in 1960, with Reading as director. Even before it became a museum, the haunting of the Whaley House was a local tradition. Reading says, "The Whaley family acknowledged that there were things that were unexplained. They heard footsteps in the house and so on. I seem to be sensitive to ghosts. When I was a child I would see figures and then they would fade away. When I came here the whole thing hit me. I kept trying to ignore it and go about my business of creating a museum, but it was just determined it was going to be present."

Identities of ghosts: Thomas and Anna Whaley; Annabelle Washburn, the little girl who ran into the clothesline; and Yankee Jim.

Anna has been seen by many visitors, most publicly by Regis Philbin, a TV talk show host who at that time worked for a local station. In 1964 Philbin and a friend decided to stay in the house overnight, and about 2:30 A.M. Anna supposedly floated into the parlor from the study. According to material put out by the management of the house, this caused a great deal of "nervous excitement" on the part of Philbin. He pointed the beam of his flashlight at the image, and it disappeared. Since then, night visits have not been permitted.

Annabelle Washburn's traumatic death is typical of many instances in which ghosts of the victims manifest. After she ran into the clothesline, Thomas Whaley is said to have carried her into the kitchen of the house, where she died. June Reading tells of parapsychological activity in the kitchen, which is attributed to the little girl. "There is movement of utensils, and rocking chairs once in a while rock," she says. "And children say they have seen her in there."

Poor Yankee Jim's story is a sad one. Imagine being hanged just for trying to steal a boat. And he didn't even get away with it! Apparently, though, the natives were getting pretty restless about people stealing boats around there, and they made an example of Jim. It was like what happened to horse thieves in the Old West. Jim was not even properly hanged, and he strangled to death. He was not given a proper religious burial; he was just shoveled into an unmarked grave. Wouldn't *you* be furious and haunt the place, even though they built a house over it?

Personalities of ghosts: They're just there; none seem to be troublesome. In fact, they're probably good for attendance.

Best time to witness: They seem to operate around the clock.

Still haunted?: The chief ghosts seem to be still around, although some minor spirits, such as children and the family dog, seem to have lost interest over the years and haven't been heard from for a long time.

Investigations: Hordes of psychics have tuned in at Whaley House. It's one of the best-known haunted places in California.

Data submitted by: June Reading, Anita Kirwin, Millicent Brabant. Material provided by Whaley House. Thanks to Rich Bolton and George Mroczkowski.

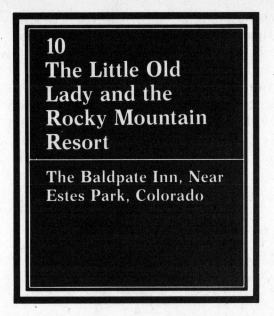

10
The Little Old Lady and the Rocky Mountain Resort

The Baldpate Inn, Near Estes Park, Colorado

Location: The inn is situated on Route 7, about seven miles south of the resort town of Estes Park, which is about seventy miles northwest of Denver. The town, with about five thousand permanent residents, swells to some 150,000 in the summer. It is adjacent to Rocky Mountain National Park.

Description of place: Mike Smith, present owner of the place, says the design of the building is called "stick architecture," a Western style popular in the early part of this century. "Many old lodges in the West," Smith says, "were built from logs and timbers. Debarked logs were used for much of the construction, and then rough planed boards were used for a kind of clapboard effect."

The place was built in 1917 by Gordon and Ethel Mace and was in the Mace family until very recently, when their granddaughter, Leean Mace, lost the ownership. Mike Smith bought the place in December 1986.

There are a dozen rooms for guests and nine rooms

for staff. There is also a restaurant, available to the general public. One of the features of the place is what Mike Smith says is the largest key collection in the world.

Ghostly manifestations: I was given this account by Suzanne Jauchius, a psychic I met while writing *The Ghostly Register*. She lives in Beaver Creek, Oregon, with her husband, Dan, and daughter, Jill, now eleven. Five years ago they were visiting friends in Estes Park.

"Our friends," Suzanne relates, "suggested we see Baldpate Inn, it was so unique, so we all went up and had dinner there. It's very quaint and really nice. It was during the week and off-season. There was just our group there. The waiter wanted to know if we'd like a tour of the key room. It's really neat.

Baldpate Inn.
PHOTO BY SUZANNE JAUCHIUS

"Off the key room is a door. My husband never stays with a group; he's very nosy. He had wandered over and opened that door and peeked in. He came back and said to me, 'You ought to check that little room out.' So I wandered over there by myself and looked in.

"It was a storage room but apparently had at one time been something else. There was a small fireplace and a wing-back chair in front of the fireplace. When I opened the door, I saw an older woman—a grandmotherly type—sitting in front of the fireplace in the chair reading a Bible, and she had her feet up on an ottoman. She had gray hair and a high collar dress on. Just as quickly as I saw her, she disappeared. I closed the door and went back to my husband and told him what I had seen. He hadn't seen this, but he had sensed something in the room and that's why he wanted me to look. He's pretty intuitive.

"In the meantime, my daughter needed to go to the bathroom. It was up on the second floor. The waiter said we wouldn't be imposing on anyone because there were no guests in the hotel. We went up. You had to go through a corridor to get to it. We had just shut the door when we heard someone shuffling outside in the corridor and a knock, knock, knock on the door. What caught me was that we had just been in that corridor and hadn't seen anybody. I said, 'Just a minute; we'll be right out.' We never heard anyone leaving; nobody said anything. So after a while we went downstairs, and I said to the waiter that the bathroom was free now. He said no one had gone up to use it.

"As we were going back to town, I told our group what I had seen. The next day my husband and I decided to go up there and ask about it. I told a young girl at the desk that I was a psychic from Portland and that I would like to talk to someone about the ghost. She had apparently heard of it. Her eyes got wide and she said, 'You've seen it?' She said, 'Let me get somebody who has seen it.' So this young man who worked there came and talked to us, and he said, 'Oh, you've seen her?' He said he would show us a family picture that was in the key room. The key room is off the lobby and is entered by a pair of French doors. We went into the key room, and as we approached the photo album a wind came up. It wasn't just a light breeze, and it wasn't a draft—it was a wind. It blew one young lady's dress up, and it slammed the French doors shut. There were no windows or doors open.

"The young man showed me the album, and I saw the woman I had seen. He said, 'Well, that is Grandma.' Then he said he had to get the owner, who would be very interested in talking to me. Leean Mace came down, and everyone was telling her what had happened with the wind and everything. She told other stories about the ghost. She said people had often been aware of such things. She said the old caretaker had talked about hearing footsteps at night when no one but him was in the building.

"She said someone would order a drink and would put it down and then reach for it and it would be gone. She figured that was Grandpa. She thought that both Grandpa and Grandma walked the place. People would find their cigarettes smashed or stolen. Apparently Grandpa didn't like cigarettes. She had quite a few stories.

"I told her about the shuffling feet upstairs, and she said, 'Let's go up, and I'll show you where Grandma's room was.' It was right near the bathroom. So now we were about seven or eight people; the group just kept growing. So we went past the bathroom, and just as we were approaching Grandma's room the wind came up again, and it slammed one door shut and blew another door open. The young girl who had had her dress blown up the day before exclaimed, 'That's it, I've had it!' and went running back downstairs.

"It was one of the few places I've been where the phenomenon actually presented itself. Usually nothing happens when a psychic is around. But it was like Grandma wanted us to know she was there."

The caretaker referred to above is Paul Hamilton, who worked at the inn in 1965 and has also worked there for the past five years. He says, "I was here when the psychic was here. I remember her, oh yeah. We had an old rocking chair that belonged to Ethel Mace, and the psychic said there's somebody sitting in that rocking chair.

"There has always been some talk about ghosts at the inn, but I've always discounted it. It's always been on the kidding side. Sometimes at night when nobody was in the inn except me and my dog I'd hear somebody running up and down those stairs. I just cast it off as being wind or something like that."

History: The history of the hotel is most intriguing. It is named after a bestselling novel, *Seven Keys to Baldpate*, written early in this century. The book has had incarnations as movies and as a Broadway play. The author was Earl Derr Biggers, who also wrote the Charlie Chan series. The novel was in great vogue at the time the inn was being built. Biggers happened to be visiting Estes Park, and when he saw the new building he said that it was the sort of place he had envisioned when he wrote the book. The Maces decided to call their new venture Baldpate Inn.

The plot of the novel was that the owner of an inn had given out seven keys to seven people. This was in the winter, when the fictional inn was closed. Each of the people believed he had the only key, and each had a reason to go there to get away from the world.

The Maces had another bright idea, and that was to give a key to every guest. Before long, however, they discovered this was more fun in concept than in practice. In 1923 Clarence Darrow, the famous lawyer, was a guest at the inn, and the Maces were lamenting to him how expensive this key giving had turned out to be. Darrow's suggestion was that instead of giving away keys, they ask their guests for keys, and he gave them one of his own to start them off.

It became an in thing to contribute to the key collection at Baldpate Inn. "Many of the keys are from famous people," says Mike Smith. "We've got the key to

Mozart's wine cellar; he wasn't here, but his key ended up here. We've got Jack Benny's dressing room key; he was a guest here. We've got the key to Edgar Allen Poe's college dormitory room, number 13. We've got the key to the hotel room where Stephen King wrote *The Shining.* We've got the key to the first bank that Jesse James robbed, the Southern Bank of Kentucky. We've got over twelve thousand keys, and we still get a couple of hundred a year."

Identities of ghosts: They seem to be Ethel and Gordon Mace, builders of the inn.

Personalities of ghosts: Mostly inoffensive, wanting to be noticed, although at least one of them seems to like to inconvenience guests who smoke and drink.

Witnesses: Suzanne Jauchius; Dan Jauchius; their daughter, Jill; Paul Hamilton, caretaker; various guests and members of the staff.

Best time to witness: Phenomena seem to have occurred around the clock.

Still haunted?: Mike Smith says he has not been aware of any manifestations, nor have any of his employees, to his knowledge. His employees are all new; none except Paul Hamilton are left over from the Mace ownership.

I suggested to Suzanne Jauchius that perhaps Grandma and Grandpa had lost interest in the place when its ownership was no longer in the family. Leean Mace had lost the place shortly after Suzanne's adventure there.

"My thought," Suzanne says, "is that they were so active because they knew she was going to lose it. She was going through a divorce and having some major changes in her life. It was really sad that the inn had to go away from the family."

Investigations: The visit of Suzanne Jauchius.

Data submitted by: Suzanne Jauchius, Mike Smith, Paul Hamilton.

11
The Haunted Advertising Agency

In an Eighteenth-
Century House in
Farmington, Connecticut

Location: The agency's address is 304 Main Street in Farmington, a suburban village west of Hartford, Connecticut.

Description of place: Farmington is a posh, historical village, an impressive address in central Connecticut. Main Street is quaint and very attractive, lined with historic houses, many now converted for use by businesses or institutions.

The house in question is occupied by Keiler Advertising, one of the largest ad agencies in Connecticut. It employs about seventy-five people. When the agency bought the place in the mid-1970s, it included two buildings. One structure was built in 1710 as a farmhouse. The other building was a 1950s Cape. The agency has linked the two houses together by way of a glass corridor and put on an addition with six wings that range from two to three stories. The entire complex provides twenty-five thousand square feet.

Dick Keiler, owner of the agency, describes the place as follows: "The old building is a typical eighteenth-

century center-chimney Colonial, with the shallow fireplaces and the beehive ovens. We've saved all the chest-
nut beams and posts and all the original hardware, the
low ceilings and the funeral door and everything. It's a
pretty interesting, well-preserved replica of the eighteenth century. And that's the area where the ghost
presumably patrols. When you walk from the part that
is almost three hundred years old into the part that is
six months old there are aspects that make it hard to
tell where you cross the dateline."

Ghostly manifestations: Everybody at the Keiler
agency seems to talk about the ghost, but only three
people and one dog seem to have actually been person-
ally aware of it. One person claims to have seen it, two
claim to have sensed it, and Tess, a golden retriever and
the in-house mascot, gives strong evidence of being
very much in the picture, ghost-wise. (Isn't that the
way they talk at ad agencies?)

Keiler Advertising Agency. PHOTO BY ARTHUR MYERS

Rita Quinn, who has been with the agency for five
years in the public relations department, seems to be
the star witness. She says she's actually seen the ghost,
or as she puts it, "envisioned" it. "I use my sense of ESP

and psychic intuition a lot," she says. She says she has a ghost in her own house, namely her grandfather, and that her son, when he was young, would also see him.

Rita says, "The public relations department was mostly on the third floor of the old part of the building. For the first couple of weeks I worked there I always felt that presence, and I knew the building had some kind of a spiritual entity within it. But it was a very comfortable feeling.

"We had this little doorway that went into a crawl space in the attic where we used to keep our supplies. Every time I would go in there I could feel an extra chill, and I knew that whoever the entity was, this is where he belonged. One day I was in a big rush. I had my arms full of envelopes and papers and I was just going to stoop and sneak out of the crawlway and back into the working area, and I happened to look quickly to the left and what I quickly envisioned was an old black man lying under the eaves. He was covered with an old horse blanket.

"When I see things it's not like seeing a real physical image. It's like when you're leafing through a magazine quickly and you see something but it isn't real, it doesn't last long.

"I saw this old black man, and after I blinked my eyes a couple of times it was gone. He had black hair, but it was gray along the sides. He seemed to be very frightened. I felt he was hiding from something and that he was going to die there. I felt he was a slave, that somebody was hiding him, and he died. I always felt he was a comfortable spirit, who was kind of watching over the building.

"Farmington is well-known as part of the Underground Railroad, but at the time I didn't know this. After this happened to me, people would go up into the attic and poke around to see if they could see him, but nobody else did."

Tommilee Phillips, media director of the agency, also

says she has been aware of the presence of the ghost.

"I've had such feelings before, elsewhere," she says, "but they are usually negative. This one is not.

"It felt like a black man, short, youngish," she says. "He seemed to be lying on hopsacking material [old-fashioned cloth bags]. I felt that the reason he's hanging around is that his family never knew what happened to him. He's very restless because of this."

Tommilee also feels the entity's presence in the basement. She feels that if the old chimney were ripped open there would be found a space in its center where a person could climb up to the attic. She, like Rita, has a feeling that the ghost is restless.

A third human witness is Steve Conroy, who used to be head of the public relations department of the agency. He is now with Della Famina McNamee agency in Boston.

Conroy feels that the spirit is a benign one, with concern for the people who now inhabit the building. As a department head, he often worked into the evenings and on weekends and was most aware of the presence at those times.

"I would be leaving the building," he says, "going down the stairs, and I would have the distinct feeling I was being escorted to the back door. One time, I can remember going out that door and turning around and looking through the glass windows and having the feeling that there was somebody or something standing on the other side of the windows, in the lobby of the agency.

"I did not see, feel, or smell anything. But one time I took my kids there on a weekend, and I was telling them about it. We were down on the first floor, and I quite distinctly heard walking around on the third floor. And there was nobody in the place. Rita told me that whatever was up there was confirming my beliefs and was trying to show the kids that it was not just a ghost story."

All of my human interviewees spoke of Tess, who seems to be as clairvoyant as the next dog. When the third floor was in use, Tess tended to do a lot of determined barking at the attic area the ghost is believed to inhabit and where it probably died. Now the third floor is not in use; there is a door to the stairs that lead to it. The dog will often go up to the second floor around lunchtime to cadge sandwiches from the people who work there. But she's still aware of something interesting in the attic.

Rita Quinn says, "The dog has been known to stop in the middle of being fed snacks and run over to the doorway to the attic and stand there for five minutes and bark."

Does the ghost move things around, as spirits are sometimes wont to do? "Sometimes stuff you leave around isn't there when you look for it," Tommilee says, "but I think it's the cleaning people."

History: The 1710 house was built by Simon Newell, later passed through the hands of two other families, and was sold to Moses Hills in 1795. In 1810 Moses's son, Lucien, became the owner. He died at the turn of the twentieth century. For many years the place was known as the Lucien Hills House. The house had a number of owners during this century. Preceding the ad agency's occupation, the buildings were used, Dick Keiler says, by an interior decorator and by "some financial types."

Ann Arcari of the Farmington Library, who did a title search for the above information, says that although a number of Farmington houses are known to have been stops on the Underground Railroad, this particular house is not one of them, although some of these refuges for escaped slaves were not recorded in history.

Identity of ghost: The consensus seems to be that it is an escaped slave who was being hidden in the house during the era of the Underground Railroad.

Personality of ghost: He is sensed to be restless but benign.

Witnesses: Rita Quinn, Tommilee Phillips, Steve Conroy, Tess the retriever.

Best time to witness: Perhaps outside of regular working hours, when the building is quiet and manifestations are more readily noticeable, but much of the awareness has been during the ordinary working day.

Still haunted?: Seems to be.

Investigations: No formal psychic investigations, although two employees of the agency profess psychic sensitivity.

Data submitted by: Rita Quinn, Tommilee Phillips, Steve Conroy, Dick Keiler, Ann Arcari of the Farmington library. Article in *Adweek*, June 8, 1987. Tip from Jim Cooke.

12

"There's a Ghost in That Bedroom Who's a Real Bastard!"

The Old Stone House, in Washington, D.C.'s Georgetown

Location: The Old Stone House is a former residence dating from the mid-eighteenth century, now a small museum administered by the National Park Service. The address is 3051 M Street NW, Washington, D.C. It is open to the public, free of charge, Wednesday through Sunday.

Description of place: The house was built in 1765 by Christopher Layman, a cabinet maker from the Pennsylvania Dutch country, and the architecture is reminiscent of houses in that region. It is constructed of stone, has three stories, and is L-shaped. Rae Koch, the park ranger in charge, says, "It looks like an old German farmhouse." Georgetown is a posh section of Washington, replete with restored old homes and fashionable boutiques, coffee shops, and bistros.

Ghostly manifestations: Ghosts seem to be rampant in this old house. One, dubbed George by the staff, inhabits the third-floor bedroom and seems to be the star performer. He gets violent. He hates women and among other things has, according to some accounts, tried to push some of them over a railing outside his room or down the stairs. He is accused of strangling women, knifing them, and raping them. At least, that's what the people at the Old Stone House tell me.

"He rapes them?" I asked one of my informants, Karen Cobb, a longtime volunteer guide. "How does he do that?"

"I probably shouldn't have said that," she demurred, "but there have been several instances of sexual assault in that house."

You mean he actually . . . uh . . . ?

"Yes."

Rae Koch, their leader, puts it this way: "There's a ghost in that bedroom who's a real bastard. He's one of those self-righteous, you-do-as-I-say types. It's not a nice feeling there. A friend of mine who's very psychic came in, and she said to me, 'Who is that son of a bitch on the third floor? I refuse to go up there as long as he's there.'"

Rae is one of the women whom George purportedly tried to push over the railing. "I was standing by the railing there one night with my ghost hunter," she says, "and I got an effect of being pushed over the rail, that someone was trying to push me over."

The "ghost hunter" is a parapsychologist who spends a lot of time at the Old Stone House, whom I will call by the pseudonym Stuart. He asked me not to use his real name, stating, "Routinely, I tell people their anonymity is guaranteed, and I would have a very hard time doing that in the future if I were to appear in public print."

Stuart isn't sure Rae was in danger, but he says, "We could sense the presence of the entity. It had form. I could feel the thing. Rae was complaining of a pressure on her right side, and I grabbed her and pulled her away from the railing."

Karen Cobb says of an encounter with George, "He almost killed me. I worked there a number of years and

The Old Stone House.

I had a lot of strange things happen to me, but this was unusual because it was so violent. I was up there one night with this woman from England who worked there for a while. Stuart says she's like a catalyst for a lot of this stuff. We were sitting together on the bed, and I suddenly felt this impression on the bed next to me. I said, 'Evelyn, do you feel that?' And she said, 'Yes.' We both reached over, and it was very cold—ice cold. She said, 'I don't like this. I'm going to get out of here.' And the next thing I knew there were hands around my throat, strangling me, like from behind, and I couldn't get loose. Evelyn was trying to pull me loose, but I could not get loose. I ended up just struggling and breaking free. I ran downstairs. I ran outside the house and it was like it was pursuing me till I got outside in the yard. I just collapsed on the bricks outside. My throat was bruised badly. Finally I got my breath back, and I thought, I'm not going back up there. I *have* gone up there since, many times, but not with Evelyn."

George might have gotten his hands around the wrong neck, but perhaps any female neck would do.

Rae says, "I had a young English girl, Evelyn, who was with me when she was about eighteen. Her mother and father were at the British embassy. Well, when Evelyn would go into that room you could actually see her being pushed out. Whoever was in there never wanted her in that room. The man is very intimidating, a real stinker."

Some visitors have reported seeing George, although none of the staff have. "This character," says Stuart, "seems to be more interested in pressure effects than in manifesting apparitionally. He'll try to prevent people through pressure from coming into the room, leaving the room, things like that. People report being shoved, strangled, knifed."

"Knifed?"

"Not drawing blood," says Stuart, "but they felt the effect of a knife going in. And this is more than one person. Some were visitors, who did not know any of the other people who have reported this."

George seems to be just one of a crowd of spooks in this old house, although the others are better behaved. Rae says, "So far, in the twenty-four years I've been here I've seen eight ghosts in the house. They're all different kinds, all different time periods. The other day I was sitting in the kitchen and all of a sudden out of the corner of my eye I looked at the staircase and caught part of a skirt. She never materialized that much, but I could feel her there with me in the kitchen.

"There's a woman on the third floor, sitting in a rocker. In fact, she looks similar to me, it's really funny. I'm a brunette about five foot three and I used to be slim and trim, and she's slim and trim. Her hair is dark like mine. I'm sixty-nine now, but when I came here I was thirty-six. I just happened to see her one time, and I said, 'Hi.' I tried to talk with her, but you don't get anything out of them. She's a different time period from the man there.

"There was a little boy, he was four years old, who

was here with his mother and father and grandmother. I was in my office in a black jump suit. And I heard the little boy say—it's a small house and you can hear things all over—'Oh look, there's a lady standing by the fireplace.' And I heard the adults say, there isn't anyone there, it's your imagination. And he said, 'Don't tell me I don't see anybody there.' And I'm coming out of my office, and he said, 'There you are. How did you change clothes so fast?'

"The woman he saw was wearing a brown dress, eighteenth-century style. I said, 'That wasn't me; that was just a little apparition. You're seeing what they call a ghost or a spirit.'

"Well, the adults got all bent out of shape. So I said, 'Look, he happened to have a nice, pleasant experience. It's not scary. He's been gifted. He's a very gifted little boy, and there's nothing wrong with him seeing things.' I said, 'I used to play with a little girl when I was around three years old in an apartment my mother and father lived in in an old house in Baltimore. One day my mother saw her.'

"The little ones are so innocent, and they're much more open to all of this because they have no inhibitions. We haven't stomped anything into their minds yet.

"Lots of times people say to me, 'How did you get down here? I just saw you upstairs.' I don't know why this woman looks so much like me.

"One night in the winter I was down in the kitchen, and I put my legs up on the table. All of a sudden I caught something out of the corner of my eye and I turned, and there comes this full woman, a different woman, down the staircase into the kitchen. By full, I don't mean fat; I mean she was solid. She looked like a person; she was fully developed. Her dress was around the Civil War period. I stood up and went over by the fire. She walked right through the table and stood right beside me. And I thought, I'm going to put my hands in her. And when I did, I got hit with an electrical shock. My ghost hunter said, 'Don't ever do that again.' I said, 'Well, I was curious.' When I touched her she faded out.

"Another time I was sitting over by the window and I was reading Park Service statistics, which is boring as hell, and all of a sudden out of the corner of my eye, like about three o'clock, there was a man standing there. He had his back to me. His hair was to his collar. He had like light tan hair. He had on a blue colored jacket and his pants were walnut color. I said, 'Oh, hi.' And he starts fading. I said, 'No, don't go.' But you know, I've never seen him since; I only saw him that one time.

"There is another man who's always in the kitchen with me. I had this class of little children come in. There was a little boy whose name was Nathaniel. He was a very bright little boy. He asked the most questions. You know how you always have one child in the class who's the leader? Well, Nathaniel was asking me questions about the house and different things. When they're ready to go, he's in the front room and the teacher is reprimanding him for something. All of a sudden I felt something near me. I looked, and I didn't see anything, but I knew it was one of my ghosts. Nathaniel's standing there, and he's fighting the teacher off and saying to me, 'Come here, come here!' He's all excited. He said to me, 'Who is that man with you, dressed in the funny clothes?' And I said to the teacher, 'Oh, he has seen one of my ghosts.' And he said, 'He only had pants to his knees, and he wore stockings like a lady. He just had a shirt on.' The little boy had seen him full."

Among other apparitions reported are a little boy who runs up and down the third-floor hall. Rae says a live little boy, Stevie Beach, used to see him continually when he would come with his mother, Peggy, a friend of Rae's. But the last time he came, several years ago, he said, "Mommie, Joey isn't here anymore."

Stuart says, "There is a German-looking craftsman. A young boy saw him back in the mid-seventies, and he has been reported off and on for the past ten years.

"We had two Colonial-period men. One tended to appear in the bedroom. He was a partial manifestation. The other one tended to appear on the second floor. He started appearing during the late seventies and has persisted for several years. He's been observed by many people.

"And there's one that appeared around 1980. Rae stays in the house overnight occasionally, and she would see this woman, a younger woman, flitting up and down the staircase. Rae would chase her, trying to get a good look at her, but she'd always disappear around a corner. She had ringlets in her hair, which leads us to believe she belongs to the late eighteenth or early nineteenth century.

"There has also been a black boy who appeared on the top floor. This was of very short duration. He appeared to Rae and one other person. We feel he belongs to the Civil War period."

History: "This house was preserved by mistake," says Stuart, "at some cost to the taxpayer. There was a lady in Alexandria who was convinced that the Old Stone House was Sutter's Tavern. Sutter's Tavern was the place where supposedly George Washington laid out the city of Washington, along with Pierre L'Enfant. Due to a records mix-up, it had always been very difficult to pinpoint where Sutter's Tavern had been. There was even, prior to acquisition by the Park Service, a sign posted on the Old Stone House: ONE-TIME SITE OF SUTTER'S TAVERN.

"The Park Service acquired the building in 1950 by act of Congress. Congress felt they should do something before the building was demolished. Park historians went to work and within two years discovered it was not Sutter's Tavern. In point of fact, Sutter's Tavern had been several blocks away and was at that time an oyster house. About that time that building was demolished. There's a marker roughly where it was, and that's it."

(To give the Old Stone House its historical due, it might be noted that the newsletter of the National Park Service terms it "possibly the only surviving pre–Revolutionary War era residence in the District of Columbia.")

"The house was primarily a residence on the upper floors, and the lower floors were rented out to tradesmen," Stuart says. "This was very common in the period. So typically there were two groups of people in the house at any given time. Some, especially around the time of the revolution, were quite colorful. Early on, the house was bought by Robert Peter, who was then mayor of Georgetown, a very powerful man. He placed the house in the hands of his mistress. Her name was Cassandra Chew. She left the house to one of her daughters."

Karen Cobb has some intriguing historical touches to add. "That house has been everything," she says. "Back in the thirties it was a whorehouse. It's been an auto body shop. When the Park Service bought it there were still oil stains on the walls. I'm very good at psychometry, and one time I picked up a candlestick and I sensed that somebody had split somebody's head open with the thing. It might have been George. I believe it was in the kitchen. There was a lot of blood."

Identities of ghosts: Rae Koch has an interesting theory as to who the redoubtable George might be. "I've never seen him," she says, "but one time I had a woman come in who is psychic and she said, 'Who is that man on the third floor with suspenders?' Now Peggy Beach, who comes to do volunteer work for me once in a while, her family, her ancestors, lived in this house for four years. They rented it. And she says that a great-great-grandfather of hers wore suspenders, and he was a real **SOB**. She says he was one of those self-righteous-type men. And he's probably the one we're picking up."

Stuart suspects that the woman on the third floor who looks like Rae might be the second mistress of the house, Mary Bromley, judging from descriptions of her appearance. Another spirit, Stuart suspects, might be that of Robert Peter, onetime mayor of Georgetown. Stuart also suspects that Christopher Layman, the builder, who died in the house, is there too.

Personalities of ghosts: George is a caution, but the rest of them seem harmless enough.

Witnesses: Rae Koch; Karen Cobb; Stuart; Evelyn, the young English woman; a host of visitors to the house, especially children.

Best time to witness: They seem abroad at almost any hour.

Still haunted?: They seem to come and go, but there is usually a spirit or two about.

Investigations: Stuart, an experienced parapsychologist, has made a study of the place for the past ten years, and many psychics drop by from time to time. For some reason, the staff itself seems to include an unusual number of psychic people, such as Rae, Karen, and Evelyn. I asked Stuart why the place seems so haunted, and he replied, "I think every site has a potential for activity, but I think what has happened here is a set of circumstances. You have an individual, Rae, who from her childhood has had many psychic experiences, placed square in the middle of a site where much living has occurred. Also, other people have come into the site—volunteers, tourists, and so on—who interact well with Rae on a spiritual level and also with the house.

"In addition, the place is in a very pristine condition. I think that a lot of it has to do with the level of upheaval of a site. I don't think age is as critical as how intact it is. The reconstruction here did very little to alter the

interior. Many key pieces are there from the original
house. There is a very pure environment there. It is as
though the life of the house stopped dead in 1950."

Data submitted by: Rae Koch; Stuart; Karen Cobb;
Priscilla Baker, assistant to the director of the National
Park Service. *Courier,* the National Park Service News-
letter, October 1986.

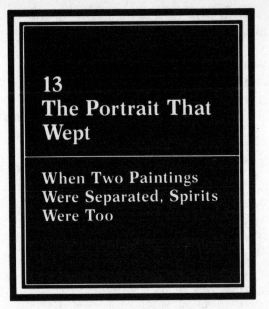

13
The Portrait That Wept

When Two Paintings Were Separated, Spirits Were Too

Location: A house in a suburb of Atlanta, Georgia.

Description of place: The twenty-year-old, two-story, spacious white brick and wood house is occupied by an affluent couple and their unmarried daughter, in her late twenties. The husband and wife are both successful lawyers. The house contains a sizable front hall, with stairs leading up to the second floor. To the right is a large dining room. Also on the ground floor is the husband's study.

Ghostly manifestations: This account was given to me by Patricia Hayes, a nationally known psychic and medium who conducts a school of mediumship and healing in McCaysville, Georgia, about one hundred miles north of Atlanta. She is often called upon to examine apparent hauntings and has developed a group of people she has trained and who work with her on investigations.

Pat says she was called by the woman lawyer and asked to come to the house and investigate an eerie and frightening manifestation. A portrait of a woman, dating from the 1700s, seemed to be weeping. Moisture trickled down from the eyes of the portrait, leaving stains that had been observed by the occupants of the house and many visitors. According to Pat, the woman had seen the "tears" trickling, had the moisture tested by a laboratory, and was told it was human tears.

The woman lawyer, although born in the United States, had an Austrian background and a considerable interest in her heritage. On a visit to Austria, she and her husband had acquired two oil portraits of an aristocratic couple, ancestors of hers. They had brought the pictures back seven years before and hung them side by side in their dining room.

Nothing unusual had happened until two years before. The woman, in the course of rearranging the decor of her house, had taken the portrait of the man and hung it in her husband's study. Then a number of unusual things began to happen.

Pat says that she and her group make a point of beginning an investigation with as little conscious knowledge as possible, and all they knew at the start was the tears of the portrait.

As their evening of investigation continued, they found out about the following manifestations in the house:

- The daughter had become depressed to the point of suicide, although she had had no previous emotional problems.
- Things were found mysteriously moved, mostly in the kitchen and the study. Papers in the study turned up missing.
- The woman lawyer had twice seen apparitions of a man dressed in clothing of the eighteenth century, once going up the front stairs, the other time going into the study. The daughter had been aware of shadows in the hall upstairs.
- The couple had begun to have marital difficulties.

Pat says, "When we walked into the house, I felt a very strong energy coming from the right, which was a dining room. They had a very large banquet table in there. The first thing you saw was the woman's picture. The energy was so strong I pulled a chair up in front of the picture, and she [the spirit of the woman in the picture] started talking. She said she was very lonely, that she couldn't find her husband, and she didn't know what to do. I began making my notes, and the rest of the people in our group started off on their own, investigating the whole house.

Patricia Hayes.

According to Pat, the picture's eyes followed her as she moved from one part of the room to the other, and the five other people noticed the same thing. Pat continues, "I went upstairs, and when I got into the daughter's bedroom I began feeling very sad and very lonely. The woman's spirit spent a lot of time there. She was stressed. I wondered why, if they were both in the house, they couldn't find each other.

"As I had gone upstairs, I could feel the man, but he did not talk with me. I could see mentally what he looked like. I saw him several times, and he was always looking out a window, as though at something far away.

"When I went into the man lawyer's study, I saw the

man spirit's picture, and I recognized who he was. I
saw him again on the back porch. Every time I saw
him, he was looking out a window. He was so preoccu-
pied with whatever he was looking at that he didn't
even notice me.

"After each of our group had done his own individual investigation, we met to consult each other's notes.
Each felt the strongest point of energy was in the dining room, where the woman's picture was. The second
strongest point was in the daughter's bedroom, where
she was again. This makes sense because she was willing to communicate with us and the man was not.

"We then did a psi session in the dining room. We all
hold hands and alter our state of consciousness and lift
into the psychic realm and begin to interpret the energies we feel. The woman came in, couldn't find her
husband, and was in a depression. Later on, the man
came in, but he wasn't communicating with her, he
was communicating with us. He was more difficult to
communicate with because he was obviously preoccu-
pied; he did not want to be there, but he was reluctant
to leave because of a sense of duty. He wouldn't leave
without his wife. But he wanted to go back to Austria;
he wanted to go back to his homeland.

"He was not aware of his wife's being there, as she
wasn't aware of him. He couldn't find her because his
attention was not there, it was back in his home. It was
like somebody who is daydreaming, always thinking of
the past rather than the now.

"So what we did is explain to him that she was in the
house, and she was extremely depressed and she had
been looking for him, and we were able to bring the
energies together. And when that happened there was a
tremendous joyous feeling. They decided they would go
home to Austria, and since that time the people in the
house have not experienced anything. And from what
I've heard, the marital crisis of the couple who own the
house has cleared up."

History: Removal of the two portraits from Austria, installation in the lawyers' home, and separation into two different rooms two years before the investigation.

Identities of ghosts: The eighteenth-century Austrian couple.

Personalities of ghosts: Lost, lonely, confused, homesick, depressed.

Witnesses: The two married lawyers who own the house and their twenty-eight year-old daughter; various visitors to the house; Patricia Hayes and her investigatory group, who are Marshall Smith, Joyce Rennolds, Kimberly Hayes, Steven Smith, and Frances Milam.

Best time to witness: The manifestations took place around the clock.

Still haunted?: According to Pat Hayes, it is not.

Investigations: Pat is aware only of this one.

Data submitted by: Patricia Hayes, of the Patricia Hayes School of Inner Development, P.O. Box 70, McCaysville, Georgia 30555, (404) 492-2772.

14
A Haunted English Pub in the Middle of Chicago

The Owner Suspects His Father, Plus a Few Others

Location: The Red Lion Pub is situated at 2446 North Lincoln Avenue, on the Near North Side of Chicago.

Description of place: A three-story wooden building in a once rough-and-ready section that has been gentrified in recent years and is now a haven for yuppies. The neighborhood's former ethnic character still survives, however; many Greeks, Assyrians, and gypsies live there.

Prior to its conversion into a chic English pub, the building housed a wild West–type saloon. "It was a dump, a terrible dump," says John Cordwell, the present owner, and no one seems to dispute him. Back in the 1940s, the second floor of the building housed a thriving bookie joint, and over the years the place has seen a variety of endeavors, such as a laundry, a fruit and vegetable store, and a novelty store, as well as apartments on the upper floors.

It is rumored that at least one person was killed during the place's gaming days, although Lou Demas, whose family ran the establishment, says that happened next door at another bookie joint.

"There's a lot of bad karma to the neighborhood," says Colin Cordwell, John Cordwell's son and one of the pub's managers.

When John Cordwell bought the building in 1984, he continued use of the first floor as a bar-restaurant and renovated the second floor, then apartments, for overflow.

Ghostly manifestations: The place seems to be home to a variety of individuals who have retired from this plane of existence. Colin Cordwell told me, "The former owner, Dan Danforth, knew about the ghosts, but he never told us. The fellow who owns a video store across the street told me that Dan—they called him Dirty Dan, that was the name of his place, Dirty Dan's—used to invite him to come over and meet his invisible friends."

Colin also mentions a man who had lived in one of the apartments some years before and who tried to do some renovations. "He told me he'd padlock the place when he went out," Colin said, "but when he came back he'd find his work undone—boards pulled apart, nails pulled out of the wall, his tools scattered all over the place. He finally moved out."

I plan to touch on a number of spirits who reportedly carry on at the Red Lion Pub, but I'll start with my favorite, John Cordwell's father.

John is an Englishman, a successful architect who went to Africa forty years ago to inspect a new university he had designed. There he met Justine, an anthropologist from Chicago, and married her. "I brought him home as a souvenir," Justine told me. John built up an architectural firm in Chicago, and when he retired as chairman of the board a few years ago there were eighty architects on the payroll. He has since worked in real estate development, very successfully, but felt it would be fun to establish an English pub.

While renovating the building, John put a stained-glass window on the stairs and dedicated it to his father, an artist. "He doesn't have a headstone on his grave in England," John said, "so I put a brass plaque under the window in his memory. Everything seems to emanate from that point. I think he was very pleased by it."

Not long after, John was standing at the end of the upstairs bar, next to the stairs, and suddenly had a spell of dizziness. This has happened to him several times, and it also happens to customers. "There's no logical reason for it," John says, "but it always happens in the same place. I've talked with a doctor and a real estate guy, both intelligent people, and they have had the same experience there."

Two other people I interviewed mentioned the phenomenon spontaneously, one a psychic named Barbara Gessler who experienced the dizziness, and the other a bartender, Valerie Ciancutti, who has heard people speak of experiencing it.

Also, John said, "when I'm upstairs I frequently get tapped on the shoulder, and my pianist has had the same experience." Brenda Varda, the pianist, corroborates this. A number of other people have experienced the shoulder taps.

"I have reason to believe that it's my father," John Cordwell told me. "He was a great believer in psychic phenomena. He said to me when I was quite young, 'You know, there's another life, a spirit world here. I'll come back and contact you.' These things started to happen after I completed the second floor, which is very much in the mood of an English pub, and put in the stained-glass window and the plaque."

I mentioned to John that I had recently researched a cabin in Oregon and a restaurant in upstate New York and had run across the same phenomena, known as clairsentience. At the cabin two women mentioned they felt nauseated, as though they had morning sickness;

the presumed ghost was a woman who had been pregnant when she was killed. At the restaurant, a woman told me she had experienced unexplained throat constriction; one of the supposed ghosts there was a woman who had died during an epileptic seizure. When I told this to John, he said his father had had emphysema and had many spells of dizziness in his last days.

Whether the dizziness and shoulder taps are signals from Cordwell's father or not, there seem to be other spirits who have inhabited the place for some years.

I was told about the pub by Richard Crowe, a folklorist who has established the Chicago Ghost Tour. He is choosy about places he puts on his tours; if he ushers people to a place, you can be pretty sure it's haunted.

"John Cordwell is a well-known architect," he said. "The restaurant is just a hobby. They're very successful; they don't need me, so you know they're not looking for publicity."

Crowe told me that he had had an experience himself at the pub. It was in October 1987, and he had gone there to see Colin to work out a time for the tour. They were sitting in the second-floor dining room, talking, when they both became aware of a very strong scent of lavender. "It lasted ten minutes or more," Crowe told me.

This is one of the building's standard manifestations. "It's usually attributed to a girl who died on the premises at the age of about twenty," Crowe said. "She was retarded. The theory is that perhaps she didn't know how much perfume is too much. The perfume thing happened to me later in the same month, while I had a group in there on a tour. A number of people had the same experience."

Legend seems to have it that this was a glamorous young woman, but Lou Demas told me that is pure romance. His family owned the building before Cordwell, and he has lived in the house next door much of his life. He said he often saw the girl sitting on the porch with her parents. She was named Sharon, and she was a plump little person, not attractive. Her elderly parents also died in the house.

Mysterious footsteps are another aspect of the pub's mystique. They are heard both upstairs and downstairs. And strange things also happen in the ladies' chamber.

"One of our waitresses," John told me, "who is not given to hysterics, was in the women's bathroom upstairs, and when she tried to come out the door would not give. It was wedged tight. She couldn't open the bloody thing. She tried for fifteen or twenty minutes and was close to crying, and all of a sudden it opened by itself and let her out. This has happened with a number of other women."

(As I write this, I am bemused by the amount of ladies' room spirit activity I have encountered in the course of writing this and similar books. What is there about powder rooms that so appeals to female spirits?)

There seems to be more auditory, tactile, and olfactory phenomenon than visual, although one account of an apparition comes from Joe Heinan, John Cordwell's former son-in-law and also a manager at the place. He was not aware of the building's hidden agenda when they opened, but one night he was introduced to it.

"I was tending bar downstairs," Joe recalled. "It was slow and I had only one customer, a guy named Steve Walker. I was closing out, and I went to the bathroom. When I came back, he said, 'You never told me this place was haunted.' He said he saw something that walked down the middle of the bar and went up the steps. I thought, if you've seen any ghosts it's the ghost of Johnnie Walker. But then we became aware of footsteps upstairs."

And, of course, on inspection there was no one up there.

One psychic who visited the place, Sheila Bitely, said

she saw a rough-looking man walking through the upstairs bar. "He looked like a cowboy. He had Western clothes, cowboy boots. He was unshaven, young, in his late twenties."

Justine Cordwell told me she is psychic and has gotten pictures of a young man with black hair, a beard, and a black hat; a woman dressed and groomed in the style of the 1920s; and a blond man with a Slavic face. She later used a Ouija board, and she said, "What came out was that the man with the black hat had been killed by the Slavic man over a bad debt."

Colin told me, "You'll hear your name called every once in a while when there's nobody there. I hear a female voice, as clear as a bell." A number of other people have had this experience, he said.

One night while Colin was tending bar downstairs, there was a terrific crash upstairs. No one was up there. He went up and found a cricket bat, which had been hung against a wall as a decoration, had been flung across the room.

An Anglophobic ghost, perhaps.

A place seemingly as haunted as this would not be complete without a dog story. One comes from Janet Davies of Chicago TV station WLS. She was doing a program on haunted places, and at the Red Lion Pub she was particularly impressed by the fact that Colin's dog refused to go up to the third floor, now used for storage. "The dog was deathly afraid to go up there," Janet told me. "He'd follow Colin all over the place, but when he went up to the third floor the dog refused to follow."

History: A building dating from 1882, erected on what was then the northern edge of Chicago. Originally farm country, it became densely urban over the years. Across from the pub is the Biograph Theater, where John Dillinger saw his last movie. G-men were waiting for him outside, with fatal results. The Biograph, incidentally, still flourishes; it now has three screens. During the Prohibition era, Al Capone and many of his associates lived in the area.

Identities of ghosts: Possibly John Cordwell's father, plus a variety of people who have lived, eaten and drunk, worked, and gambled in the building.

Personalities of ghosts: They don't seem hostile, although whoever flung the cricket bat may have been a bit piqued at the moment.

Concerning the elder Cordwell, John Cordwell says, "My father probably wants to borrow some money."

Witnesses: John, Colin, and Justine Cordwell; Joe Heinan; Richard Crowe; Stephen Walker; Brenda Varda; Barbara Gessler; Sheila Bitely, Janet Davies.

Best time to witness: Seemingly late at night or on Sunday, when there are few people about. Things are more likely to be noticeable at those times; also, psychic Sheila Bitely mentioned that spirits tend to shy away from the vibrations of large groups.

Still haunted?: Apparently.

Investigations: Psychics such as Sheila Bitely, Barbara Gessler, and others have been brought in. All three of the Cordwells have psychic tendencies. The pub is a regular stop on Richard Crowe's tours.

Data submitted by: Richard, Colin, and Justine Cordwell; Joe Heinan; Lou Demas; Janet Davies; Richard Crowe; Valerie Ciancutti; Brenda Varda; Barbara Gessler; Sheila Bitely.

15
The Return of the Famous Palm Reader

A House in Indianapolis Once Frequented by Celebrities

Location: The house, called Tuckaway, is in an old residential area on the north side of Indianapolis, Indiana.

Description of place: The house was remodeled in 1910 from a 1906 bungalow. "It's an overgrown bungalow," says Kenneth Keene, Jr., its owner. "It looks like a little one-and-a-half-story house set in a forest of trees that are three hundred years old, but you walk in and the living room turns out to be a two-story, beamed-ceiling drawing room. The dining room is forty feet long."

The bungalow was bought and expanded in 1910 by George Philip Meier and his wife, Nellie Simmons Meier. George was a women's dress designer of some reputation in the Midwest; Nellie was a famous palm reader. The world beat a path to her door.

Flocking to Indianapolis for readings were such celebrities as Carole Lombard, Mary Pickford, Ramon Navarro, Marie Dressler, Joan Crawford, Walt Disney, Rudy Vallee, the Douglas Fairbanks senior and junior,

Helen Hayes, Alfred Lunt, and Lynn Fontanne.

"Eleanor Roosevelt came here for tea," says Ken Keene. "Serge Rachmaninoff gave concerts in the living room. Gershwin would play for parties. During the Roosevelt years, Nellie was often a guest at the White House."

George died in 1931, Nellie in 1944. They left the house to their niece, Ruth Austin, a dancer and dance teacher of considerable note. In 1972 Austin sold the house, somewhat rundown, to Keene, a young interior designer. He refurbished it with loving care, filling it with art objects and furniture of the 1920s and 1930s. For two decades it has been something of an informal social center in Indianapolis. Keene gives many parties and benefits and encourages his friends to give parties there.

Ghostly manifestations: George and Nellie Meier apparently are still inhabiting their beloved Tuckaway. Apparitions of them seem to be constantly observed by Ken Keene, as well as numbers of people who visit the house. Ruth Austin's apparition is also frequently reported.

Tuckaway, with Ken Keene standing on the steps.

I became aware of Ken Keene and Tuckaway
through Lynn Gardner, a well-known psychic who lives
in Indianapolis, with whom I became friendly while
researching *The Ghostly Register*. She is a friend of
Keene and enjoys being at Tuckaway.

"It's a lovely experience," she says. "This is one of
those things that points out the positive energy of spiritual essences who loved where they lived and who are
trying to do everything possible to help the person who
lives there now and who loves the place as much as
they did. Being there is like stepping back into a time
warp, a place where people who had a wonderful life
there like to drop back and forth."

Lynn says she has seen the Meiers at various times.
Once they were on a balcony looking out over their
yard. "They turned and smiled," she says. "They were
very peaceful, wonderful energies. Not threatening,
just 'We're here, we love it here, and we like coming
back to visit here.'" Once, Lynn relates, she was at a
gathering at Tuckaway and she saw Nellie standing off
in a corner, smiling.

One time, she says, she sensed a big dog, a Dalmatian, she believes. She asked Ken if the Meiers had had
a dog, and he replied that they had.

Nellie's spirit, Lynn believes, has a gentle way of
influencing people. When Keene first bought the house,
he says, he was often impelled to acquire old furnishings, only later to find out, sometimes through old photographs, that they were similar to furnishings the
Meiers had had in the house. He even discovered that
he was putting these furnishings in the same places
the Meiers had had them.

Shortly after he bought the house, he says, he was
driving to work one morning and somehow the car
seemed to have a will of its own, delivering him at an
antiques shop he had never been in before. He bought
a floor lamp dating from the early twentieth century. "I
took it home that evening," he says, "and was rewiring

it in the middle of the living room floor. Suddenly a voice seemed to tell me to get out some early photos of the house. In a snapshot of the dining room there was this lamp and its mate. I took it back to the antiques dealer and he said he had bought it from a family who had gotten it from an old house on the North Side. Many years later a visitor to the house told me she recognized the lamp; it had been there when the Meiers were there."

With some sites of supposed hauntings, the earnest investigator has to rather frantically beat the bushes to come up with indications that the places are really being visited by spirits. With Tuckaway, there is a glut of riches. My method was simply to ask Ken Keene to start talking and also to point me toward some other people who had had experiences or who could corroborate stories he told me. He mentioned Lani and Ned Rosenberger, who now live in southern California. Lani attended Butler University in Indianapolis, where Ned was then chairman of the theater department. They assent that they had experiences at Tuckaway.

"The one that stands out the most in my mind," Lani says, "is the night we were all up quite late. We kept feeling kind of a cold draft. We'd been talking about Nellie and Ruth. We turned around, and George was standing on the stairs, obviously very put out that he had been left out of the talk. It was really quite vivid; we all saw him standing three or four steps up. Ned and I were there and Kenny. My son, who was about four, was with us, but I think he had fallen asleep on the couch by that time.

"Another time, not long after Kenny moved in, there was an open-house party, well over one hundred people. A lot of them were out in the backyard. I looked out the window, and I definitely saw George and Nellie out there, really being just tickled that the house was being lived in and taken care of and there was joy and happi-

A view of Tuckaway. That's Ken Keene in the window.

ness in their home again. It was like they were guests at their own party. A lot of us had dressed in the clothes of the twenties and the thirties that George had designed. A lot of the clothes had been left in the house. Nellie was wearing one of those shapeless kinds of twenties dresses with one of those silly headbands with a big feather coming out the front. They were having such a great time."

Ken Keene says when he first bought the house people would see the Meiers and think they were seeing some elderly relatives who were staying with him. Sometimes this would be complicated even further at costume parties where 1920s clothing was worn. Keene tells of a guest at such a party—a friend of a friend of his—who didn't know the reputation of the place.

"I told her to look the house over and don't miss the upstairs," Keene relates. "Within three minutes she screamed and came running down the stairs, ran through the drawing room and out the front door. Her girlfriend ran after her. She got in her car and drove away with a screech. Her girlfriend came back and said her friend had gone onto the sleeping porch and had noticed an oddly dressed couple, but she thought they were just in costume. But they seemed much older than everybody else. The man was in a white summer suit and had a monocle and a mustache and silver hair. The lady was very short and rather plump. They seemed to be talking to each other. The girl walked up to them to introduce herself; they turned to her and smiled and evaporated."

I asked Ken to lay another story on me, and he told me this one: "Last Halloween I had a costume party. A guy showed up early who was alone but who had been invited by a friend of mine. We chatted and he said he was in the contracting business. He said the place was fascinating to him and asked if he could go down and inspect the basement to see how the house was supported. I said sure, and he went down. When he came up, he told me an attractive woman in 1920s costume had come up to him. When he spoke to her, she disappeared. He said he wasn't frightened, because he had once lived in a haunted house. He described her, and I got out a photo of Ruth Austin that was taken in the twenties, and he said, 'That's her.'"

Keene says an apparition of Austin once came into

the living room when he was alone and spoke briefly to him. She had died a few months after selling him the house. He had become very fond of her, he relates, had been thinking of her, and had in fact spoken her name out loud. He said she asked him not to do that, as it was very difficult for her to come back. Then she disappeared.

Keene often has people living in his house, and at one time his guests were Robin and Amber Faith. The Faiths were devotees of the Ouija board and apparently were constantly in touch with the Meiers, according to Keene. "Nicknames and incidents would come through that I'd do a little research on and find out they were true," Keene says.

A girl student roomer named Beth Marker, he relates, once dreamed that her covers were being pulled off her and were flying around the room. When she woke up, she found that the bedclothes were indeed draped all over the place. "It took a long time for her to tell me that," Ken recalls, "about a year. But she said she wasn't really frightened, because there was a playfulness about it."

History: Built in 1906. Acquired in 1910 by the Meiers; owned by their niece, Ruth Austin, after their deaths, and acquired in 1972 by Ken Keene. The house is currently on the National Registry of Historic Places.

Identities of ghosts: George and Nellie Meier, Ruth Austin, and possibly a Dalmatian dog.

Personalities of ghosts: Apparently loving, pleased that the house is being used by people who enjoy and appreciate it.

Witnesses: Kenneth Keene, Jr., Lynn Gardner, Ned and Lani Rosenberger, Robin and Amber Faith, Beth Marker, numerous visitors to the house.

Best time to witness: Many accounts involve the evening hours, since that is when most social occasions occur. However, Keene says, when he is home during the day he often hears the front door slam and footsteps on the stairs. "But," he says, "after living in a haunted house all these years, you don't pay any attention to it. This happens all the time, especially in the late afternoon."

Still haunted?: Although Keene says he thinks the height of the manifestations was during the 1970s, not long after he bought the house, there seem to be plenty still going on.

Investigations: Psychic Lynn Gardner is a frequent visitor and once, accompanied by the writer and parapsychologist Nancy Osborn, did a TV show on Tuckaway that was rebroadcast nationally. Many newspaper articles have been done on the place, and other psychics have visited.

Data submitted by: Ken Keene, Lynn Gardner, Lani and Ned Rosenberger.

**16
Total Mayhem on
Superbowl Sunday**

**Wild Times in Melrose,
Massachusetts**

Location: The house is situated at 39 Linden Road in Melrose, a working-class town about a half hour north of Boston.

Description of place: A big barn of a three-story, brown, clapboard house, in a dilapidated state of repair. Once probably a single-family house, it is now cut up into apartments. On the day of my visit, empty beer cans decorated the lawn. As one enters the side door, one is confronted with a large metal sign, possibly purloined from some construction site, propped against the wall, stating DANGER, KEEP OUT. "Aw, somebody put that there last year," says Dave Fortier, one of the three live people in this chapter. "That was *last* year," he adds, the implication being that life in the big old house isn't quite as wild as it used to be, at least as far as he's concerned. The occupants of another apartment, he explains, threw the cans there, and as he gathers them up he grumbles that if this keeps on he's going to start turning the cans in for the refunds himself.

Fortier, who lives in an apartment on the second floor, is a tall, blond, good-looking man who looks younger than his thirty-three years. He's a carpenter but fell twenty-five feet on a job five years ago and has not worked since. He seems vigorous but points out long surgical scars on his legs. Sometimes, he said, he wears braces.

Dave Fortier. PHOTO BY ARTHUR MYERS

Ghostly manifestations: The big explosion, Fortier relates, happened two years before on Superbowl Sunday 1987. He and a friend, Mike Costello, who lived in the third-floor apartment, had gone to a friend's house to watch the game on TV. "We came home," Fortier relates, "and it was like total mayhem around here. Mike's apartment and mine were totally disrupted. Every drawer was pulled out. If a door had been open, it was closed."

The star performance involved a set of French doors in Costello's apartment. The doors separate the bedroom from the living room, and Costello always kept them open, flat against the wall. Blocking the doors from being closed was a couch, an end table, and a TV set. Wall-to-wall carpeting covered the floor and under normal conditions would prevent the doors from being swung closed.

"I put the rug down myself," Fortier says. "It was tacked down, with padding. Well, Mike comes in, and these doors are closed. He freaked out. He came down here white as a sheet. Whatever had done it had never moved the rug, and you couldn't close the doors with that carpet there. I went up and looked for drag marks. I looked to see if they knocked off the door pins. I looked to see if the screws were taken out. Nothing. And it was freezing up there."

Costello says, "I had a statue of Jesus on the dresser in my bedroom. Over my kitchen sink I had four or five beer bottles lined up. The statue of Jesus ended up over the kitchen sink in the middle of all the beer bottles. I had the front door locked with a safety chain. We were sitting there among all the debris, and I said, 'This looks like some kind of a big hoax.' As soon as I said that, we heard the front door open and close again. We went out there and the door was locked and there was still a chain on it, but there was a hole in the wall where the door handle had slammed against it."

The night of the Superbowl game was just the culmination of many strange happenings, according to Dave and Mike. They both had heard constant footsteps on the stairs. "It didn't matter if we were having a party or not," Dave says. "I could be here with my girlfriend, he could be in his place with his girlfriend, or we could be alone—it didn't matter. You would hear footsteps coming up the stairs. People in my place would go and answer the door. I'd say, 'Don't bother, there's no one there.' I'd be sitting here and BAM!—that door would slam. My telephone would ring. I'd go answer the phone, and the doorbell would ring. No one on the phone, no one at the door.

"They did a lot of electricity stuff. They would make bulbs go on and off. I put a medicine chest in Mike's apartment. It has a strip light across the top, but I never wired it. A friend came in, and the kid goes into the bathroom and flips the switch on the wall, the one for the overhead light. But the light on the medicine chest comes on. And it was a dead end wire. They messed with my stereo, they messed with Mike's stereo. All of a sudden, like two in the morning, the stereo would come on blasting."

Mike had set up the basement as a little bar, and constant manifestations ensued in this grotto of delight. Pipes would bang—in the summer, when no heat was on. A rocking chair would rock with nobody visible in it. "Something was always strange around here," Dave says. "I've lived in this apartment about seven years, but before that I lived downstairs with a kid, Bob Bryant. We'd be working on our motorcycles in the cellar, and all of a sudden there'd be an air—I mean a strange something. You'd feel like something was there. Bob wasn't surprised when he heard what happened to Mike and me. He wasn't surprised at all."

Did other tenants of the building have unusual experiences? At first Fortier said they had not, but when pressed he seemed less certain. "The girl downstairs just doesn't want to know about it," he said. "She won't talk about it. She's frightened." The couple in the apartment next door hasn't had any experiences, as far as Dave knows, and the young man who now lives in Mike Costello's apartment hasn't either. Dave and Mike seem to have been the main target.

Psychic Juliana Kallas.

Investigations: Mike had a Ouija board in his closet, left by his sister, who had formerly lived in the apartment. He had never used it. "I had never even seen one before," Dave says. "We put it on the table, and Mike goes to touch the little thing that moves around. His fingers get about two inches from it and it goes— eeeeep!—right off the board. The thing skated right off the board. We got it back, and it goes to the letter L, then starts going nuts again."

Dave and Mike kept working with the Ouija board that night and say they contacted two spirits. "One," says Mike, "was a lady who had died in the apartment I was living in. She said she was there to watch over the house. The other was the one who did all the destruction and moving things around. We could feel the difference between the two spirits, the difference in the power. With the lady it was moving around real slow, and with the guy it was zipping around the board."

At this point, the boys began to feel this was no job for amateurs. They knew a professional psychic, Juliana Kallas, who lived in nearby Salem. She had once come to a party at their house but had sensed a great deal of negativity and said she wouldn't be back. When Mike and Dave called her she warned them to stay away from the Ouija board, that it was dangerous, and that she would be over the next night.

When she arrived, she meditated with Dave and Mike. "I picked up the energy of this man," she told me, "who was very upset at the way the house was being treated. I want to say he was a carpenter, but I'm not sure. Let's just say he did work on the house. He took great pride in the house and didn't like the vibration that was there now. He was literally raving mad at how they were treating his property—he felt it was still his property—the kind of lifestyle that they were living. I conveyed this to Mike and Dave. I can't remember what they said—whether they were going to tone things down or what. When Mike got married and lived up there with his wife and had a baby, the energy totally changed. All the incidents seemed to go away. The spirit I picked up was a man who seemed to be in his thirties or forties. He looked like the 1800s to me. He looked like a man who worked with his hands—and he was big. I also at times felt a woman, but she was more mellow."

Juliana suggested that the boys put salt in the doorways of each room of their apartments. When I asked her if she had known of such things as doors swinging through solid objects, she said she has not seen such phenomena but had heard of them.

History: The present owner of the building has no idea of its history, only that he acquired it from a real estate agency that had bought it shortly before from a little old lady. The assessor's office in Melrose says the house was built in 1894 but has no idea by whom. The public library offers the information, gleaned from the town directory, that many people have lived at the house. "No one stayed long at that address," the librarian said. "I don't know the reason."

Identities of ghosts: Seemingly a man who either owned or had some sort of interest in the house and who didn't like the current goings-on there. There was also the quiet spirit, the woman who had died in Costello's apartment at some time in the past.

Personalities of ghosts: The man, "raving mad;" the woman, "more mellow."

Witnesses: Dave Fortier and Mike Costello, Juliana Kallas, various other people who have visited the house.

Best time to witness: If this were a couple of years ago, the best bet might have been to get invited to one of Dave and Mike's parties.

Still haunted?: Since Dave and Mike have reformed, the house seems to have quieted down.

Data submitted by: David Fortier, Mike Costello, Juliana Kallas.

**17
Knock, Knock,
Who's There? The
Playful Ghosts**

The Dillingham House
in Sandwich, Cape Cod,
Massachusetts

Location: The Dillingham House is situated at 71 Old Main Street in the quaint, historic village of Sandwich, on the North Shore of Cape Cod.

Description of place: A three-story wooden house, now empty. Dugan Realty of Sandwich, currently seeking a buyer who doesn't mind the odd rap or apparition, states in a brochure, "This gracious home would make a lovely B & B or spacious family home."

Ghostly manifestations: The place has long had a reputation for being haunted. Police are constantly responding to burglar alarms there, possibly set off by the milling about of unearthly residents. One local policeman, Jim Foley, who has several times answered alarms in the dead of night, wrote in the town archives the following evaluation of his experiences: "It is highly recommended that any officer entering this house act according to his or her feelings. In other words, if you feel like running, please do so. Screaming will also be allowed. It is requested, however, that upon exiting the house you at least slow down long enough to open the door and not go through it."

The Dillingham House. PHOTO BY ARTHUR MYERS

Chrystal LaPine is a former cop. She is a small, attractive, very feminine-appearing woman of thirty-two, who served as an officer with the Sandwich police force for ten years, until she retired to raise a family. She gives the following account of a night at the Dillingham House: "I didn't tell anybody what happened at the Dillingham House for a long, long time. I kept it pretty much to myself, except for my husband and my mother.

"One night, it must have been in '80 or '81, I got a call to go to the house for a burglar alarm. I pulled into the drive, got out of the cruiser, and went to the door. The door was locked, and I remembered I didn't have a flashlight with me. So I went back to the cruiser to get my flashlight, and as I turned around to go back into the house all the lights had come on upstairs, and the front door was open. I didn't let it bother me. I kept making up excuses in my head.

"I went inside the house and started to walk around. As you first go in there's a little kitchen, and as I was walking through there the microwave came on. I thought, well, that's certainly strange. I walked on through to the living room. I could hear rustling noises, and I looked over to the windows. All the curtains were blowing back and forth. I looked around to see if I'd left a door open or if any windows were open, but I couldn't see anything open. I opened a door and looked down into the cellar, and I decided I was *not* going to go down into that cellar. No, no, no, no!"

Chrystal thought she could hear footsteps upstairs, and unlike the course of action most of us would take at this point, she ran up to investigate. She found nothing, but she could hear further developments downstairs—a creaking noise, like a rocking chair. In the meantime, her backup, the aforementioned Officer Foley, had shown up and begun walking around the house. He looked into the living room window and saw a rocking chair rocking back and forth, empty of an occupant.

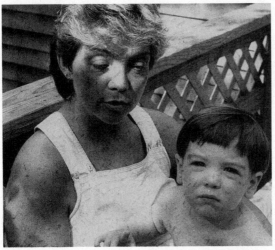

Chrystal LaPine and son Joshua.

PHOTO BY ARTHUR MYERS

"There was nothing really dramatic," Chrystal says, "just enough. Enough to scare the pants off you at three or four o'clock in the morning, that's for sure."

The Bryden family moved down to Sandwich about

twenty years ago from Boston's South Shore and lived in the Dillingham House for three years. The materfamilias, Marilyn Bryden, now lives in a modern house in Sandwich. She says, "We'd lived in another old house in town in which strange things happened, and after living in those two old houses I decided I was going to make my own memories in a much newer house and not live in old houses with other people's memories."

She and her husband bought the Dillingham House from a friend—"She never breathed a word to me," she comments. Any Bryden—in fact, probably any former resident who has no current financial interest in reselling the house—has stories to tell. One of the most articulate is the eldest of the Bryden sons, Willard, who is forty-two. He says, "My first experience there was when I was about nineteen, when my parents were buying the house. My mother and I rode down to see the house. We pulled into the driveway, and my mother went in to meet with the people who owned the place. I saw a little girl looking at me out the window on the top floor. A couple of minutes later I was invited in too, and we went through the whole house and I didn't see anybody. I asked about the little girl, and they said there was no little girl.

"The first weekend I was there I slept on the third floor. There's a bathroom on the third floor, with one of those string-pull lights. I was sitting there, and all of a sudden the cord started to move and the light went off. I pulled the cord and put it back on. And it went back off again. And I pulled it on. This time I held onto the cord. Then the latch door opened and shut, as though someone had entered or exited, which was quite exciting.

"Later on I went to bed. My fiancée was staying downstairs. No sooner did I turn off the light when I heard someone walk into the room. I didn't know if it was my fiancée or what was going on. I turned on the light, and there was nobody there. I turned off the light—and footsteps again. And it just kept going on and on and on. I'd turn off the light—they'd start. I'd turn it on—they'd stop. It sounded like someone was walking around the bed. I went downstairs and talked with my fiancée and her brother and my parents, and they said they could hear the footsteps downstairs. What happened is that I slept up there with the light on.

"The bathroom lights was an on-going thing. They seemed to like me when I went into the bathroom, but it happened to other people too in the bathrooms on the second and third floors."

Rappings were a big feature of the house, Willard Bryden says. "Constantly, there was someone with you. It was as though someone else was living there at the same time. We used to go up and down the back hallway, and we'd rap on the wall and they'd rap back. This would happen anytime you wanted to do it. You could do it for friends—anyone who was there."

Bryden feels there was a childlike quality to many of the manifestations. At one time, according to town historians, a family of children lived there without adults. There are carvings on the back staircase that are dated over a hundred years ago. However, Bryden tells of seeing, with his younger brother, Rick, an apparition of an adult man. "We were standing at the foot of the stairs, and we saw a man go by in the corridor at the top of the stairs. He looked as human as anybody else, but I went up to see who it was and there was nobody there. He was in a suit, a fairly modern-looking suit. He didn't pay any attention to us whatsoever."

It's always nice to get the local animal reaction in accounts like this, and Willard says the two family dogs would not go upstairs except under extreme duress. "One was a collie," he says. "If you'd carry her up the stairs, she would just cower and tremble and go tearing back down the stairs again the moment you put her down."

Both Willard and Marilyn Bryden tell of latches going up and down and doors opening and closing with no perceptible human agency. "That went on all the time," says Willard. "It was an active house. After a while you just learned to live with it."

History: A plaque proclaiming that the house dates from 1650 hangs in front, but former Sandwich archivist Russell Lovell says this is in error, that the house was originally built about 1790 in the nearby village of Sagamore. In 1810, he says, it was moved about a mile to its present location.

The house remained in the Dillingham family until the twentieth century. In 1813 the resident owner, Branch Dillingham, committed suicide. His wife, Ruth, died a few weeks later, of causes that are unrecorded. They left nine children, who seem to have lived there by themselves, under supervision of the older siblings, who were teenagers.

Identities of ghosts: The indications are that many of the manifestations, particularly the responsive rappings, are caused by the spirits of children. Most of the children of Branch and Ruth Dillingham lived long lives; one lived to be a centenarian. But a psychic told me that after death they may have reverted to the time of their childhood: "Those were their happy years; they're reliving their lives when they were together and happy."

Personalities of ghosts: Willard Bryden puts it this way: "The house was a fairly friendly place. The ghosts were just there; they weren't doing anything hostile or even particularly scary if you were used to it."

Witnesses: Sandwich police officers, the Bryden family, other residents and visitors. "Even now," Willard Bryden says, "the neighbors insist that they hear noises and see lights go on and off." Marilyn Bryden tells of a sister-in-law who, given use of the house for the winter when the Brydens first bought the place, left after two nights. Marilyn says, "She wouldn't go back in the house even if we were there."

Best time to witness: It seems to be a twenty-four-hour operation.

Still haunted?: Seems to be.

Investigations: No formal psychic inquiries were reported.

Data submitted by: Members of the Bryden family; Sandwich police officers Chrystal LaPine and Jim Foley; Russell Lovell, former town archivist; Barbara Gill, current town archivist.

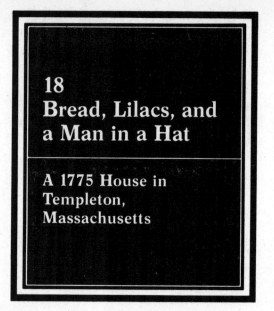

18
Bread, Lilacs, and a Man in a Hat

A 1775 House in Templeton, Massachusetts

Location: Templeton is a village about fifty miles west of Boston. The house, owned by an elderly couple, Al and Adeline Whitaker, is on Athol Road, a couple of miles out of town. The Whitakers are antiques dealers; there is a sign by the road in front of the house. Their shop is an adjacent one-story building, and the house itself is full of antiques. The Whitakers are friendly people who seem to like to talk about their experiences with haunts in their old house.

Description of place: A three-story, wooden house, dating from the Revolutionary War. It is strikingly similar to the Dillingham House in Sandwich, Massachusetts, also built around that time. "We've got the original wainscoting and paneling," Al Whitaker said, "and there used to be a ballroom up there." At one point during my visit, Al took me upstairs and showed me a small room under the stairs leading to the attic that he said was once a stop on the Underground Railway of pre–Civil War times.

Ghostly manifestations: "I'm a disbeliever, frankly,"

128

The Whitaker home. PHOTO BY ARTHUR MYERS

says Whitaker, who is eighty but looks much younger. "But I can't account for some of the things that have happened here. To start with, at times you can smell flowers all through the kitchen."

"We smell lilacs in the den," Adeline says.

"You mean in the kitchen," Al says.

Adeline smiles. "Well, they're supposed to be in the den."

"One time," Al continues, "my wife woke up in the front bedroom, and a man was standing in front of the bed with a tricorner hat, one of those early hats."

"He seemed to be peering at me," Adeline says.

"She just lay there and looked back," Al says. "He was apparently not trying to do anything. He was just standing there, and all of a sudden he just disappeared. Now my wife is not the type of person who believes in this stuff, either. And I'm like an attorney—I have to have proof. It's not enough proof that my wife says she saw something.

"I'm not much of a Bible believer because I have to have proof. But once I saw an angel hovering over my daughter's bed. She was about fifteen at the time, a good many years ago. I said to myself, hey, I'm sleeping, I'm still half asleep. I was going to the bathroom. So I went to the bathroom and I came back and I knew I was awake, and I looked and it was still there. It looked like an angel."

"Did it have wings?" I asked.

"I don't recall that it had wings. It was just stationary, right over her head."

"Was it male or female?"

"I wasn't able to tell. I didn't get that close."

Al tells of hearing footsteps walking up and down the stairs, when nobody is around except him and his wife. One of their middle-aged children, Chuck, also said he has heard such footsteps. The other children deny knowledge of anything out of the ordinary. The oldest son, Dr. Albert H. Whitaker, Jr., is the archivist of the commonwealth of Massachusetts, and I was hoping for some good tales. I was disappointed, however. "I never enjoyed the experiences that my mother and father did," he said. "I'm not a skeptic. I don't scoff at people who have had psychic experiences. I wish I could say I've had such experiences, but I haven't."

"I don't know what the hell it is," Al Sr. said, "but they're there. And I'm pretty much of a disbeliever in that sort of thing."

The Whitakers say a number of their visiting friends have had psychic experiences in the house. One, Bud (Henry Clay) Foster of Wexfield, Pennsylvania, told of seeing a ghostly man at the foot of a bed. Bud had died a few months before I began to research this chapter, but I interviewed his wife, Tommy.

"I wasn't aware of things going on at the Whitakers,'" she said, "but Bud was. He spoke of seeing a man in the bedroom upstairs. When he mentioned it to the Whitakers the next morning they said it wasn't unusual, that they'd had experiences there. Bud just shrugged it off. He was used to this sort of thing."

They occurred constantly, she said, in Bud's child-

Al and Adeline Whitaker. PHOTO BY ARTHUR MYERS

hood home and in their house in Wexfield. "Bud was psychic," Tommy said. "He experienced things I didn't see. Our house is furnished with eighteenth-century furniture. One time he walked into a guest bedroom. There was a connecting bathroom, and he walked through. And there was a woman lying on the bed. She looked up. He didn't recognize her. Then she disappeared. Bud was very psychic. I'm not surprised he saw things at the Whitakers.' "

My star witness, it turned out, was the man who owned the house prior to the Whitakers. He is Thor Carlson, an accomplished artist who now lives in Charleston, New Hampshire. Carlson is a graduate in fine arts from Yale; he studied in Florence, Italy, under a Fulbright grant. He has sold paintings to such varied celebrities as Vincent Price and the late Eamon de Valera of Ireland.

Carlson sold the house to the Whitakers in the early 1960s. "We did not tell the Whitakers anything about the house," he said. "While we had the house up for sale my wife and I decided we wouldn't talk about such things, because people get really put off by it. It was they who came to us within a month and started telling us what was going on, and we told them what experiences *we* had had.

Carlson bought the house in 1958. It had, at that time, been cut up into four apartments. He married shortly afterward, and as he and his wife began restoring the house a lot of strange things started happening.

"But even before that," Carlson said, "the day I passed papers on the house, I had a snoopy aunt who wanted to see what the house was like, and something pushed her as she was peeking in the windows in the back and she fell and broke her arm. She was going to try to sue me, but I didn't own the house when this happened. That was the first thing, the first indication of anything going on.

"In each of the rooms there were pitchers of holy water on the mantels and pictures of the pope all over the house. I didn't think too much of it at the time, but a number of years later, after I had sold the house, I was doing some private teaching. One of the women who came for lessons had worked at the mental hospital in Gardner, and she told me about the woman who had owned the house before me. I had never met her; I bought the house from her estate. She had been declared *non compos*. At any rate, they thought she was just raving mad when she told of all the things that had happened in the house and how frightened she was of it. So that sort of fit the pattern as to why the holy water was around. She was a French-Canadian.

"My wife and I had a lot of experiences of odors—the smell of lilacs in January or the smell of baking bread. There had once been a large oven in the kitchen. While I was living there alone I heard this terrible rapping noise in the main hall. It woke me out of my sleep. I had two cats and they rushed right off, so I knew it wasn't just me hearing it. It was as though somebody had a cane and was slamming it against the wall in the center hall.

"We got a lot of manifestations when we began renovating but nothing negative. I think there was a sense of approval that the house was coming back to what it had been. The smells became much more frequent and noticeable, for one thing.

"One time some friends came for a visit and brought their two-year-old daughter. She was walking, but she couldn't talk yet—that is, so you could understand her. We were sitting in the parlor and the little girl was out in the hall babbling away and looking up the stairs at somebody, with a big smile. It was obvious that there was someone conversing with her. She kept running back in to us and laughing and then running back out again. This went on for some time.

"A couple of our friends had experiences. We had a guest room, and in one case our friend, a man, was in the room and the door swung open. It was a door that normally swung the other way because of the pitch of the floor, so it wasn't just gravity pulling it; it was swinging against gravity.

"The other case was a woman friend who had just broken an emotional attachment, and my wife was commiserating with her. Our friend felt someone put an arm around her as if to console her.

"I have a certain psychic sense myself, and I had a couple of experiences with my father, seeing him. He had died about a year before we sold the place. He was a carpenter, and the smell of fresh wood would permeate the place every now and then. We had a close friend who was quite psychic, and she saw things in the house. She described apparitions of my great-uncle. He was very good to me as a child, so it's not surprising he would be around."

History: The house was built by Ebenezer Goodrich and is still referred to in Templeton as the Goodrich house. Goodrich was a prosperous tanner, who probably made his money during the Revolutionary War. He built the house for four hundred pounds sterling, a considerable amount of money in those days. The original land grant was one hundred acres. Goodrich had four children, one of whom became a miniature painter who studied in Boston with John Singleton Copley, the most famous painter of the time. Two of the others became piano and organ builders.

Identities of ghosts: Could the man at the foot of the bed have been Ebenezer Goodrich, known as Captain Goodrich in those parts? It kind of depends on the hat. Thor Carlson suspects that the man Adeline Whitaker and Bud Foster saw was his father. "From their description," Carlson said, "I know that's who it was. My father often wore a felt hat and a long coat, and that was their description." When told that Adeline had described the man as wearing a tricornered hat, he replied, "Well, that's an addition to the story from the last time I heard it." Could it have been two different ghosts with two different hats?

Carlson has theories about the other entities. "I always had the impression," he said, "that they might be some of the women who had lived in the house. There was a mother and daughter who lived in the house, and they had a very unhappy relationship. I think that at three different times women owned the house, and it was through some catastrophes that that came about. It seems that each time this happened the women were declared *non compos*, and the management of their affairs was taken over by somebody else."

Al Whitaker said, "Someone told me that one of them is a little girl about nine or ten years old. She died here many, many years ago." Could that be the entity that the two-year-old in Thor Carlson's account was conversing with so merrily? That little girl, incidentally, Carlson said, is now married and in her thirties, and the house she lives in is haunted. So perhaps she is a psychic person who sees a dimension that most of us don't see.

Personalities of ghosts: "Nothing has ever tried to hurt me or my wife," says Al Whitaker. Possibly Thor

Carlson's aunt might have a different impression.

Witnesses: Al and Adeline Whitaker; Chuck Whitaker; Thor Carlson and his wife, not to mention his unfortunate aunt; Bud Foster; various other visitors to the house.

Best time to witness: Most of the manifestations described seem to have happened at night.

Still haunted?: "We haven't had any experiences for several years," Al Whitaker says, "but I can't remember worth a damn, and my wife is worse than I am."

Investigations: Apparently no formal psychic investigations.

Data submitted by: Al and Adeline Whitaker and their children, Thor Carlson, Tommy (Nyla) Foster.

**19
The Haunted
Movie Theater**

A Modern, Multiple-
Auditorium Theater in
Tupelo, Mississippi

Location: The theater is on Cliff Gookin Boulevard, on the outskirts of Tupelo, a city of about twenty-four thousand in northeastern Mississippi.

Description of place: The theater was put up in the late 1960s, a square, cement block building that originally housed two auditoriums and was called the Tupelo Twin. During the time covered in this account, the mid-1980s, it was expanded to four auditoriums and the name was changed to the Tupelo Quartet. It now contains seven auditoriums and is called the Tupelo Seven.

Ghostly manifestations: An intriguing, even unsettling, aspect of this story is that the primary informant, Mike Curtis, is a man who is currently a freelance writer for comic books, and one of his chief outlets is the Casper the Ghost books. I couldn't help wondering when I began my investigation where fact ended and fancy began. But as I interviewed Curtis, his former wife, his daughter, and various other people, it became more and more apparent that something strange was indeed going on in this neighborhood movie house.

Mike was manager of the Tupelo Twin, which became the Tupelo Quartet during his stewardship, in 1984 and 1985. "We figured when the construction took place we'd lose the ghost," Mike says, "but we didn't."

Mike, who now lives in Conway, Arkansas, where he grinds out adventures for Casper, was the first person I contacted. I had noticed a short article by him on the theater in *Fate* magazine. But perhaps the most vivid accounts were given by his ex-wife, Vicki Gillard, and nineteen-year-old daughter, Ann Gillard.

Mike Curtis.

(Incidentally, mother and daughter have the same name because they married brothers. Does that make them sisters-in-law? Keep reading; this chapter is filled with offbeat little touches.)

Possibly the reason Vicki and Ann were so aware of spooky doings at the Tupelo is that they are apparently very psychic. One of their accomplishments is that they do not have to be together to speak to each other. All they have to do, they say, is think of each other. Once mental contact is established, however, it seems it does help to go to a phone and call the other person.

Vicki is now a theater manager in the Washington, D.C., area. She enthusiastically supported Mike's story.

"I don't know what it was," Vicki led off, "but something wasn't right in that theater." She told of an adventure she had with their Doberman pinscher, Raven, who is also psychic.

"One night," she related, "I went to the theater to clean it, and I took Raven along because I didn't like going there alone at night. Everything was OK downstairs, and I started to go upstairs to check the projection booth. When I started up the stairs, every hair on that Doberman's back stood up. I didn't hear or see anything, but she started growling and showing her teeth, and that's something this dog never does. But she just went crazy that night. I had her on a chain and had the chain wrapped around my hand. That dog tore the chain off my hand and just cut my hand all up. She took off and she hit the heavy glass front door so hard that she shoved that thing open—and those things aren't easy to open. She ran outside, clear down to the road. I finally caught up to her and got her into the car. I went back into the theater because I had to turn the lights out and lock the door. She would not get out of the car, so I didn't even try getting her out. She stayed in the car, and she barked, and she howled, and she growled the whole time I was in the theater. I could hear her while I was inside; I had left the door open— I wasn't going in there with the door closed. And I had to take her home. The next night I took her and she never did a thing. It wasn't that she was frightened of the theater, because she was in the theater almost every night with me."

I asked Vicki if she had checked to see if anyone was in the theater, and she said she hadn't, but added, "Raven wasn't afraid of people; she wouldn't have barked and growled at a person."

Vicki had another dog story to offer, one Mike also told me. He said she had opened a closet in the projection booth and could hear the sound of dogs barking. Vicki concurred, "Yes, there were dogs barking. My sister was with me that night. You'd close the broom closet and you wouldn't hear anything. Open it and it would sound like seven or eight dogs barking. It was just your normal closet; all it had in it was brooms and a utility sink. It just happened that one time."

Vicki and Ann gave me similar versions of the moving-curtain story that Mike had originally told me. The fact that when interviewed Vicki was in Maryland, Mike in Arkansas, and Ann in Tupelo buttressed these accounts, which never conflicted factually.

"One night," Vicki related, "my daughter, when she was around eleven, was playing down near the screen. She yelled, 'Mom, there's no ghost here, this is crazy.' You know how kids are. I went upstairs, and I heard her scream. I ran downstairs and she said, 'Mom, Mom, the curtains are moving, the curtains are moving!' Those curtains are so heavy there's no way a breeze could move them, but they were swaying. She was screaming and crying and running up the aisle. There was something behind her, making coughing, weird sounds. It was like following her, and she just ran screaming out of the auditorium."

I asked Vicki if she checked behind the curtain to make sure there was no live person there, and she said she had.

Mike, Vicki, and Ann all told me about ghostly laughter they heard while previewing the film *Sweet Dreams*. He routinely checked films before showing them to make sure everything was in order. The viewers, according to Ann, also included a doorman and janitor, George Faught, and his ex-wife, Mary.

In his *Fate* article, Mike says it sounded as though the laughter was coming from about three rows back, but there was nobody else in the auditorium. It happened throughout the film, Ann told me, even though nothing funny was happening on screen.

When I asked Bill Towery, the present manager of the theater, if he'd ever noticed anything strange, he replied, "No, not really. I think Mike has a pretty vivid imagination. He would have *loved* for the place to be haunted."

Towery worked hard at trying to tout me onto another theater in town, the Lyric. "That would be a more likely place," he argued and went on to relate various rumors. However, several weeks before, I had checked out the Lyric pretty thoroughly and given up; I had been unable to find anyone who had witnessed anything firsthand or who could even pass me on to someone who had. I had investigated the old Lyric by accident. I had originally seen Mike's article and filed it—actually lost it—and I just got mixed up with the wrong theater. I had already scratched the Tupelo, Mississippi, mission when I found the article and discovered I had zeroed in on the wrong place. Instead of the creepy, romantic old Lyric, it was this modern, prosaic, cement-block movie house that was spooked!

Mike retold a story about George Faught, the doorman-janitor, that he had put in his article. "One night," Mike said, "George was cleaning, and he sat down in a seat. He's very nervous, kind of like a Don Knotts–type character. Another seat nearby went down. This had evidently happened before. This time he didn't get scared; he just cursed and hollered at it and the seat went up, and this sort of thing never bothered him again."

I contacted Faught, who still works at the theater, and found him a rather reluctant witness:

Did the seat actually go down?

"Yeah, that was a long time ago," Faught replied.

But it really happened?

"Well, I couldn't really tell you that because I was pretty tired. I could've just imagined it."

Did it happen a number of times?

"No, it just happened that one time, and I was real tired that night; I'd been up about thirty-six hours. So I couldn't definitely tell you on that."

Did the seat move?

"It seemed to be moving."

Did it actually go down?

"Yeah, it seemed to, yeah."

Was there a movie going on?

"No, I was cleaning up that night late. I was resting on a break."

Did you have any other experiences in the theater?

"No sir, I never did. That's about the only one I had."

According to Mike Curtis, a constant phenomenon was footsteps upstairs in the projection booth–storage room, as well as voices. "We heard two or three voices at different times," he said. "After a while everyone got used to it, and we weren't scared anymore. We would just try to understand what they were saying, but we could never make it out clearly."

Now and then Vicki and her daughter or her sister would be cleaning up late at night and the spooky voices would get to be too much; they'd bolt for the parking lot till things quieted down or they got their courage up, whichever came first.

History: The building dates from the late 1960s, with two additions during the 1980s. Mike relates that he researched the site to see if he could get a hint on where the ghosts came from but that it had just been woodland.

Identities of ghosts: Definitely up for grabs. Mike speculates that there might have been an Indian burial ground in the nearby woods or that someone might have been killed on the site. Also, a young woman box-office employee had been killed in an auto accident,

Mike says, and for a time he suspected her, but then he was told that the manifestations well preceded her death. Vicki mentioned a former manager, now deceased, but the same consideration, reports of happenings predating his death, seem to apply.

Mike, warming up, mentioned a theater in Memphis that is believed to be haunted by a ghost named Mary who had nothing to do with the place in life—she just likes movies. He speculated that the Tupelo theater ghosts may just hang around because they like it.

And then there is the dummy coffin.

"One thing may have aggravated it," Mike said pensively, "I don't know if it did or didn't. I kept a coffin up there in the projection room."

A coffin?

It seems Mike had a sideline; he sometimes set up "ghost houses." He would provide them for the local police department on Halloween, at a community center, for example. He also used to use the coffin when he'd set up a display at the theater, to promote a horror show.

"This is what they call a shipping casket," he explained. "Basically it's a dummy, a plywood casket covered with gray felt and with tin handles. It looks like a nice casket. I understand some people have been buried in those things. It's something that's very cheap, and they ship corpses across the country in them. After ten or twelve times they consider it unsanitary and dispose of it.

"I bought a used one for ten bucks and used it for displays. This one had been used, all right. There was blood on the pillow, for that matter. It may have aggravated whatever was there, but the thing is that we heard reports of noises and things from people who worked at the theater before we ever got there, so whatever it was had apparently been around a while. I kept the coffin upstairs in the booth on occasion and sometimes down in the lobby on display, but I also had it in my own houses, and nothing was ever agitated there."

Could Mike be making a "ghost house" out of the theater, I hinted delicately. His reply: "I've been scaring people in spook houses for years, but if I was making this up I think I'd make it a little more scary than it was. It was interesting; it was just kind of fun to have, a haunted theater."

Personalities of ghosts: "They seem playful and seem to be fascinated by the machines," Mike says. A great deal of footstep-and-mumbling activity seems to be concentrated in the projection room.

Witnesses: Mike Curtis, Vicki Gillard, Ann Gillard, Raven the Doberman, Vicki's sister, George Faught, various people who worked at the theater, and possibly some who just go to the movies.

Best time to witness: "In the late hours, after midnight," Mike says, "and sometimes early afternoon. I'd come in early and start setting up for the five o'clock show. I'd be in the concession stand, and I'd hear things walking around up there in the booth. Of course, things may have been going on with the customers there, but you wouldn't be able to distinguish it."

Still haunted?: Mike says he doesn't know. Current employees tend to deny everything.

Investigations: During Mike's tenure, some employees of the theater held a séance in the projection room. According to Ann Gillard, who was not at the séance, "They used a Ouija board. They thought an Indian came through who had something to do with some burial ground around there."

The séance was held on a Wednesday. The spirit was supposed to have said that the projectors would not work on the following Saturday. Mike reports that this happened, although he did not know about the séance till some time later, after his experience with the disabled projectors. He found that the fuses had been turned off, although no one had been in the projection room but him. This happened frequently after that, he reported in his *Fate* article. "Apparently," he wrote, "the ghost liked playing with projectors."

Data submitted by: Interviews with Mike Curtis, Vicki Gillard, Ann Gillard, George Faught, Bill Towery, various other employees of the theater. Short article by Mike Curtis in the October 1988 issue of *Fate* magazine.

**20
The Phantom
Steamboat of the
Missouri River**

Bucking the Current
Where the Missouri and
Osage Meet

Location: The confluence of the Missouri and Osage rivers, about twenty miles down the Missouri from Jefferson City, the state capitol.

Description of sighting: An apparition of an early steamboat.

Ghostly manifestation: "I was down there fishing when I saw it," says Russ Hawkins, the man who says he saw this ghostly boat. He had been described to me as a good old country boy, and he sported a down-home accent as thick as that of a character actor in a Hollywood movie of the life and times of Daniel Boone. This is Boone country we're talking here.

I asked if he'd seen other apparitions. Russ replied, "Oh, I can spend all day telling about the apparitions I've seen, but very few people believe it, because they don't manifest themselves with any degree of regularity. You can't set your watch by them. They can show up spontaneously and never ever be seen again. People are loathe to talk about anything like that around here. I'm considered very unique and maybe some sort of unadulterated nut. I don't give a damn. I tell it the way it is, and that's all."

Russ is a retired farmer and sometime mechanic, just turned seventy. He lives in a trapper's cabin about six miles from the village of Ashland. "My wife lives in town," he says. "My cabin is not a place that any woman would be proud to live in. But it's highly practical for the dogs and me. I'm home most of the time. If it's pretty weather I may be out with the dogs, taking a pot shot at something, whether it needs it or not."

How about that boat?

"It was just after dusk when I saw this boat," Russ said. "It was about ten years ago. It was dark, but it was a moonlit night, and I did behold an apparition of an old-fashioned boat, a steamer, with a different propulsion system from what exists now. The boat was pushing right on up the river. I couldn't hardly believe my eyes at all. I realized the thing was floating four feet above water level. Most of those things seem to hold to the same level of their time."

Has anybody else seen this boat?

"Well," Russ says, "I spoke the next morning to some old-timers on the dock and they said they'd never seen it, but they had heard of men who had. And they described it in great detail from a secondhand point-of-view, and it was just exactly what I saw.

Russ Hawkins.

"It was a unique craft. You could tell that the thing was one of the old-timers. It was just about what people who didn't know anything about steam navigation would have started up on, you know, and just kept on climbing. Apparently it had two pistons that came off a steam bore. I guess it was a low-pressure bore. It had to be. And these things pushed duck feet, first one and then the other, right and left, right and left. And these feet opened up, like a duck's foot, and got a purchase against the water. And then they'd drag them forward and they'd get another bite. They were real slow. It was just like a duck swimming. But the principle seemed to be real good, with the exception, of course, that you couldn't get much power unleashed. But you could push against the current that way. This thing was going up the Missouri.

"I've had many sightings of things as far out as that, but that just struck me because I was always a mechanic anyways, you see, and I was always interested in things such as that. I went home and started drawing out some plans about how the thing had been built. And I realized it was just the rudiments of a steamboat, the very rudiments, that's all. I'd say five pounds of steam would operate the thing.

"I saw people on the boat. It appeared to be a passenger boat. It was one of the few apparitions I ever saw that I heard the noise of the equipment. I could hear the machines working. Most of the time, you just see a fleeting glimpse. But this was much clearer than most apparitions. Most of them are translucent, you know, but this one wasn't; it was solid and you could hear the sounds of the machinery a-goin'. I didn't count the people, but I would say there were ten or twelve. I don't know how they were dressed. I didn't give it that good a look, the thing was too spontaneous. I wasn't ready for it.

"After it got about a hundred yards from me, I realized it wasn't touching the water. It went right by me. It was a-ridin' the same level it rode in its time, you know. I'd say I watched it three or four minutes. It was struggling against the current. Then it disappeared. I wouldn't say it passed into another dimension and was gone, or anything like that. It just got out of sight. It was after dark, you know. It was a moonlit night, but it was dark.

"I've gone down there many times, even went down the same night of the year, but I never could bring it back again."

History: Bill Crawford, president of the Boone County Historical Society, in Ashland, was skeptical of the phantom steamboat but was a fount of information on historical steamboating on the Missouri. From *History of Boone County*, he read me a passage on the arrival of the first steamboat in those parts. According to that tome, the steamer *Independence* was the first to attempt navigation of the river, and it first docked thereabouts in 1819. If a phantom boat is something of a legend in Boone County, Crawford hadn't heard of it. But then he said he hadn't heard of Russ Hawkins, either.

But Melody Nichols, a reporter on the *Boone County Journal*, had heard of Russ. "He used to be a maintenance man at school," she said. "He's been around here forever. I like Russell. My mother was raised down next to him. Russell's quite a character. You've got to really know him to appreciate him."

She couldn't remember ever hearing anything about a ghostly boat, she said but added apologetically, "But things like that don't register with me a lot."

Identities of ghosts: The passenger list of the boat was not available; nor, for that matter, was the identity of the boat.

Personalities of ghosts: Probably having a great time pushing up the river.

Witnesses: Russ Hawkins; as well as vague rumors of other observers in the past.

Best time to witness: Russ says that about an hour after dusk is the best time to see these things.

Still haunted?: Only time will tell.

Investigations: Russ seems to be the only observer within living memory, at least the only one to report his experience.

Data submitted by: Russ Hawkins; Dr. Fred Nolen of Columbia, Missouri, a friend and fellow psychic investigator of Russ's; Bill Crawford, president of the Boone County Historical Society; Melody Nichols, an employee of the *Boone County Journal.*

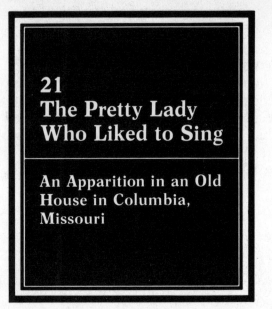

**21
The Pretty Lady
Who Liked to Sing**

An Apparition in an Old
House in Columbia,
Missouri

Location: The house is just outside the city limits southwest of Columbia, home of the University of Missouri. It has now been razed—burned down in 1983 as a training exercise for the fire department. The foundation stones are still there; the garage is collapsed. The address is 4933 Lake Valley Lane.

Description of place: "It was a two-story frame house," says Dr. Fred Nolen, a clinical psychologist who practices in Columbia and who was the last person to live in the place. It was built before the Civil War by a Boone County pioneer by the name of Sutton and was occupied for several generations by his descendants. The area, even in recent times, was pastoral, although it is now surrounded by housing developments.

When Nolen moved in, in 1972, the place had not been painted in thirty years. He painted it and did considerable other renovation, although he was renting—at five dollars a month. He had just received his Ph.D. from the University of Missouri and occasionally sublet rooms to graduate students and friends.

"There were three rooms upstairs and four down-stairs," Nolen says. "Two of the rooms upstairs were not accessible to each other, which is typical of a lot of the pre–Civil War structures around this area. There was no door between them. That was to keep the males and the females separated, to prevent midnight forays. And also, they could be used for isolation rooms for sick and crazy people." (This peculiarity of the room arrangement does not seem to have anything to do with the haunting, but it's an intriguing sociological footnote.)

There was also a hand-carved, walnut staircase leading up to the second floor, which Nolen suspects does have a connection with the haunting of the house.

Ghostly manifestations: Nolen had been living there six years before noticing anything unusual. Then, one fall morning, he says, he awoke to see a pretty little apparition glide past his bed, a petite, fine-featured young woman, with long brown hair and a simple, gray dress. She did not seem aware of him and drifted on through the closed door.

This, Nolen says, was the only time he saw the apparition, but it was not the end of his relationship with the pretty ghost. He says he gradually became aware of a presence, a sense that someone was beside him when he was most enjoying the old house, for which he had a great affection.

Nolen is an enthusiastic amateur pianist and often serenaded himself. He says he would sometimes hear a woman's singing voice, coming from upstairs and wordlessly repeating the tune he had just played. He describes the voice as "like a heavenly flute, crystal clear."

He says that to his knowledge four other people have heard this voice. On one occasion, two women guests heard it at the same time. Nolen says they were in different parts of the house and looked each other up to compliment the other's singing to his piano accompaniment. Yet at that time, Nolen says, he did not hear anything himself.

Twice, he says, something touched him on the shoulder as he played. "One time," he says, "I was playing a nice, quiet song, and on my left shoulder I felt a very kind hand. I turn around and there's nobody there. The next time, I was playing Glenn Miller's 'In the Mood.' I was kind of rocking it, and I felt a hand slip up the back of my head. I sort of felt like it was saying, 'You're not playing that very well,' or 'I don't like that kind of playing.'"

Dr. Fred Nolen.

The house had long had a reputation for being haunted, with a constant turnover of tenants before Nolen arrived. However, he says, he knows of at least one case in which people who did not know of the house's reputation saw what was probably the lady ghost. One summer afternoon a friend dropped by for a visit, bringing along her two young sons. As they drove up to the house, one of the boys exclaimed, "Look, Mama, a lady!" and pointed out a figure in an upstairs window. Assuming it was a guest, they came in but found no one home, although they went through all the rooms.

Another witness was a friend of a friend of Nolen's, Dr. Julie Stephens, a school curriculum specialist. She is apparently a natural psychic, although she has never characterized herself as such or made efforts to develop her abilities. She says she knew nothing about the ghost when she visited the house; she was just interested in antiquities, and Nolen was showing her around the old place.

"We were in the kitchen," Stephens says, "when she appeared in a doorway I was facing and toward which Fred's back was turned. My first thought was that it was a fellow guest, but in an instant I knew better. There was something filmy about her. As if in respect for a private conversation, she turned away at once and disappeared."

Nolen had various other psychic experiences in the old house. "Over many years," he says, "I heard something moving across the second-story floor—fast, regularly, and sounding hard. At first I thought it was mice, but mice don't have feet that hard and they don't run in a continuous and straight line. It sounded like marbles rolling across the floor. Some psychics have said it's the ghost of a little kid, rolling marbles upstairs."

Nolen had a wind chime in the house that often would tinkle when no earthly wind seemed to be agitating it. Sometimes tablecloths would flutter when the air was dead still. Nolen likes animals, and he says that sometimes his cats would react mildly to these phenomena, as if to a surprising but unalarming presence that their owner could not see or hear.

Nolen's landlord died, and the widow would not sell him the house. It was fated to be gobbled up by a subdivision, although as it turned out its particular space was never used.

"Just before I left," Nolen says, "I was sitting there in

the living room, and a big wind blew through the house. And I heard a big, heavy chain clanking on the front porch. It sounded like a logging chain. I went out there, and there was no wind at all. There was no one there but the dog. Something was just saying good-bye."

History: The house, built before the Civil War, was the homestead of the Sutton family for many generations. It was then rented to other families and often would be vacant. "It would go empty for a while," Nolen says, "and people would come in and party—college kids and so on."

Identity of ghost: Two Sutton women hanged themselves on the property, but whether it is one of them who is the ghost is questionable, at least in Nolen's mind. Nancy Sutton hanged herself in the barn in 1858. "Miss Virgy" Sutton hanged herself from a tree in 1940. Miss Virgy was a well-known businesswoman, and it was rumored she had buried gold on the property. Neither of them were physically like the entity reported by Nolen and others.

"I have a real strong idea who the apparition might have been," Nolen says. "There was a lady who lived there two families before I got there. Her name was Lucy Calvin."

Nolen says that when the *Columbia Missourian*, a college newspaper, published an article on the house, he got a call from a woman who said she thought the ghost was her grandmother, Lucy Calvin. "She told me," Nolen says, "that her grandmother loved that old place, and she told people that after she died she didn't want to go to heaven, she wanted to go back to the farm. She said it was the most wonderful place she'd ever lived. The woman also told me that her grandmother played piano by ear and sang beautifully. She also told me one other thing that really clicked. She told me that her grandmother built the hand-carved, walnut staircase that led up to the second floor. She said her grandmother loved that staircase and polished it every day."

Nolen mentions that several psychics who have visited the house, including Russ Hawkins of nearby Ashland (see chapter 20), has "sensed something going on with that walnut staircase."

Nolen says that the woman who called him admitted that her grandmother had not physically resembled the apparition he and many others had seen, even aside from the age factor. Nolen has an interesting, if perhaps chauvinistic, comment on the subject. "Mr. Hawkins," he says, "had a good statement on all that. He said ghosts when they manifest—especially female ghosts—they don't look like they did; they kind of look like they wish they had. Women tend to come back twenty or twenty-five years old. Male ghosts come back thirty or thirty-five—in their prime. When I described the apparition to the granddaughter, it wasn't even close. Mr. Hawkins has run into the same thing, where they look like something they didn't look like when they were alive." (If this is truly the case, I plan to come back looking like Robert Redford.)

Personality of ghost: Russ Hawkins says, "She sounds typical of spirits unaware that their bodies have been destroyed. That's what most 'spooks' prove to be, people who just don't know they're dead because they died in such a way as to never know what was happening. In some state we don't understand, these people manage to go on living the life they loved. I think she was one of these and that possibly disappearance of the house made her understand her situation and go on to the next stage of existence."

Nolen has this to say: "I think we resonated on a whole lot of aspects because I just loved the place myself. I can't sing, but I can play the piano by ear, and there might have been some affinity there that I was tuning in on."

Witnesses: Dr. Fred Nolen, Dr. Julie Stephens, Russ

Hawkins, many investigating psychics, many residents of and visitors to the house.

Best time to witness: Nolen says most manifestations were noted during the daylight hours.

Still haunted?: The house has been razed. Nothing unusual has been noted about the property.

Data submitted by: Dr. Fred Nolen, Russ Hawkins. An article by Joan Gilbert in the July 1988 issue of *Fate* magazine.

**22
The Lady and the
Time Warp**

**A Music Professor Pops
Up Posthumously**

Location: The C. C. White Memorial Building, once a music education building on the campus of Wesleyan University, in Lincoln, Nebraska. The building was torn down in 1973.

Description of place: The building, put up between 1903 and 1907, was an Italian Renaissance structure of four stories. The building housed the university's music education program, with many classrooms and practice rooms.

Ghostly manifestations: The following account was given to me by Dr. David Mickey, a retired professor of history, who is writing a history of the university. He says, "In 1963 we had a visiting distinguished professor of music education who came from the University of Edinburgh, James McCourt. He was given an office at the northeast corner of the main floor of the C. C. White Building. He was in much demand for talks to service clubs and so on, and Colleen Buterbaugh, the secretary of the academic dean, sort of handled his bookings and calls. She worked in the Old Main, a

building adjacent to the White Building. One morning
she couldn't reach McCourt by phone, so she decided
to take the message over to his office and put it on his
desk.

"Now, one morning back in April of 1940, one of our
lady professors of music theory and composition, Clara
Urania Mills, was running behind schedule and was in
a hurry. She came into her studio in the White Building and had a heart attack and died right there. They
found her when she didn't appear in class.

"Now, twenty-three years later, Colleen Buterbaugh
came to the White building to deliver her message to
James McCourt. It was at the time classes were passing, at nine in the morning—an interesting thing is that
it was just about the same time that Clara Urania Mills
had died. Mrs. Buterbaugh had to go in through the
music office. She had to go through a gate at the end of
a counter and then into an inner room where
McCourt's office was.

"The minute Mrs. Buterbaugh stepped into the music office, she said, suddenly there was no noise in the

The C. C. White Memorial Building.

building, where before it had been full of noises—people moving around and so on. And it felt cold and clammy. She thought she saw a man sitting at McCourt's desk to her left as she entered the inner room. She looked again and he wasn't there.

"Then she turned and she saw a tall lady with hair that was sort of bouffant, like they used to wear before World War I, with a lacy white blouse closed at the neck and lace sleeves. A long black skirt hung to her ankles, and she was wearing old-time buckle shoes.

"This startled Mrs. Buterbaugh. Then she thought she saw the man sitting at the desk again, and she turned back to him, and then she turned back to the woman, who was going through a rack of music, apparently looking for something.

"And then Mrs. Buterbaugh looked out the windows. The trees were no longer tall. There were at this time one or two structures across the street from the White Building, but they were not there. The library building that stood to the east was not there. It was a kind of transfer back in time to the way things were on this campus before World War I.

"Colleen rushed out of this room and back to the adjacent Old Main building. She was seen by Karen Cook, who was then director of alumni activities, as she rushed by. The dean asked her what was the matter, and she told him as best she could. Then one of our older professors said, when Colleen described the woman to him, 'Why that's a dead ringer for Clara Mills as she looked when she started to teach here.' Clara Mills came here in 1911, and she was here until her death in 1940.

"I've talked with Colleen Buterbaugh about this, and—I'll put it very carefully—I never doubted that she thought she saw what she thought she saw. And there is no doubt in Mrs. Cook's mind that this woman had had a very shaking experience. She was undone.

"I asked McCourt if he had any hesitation about

going into his office again, and he said none at all; he didn't see why Scotland should have a corner on all the ghosts."

Karen Cook also gives her version of the incident: "I had just left my office to go down the hall, and I saw Colleen Buterbaugh coming out of the C. C. White Building. She looked white as a sheet. She was obviously very, very shaken. I went back to my office, and about forty-five minutes later she came into my office. I had a bookcase that had old Wesleyan yearbooks in it, and on top of it I had some old photographs. One was labeled 'Faculty About 1914.' We talked about her experience. She said that one of our professors, Dr. E. Glenn Callen, had just identified the ghost as Clara Urania Mills. We both got up and went to the bookcase. Colleen's eyes just got enormous. She put her finger toward this picture of the faculty about 1914 and pointed to a woman in the back row and said, 'That is who I saw.' The picture wasn't labeled, so we pulled out the yearbook for 1914 and looked until we found a picture that matched the one in the group photo, and it was Clara Mills."

History: Dr. Mickey says that repercussions to this incident have been far-reaching. It has been widely written up in psychological journals and in the general press. "There has been a lot of embellishment," Mickey says.

It lent the campus a spooky aura that appealed dramatically to its youthful inhabitants. "Before the old building was taken down," Mickey says, "you had kids appearing in white robes and ghost costumes. But there has never been a repetition of the incident, except a mockery of it."

A new administration building, the Smith-Curtis Building, now stands on the site of the White building, but it seems innocent of mystery.

Identities of ghosts: If not Clara Urania Mills, who? The elusive, flickering man at the desk seems unidentified.

Personalities of ghosts: They seem typical place-memory apparitions with no awareness, like actors on a film taken around 1914 and being projected half a century later.

Witnesses: Of the primary event, only Colleen Buterbaugh. Karen Cook observed Buterbaugh immediately after her experience, and David Mickey spoke with her later.

Best time to witness: So far, just that once.

Still haunted?: No indication of further incidents.

Investigations: The psychology department of at least one Midwestern university sent representatives to investigate Colleen Buterbaugh's adventure, although which university has slipped Dr. Mickey's mind. He remembers clearly, however, that the celebrated psychological research institution Menninger Clinic, of Topeka, Kansas, sent two staff members to interview Colleen. One was the eminent psychologist and parapsychologist Dr. Gardner Murphy, who at the time was Menninger's director of research. During his career, he was president of the American Psychological Association and the American Society for Phychical Research. With him he brought a Menninger psychiatrist, Dr. Herbert Klemme. They published an extensive report in the *Journal of the American Society for Psychical Research.* Colleen's interview with the scientists varied little from the account she gave Dr. Mickey, except that she emphasized a strong odor in the room and indicated she did not actually see a man at the desk but "felt his presence." Her description of the apparition was graphic:

> She had her back to me, reaching up into one of the shelves with her right hand, and standing perfectly still. She wasn't at all aware of my presence. While I was watching her she never moved. She was not transparent and yet I knew she wasn't real. While I was looking at her she just faded away—not parts of her body one at a time, but her whole body all at once.

The investigation traced Colleen's life and psychological attributes back to birth, mentioning that she seemed "happy and action-oriented . . . a very direct, matter-of-fact, down-to-earth, and realistic person who was fulfilling very competently her life assignment as a wife, mother, and full-time professional secretary," and mentioning in passing that she had a bowling average of 152. The conclusion, couched in dense psychological jargon, seemed to be that she was no crazier than the rest of us.

Did they think she really experienced what she thought she did? The summation seemed to boil down to "who knows?" In fact, the title of the paper was "Unfinished Business."

Data submitted by: David Mickey, Karen Cook. Article by Gardner Murphy and Herbert Klemme in the October 1966 issue of the *Journal of the American Society of Psychical Research*. Tip from Dick Mezzy.

23
A New Ghost in an Old House

Lights Flick On and Pans Rattle in East Kingston, New Hampshire

Location: A house on Route 107—locally known as Depot Road—just east of the center of the village, two doors from the local library. The address is 47 Depot Road. The owners would probably chat if phoned in advance.

Description of place: The owners since October 1988 have been Keri Marshall and her husband, Rich Tucker. They are a handsome young couple, she a lawyer, he a construction worker. They are in the throes of restoring the two-story, run-down old house, which is about 150 years old. "It's no particular style," Keri says, "people just kept adding on to it." Rich says, "It was originally a Colonial Cape."

Ghostly manifestations: All seemed quiet on the supernatural front here for the first 150 years. Only recently have things been jumping, and it's really livened up conversation in East Kingston.

A star witness is Merle Straw, an auctioneer who was readying the house and its furnishings for auction. He and his wife, Judith, were checking over the premises

The house in East Kingston, New Hampshire.
PHOTO BY ARTHUR MYERS

when they thought they heard a door close upstairs. They didn't stick around; they got in their car and headed for the local police station.

"Sometimes people break into an empty house and use it," Straw says. On the way, they met a police cruiser, waved it down, and told the officer their experience. They were rather surprised when he laughed. The policeman went back with them and checked through the place but found no one.

The reason the policeman had laughed was that 47 Depot Road had recently developed a reputation. Neighbors such as Dick and Marilyn Worth—he's a retired nuclear engineer—had noticed lights going on and off. Keri's mother, Madeline Marshall, who lives next door, had too. Henry Lewandowski, the chief of police, had seen lights and investigated.

"I was driving around one evening when I saw a light in the house," Lewandowski says. He went in to see what was going on. He told me he has been involved for years in the ordinary hazards of police work but has never been as frightened as he was when he went through this empty house. There was something about the place.

"I've been shot at, attacked, and all the rest," he says, "but I've never felt as terrified as I did that night." But he persevered and turned out the light.

"After that," he says, "the police were often involved. The lights would be on, the police would investigate, and there would be nobody there."

An intriguing occurrence took place during the winter of 1987. Keri Marshall had been working late and was returning to her parents' house next door, where she was living at the time. There had been a snowstorm, and new snow thickly covered the ground. She saw the lights at Number 47 blazing brightly. There were no footsteps in the snow. Keri called the police; they came and observed the situation. They decided for reasons of their own not to enter the house but came back the next morning. Now the lights were out. The

Keri Marshall.
PHOTO BY TOM ELLIOTT

snow was still virgin, completely unmarked by footsteps. The police went in at this point and found the house empty.

Lewandowski tells of hearing an unusual noise on one of his inspection tours. By this time he knew the house quite well, but the noise was new. He finally discovered what it was. There were two old electric clocks in the house, one hanging from a wall on the first floor, the other a bedside clock on the second floor. He had never known them to be working, but now they were. They had not been set, but they were churning away.

The spirit seems to have a penchant for fooling around with timepieces. Andrew Hartmann, a friend and client of Keri's, had three such experiences. Three times, he says, he found watches he was wearing stopped after he had been visiting Keri and Rich in their house. This involved two different watches. Also, he says, one time he was visiting the place with his housemate, Scott Cadieux, and when they got home Cadieux found three of their house keys, which he had been carrying in his pocket, bent so that they could not use them.

Police Chief Henry Lewandowski.
PHOTO BY TOM ELLIOTT

Merle Straw's outstanding experience came shortly before the auction sale. He and his wife were working in the house when Richard Donovan, son of Robert Donovan, a local lawyer who was executor of the estate, showed up with some friends. They wanted to look over the house prior to the auction. They were standing in the kitchen, when, as Straw remembers it, "Somebody said, 'I understand this place is haunted.' With that, we heard this rattling of pans in the cupboard behind us. Everybody heard it. My wife opened the door of the cupboard behind us, and nothing was moving."

Keri and Rich, during their brief residence in the house, have constantly heard doors closing and are used to lights flicking on and off. They have had the lights checked by professionals, and out of this has come another tale in the legend of 47 Depot Road. An electrician went down into the cellar to do his thing, carrying with him a battery-generated flashlight that had never failed him before. But it failed then. He had to rig an alternate means of lighting, from the house's wiring.

When he finished his inspection and came up and went outside, he turned on his flashlight, and now it worked. He is quoted as follows: "I'm getting the hell out of here!"

History: The house was probably built in the 1830s, as a farmhouse and a homestead for the Philbrick family. The last person with the Philbrick name to live in the house was Eva Philbrick, married to Charles, who was the town clerk for many years. Eva was an elementary school teacher at the nearby Pound School, now the town library. Eva, by then a widow, died in the early 1950s, and the house was acquired by Arnold O'Brien, who commuted to his job in a bank in Boston. A bachelor, he lived there with his mother, Edith, till she died in the early 1970s.

Arnold, a loner and recluse, retired and became stranger and stranger, according to local testimony. His neighbor Dick Worth says of O'Brien, "He would make one trip a day out of the house, down to McDonald's to get his lunch."

Keri Marshall, who lived next door, says, "He lived alone after his mother died. I felt sorry for anybody who was so lonely. When he was sick, I'd spend hours and hours with him. He was one of the most reclusive people you could meet. He would never go out."

He died in 1987. He had no heirs, and the house was put up for auction. Keri and Rich wanted to buy the house, and Keri, being an attorney, did a title search. She found that Eva Philbrick, in the 1920s, years before her death, had drawn up a will in which she stipulated that the house was never to be put up for auction.

Identity of ghost: The story is much neater if we assume it is Eva wandering around the place, flicking the lights, rattling the pans, starting the clocks, and generally upsetting the living. So they insisted on buying the house at auction, against her wishes expressed sixty years ago—she'll show them!

But Keri thinks the ghost is Arnold O'Brien. He was so glued to the place in life, he can't let go, she suspects. And she feels he had reasons of both love and hate to hold him there. While searching the house, Keri and Rich found what they call a "Dear John" letter from a lady he had known, along with an engagement ring. Also, Keri suspects, he might be angry at anyone who would buy the house.

"Arnold was always afraid that people were ripping him off," Keri says. "He was real suspicious. He was a banker. I wonder if he felt we got the estate for less than it was worth."

Another possibility is raised by next-door neighbor Madeline Marshall, who says she has been seeing a shadow in the window facing her house for many years, "since the later days of Arnold O'Brien." Could the ghost be his mother?

Personality of ghost: A little scary but nothing overtly hostile, so far.

Witnesses: Keri Marshall and Rich Tucker; Police Chief Henry Lewandowski; Madeline Marshall, Keri's mother and neighbor; Dick and Marilyn Worth, neighbors; Merle Straw, auctioneer, and his wife, Judith;

Sitting on the front steps of the house: (left to right) Rich Tucker, Keri Marshall, and Henry Lewandowski.
PHOTO BY TOM ELLIOTT

Richard Donovan, son of the executor of the estate of Arnold O'Brien; Andrew Hartmann and Scott Cadieux; various local police and an electrician.

Best time to witness: The spirit seems to be up and around almost any time of day or night.

Still haunted?: Seems to be.

Investigations: No avowed psychics have visited the place.

Data submitted by: Keri Marshall and Rich Tucker; Henry Lewandowski; Madeline Marshall; Dick and Marilyn Worth; Merle Straw; Robert Donovan, attorney and executor of the estate of Arnold O'Brien; Jim MacLeod, an attorney and a current roomer in the house; Andrew Hartmann; Scott Cadieux. Tip and assistance from Tom Elliott.

**24
A Murdered
Woman Searching
for Her Baby**

In What Is Now a
Restaurant in Nashua,
New Hampshire

Location: The Country Tavern is situated at 452 Amherst Street, on the outskirts of Nashua, a small city about an hour northwest of Boston. It can be reached by going up Route 3, taking Exit 7 West, and going seven traffic lights. The restaurant is on a corner to the left.

Description of place: An attractive building, constructed of wood, painted red, surrounded by very old trees. Until about six years ago, when a local family bought the place and turned it into a restaurant, it comprised two buildings dating from 1741. One building was a house, the other a barn. They were combined when the place became a restaurant.

Ghostly manifestations: The ghost is called Elizabeth. According to local lore, she was Elizabeth Ford, and she was murdered by her sea captain husband. He had been on a long sea voyage, well over nine months, and had returned to find she had given birth. Infuriated, he murdered both her and the child and buried them near the house.

The Country Tavern. PHOTO BY ARTHUR MYERS

The house has long been reputed to be haunted. Many employees and customers at the restaurant tell of ghostly manifestations—including apparitions of Elizabeth.

Some thirty years ago a family named Fox was living in the house. Bonnie Gamache, a manager at the restaurant, tells of waiting on members of the Fox family when the restaurant first opened. They had moved to Virginia but had come back to attend a family reunion.

"They were telling me stories about Elizabeth," Bonnie says. "I thought it was a bunch of baloney. The mother told me one of her sons used to play ball with Elizabeth. He was there at the table. He was now thirty-five and a lawyer, and he said yes, that was true. He said when he was a child he could see Elizabeth and so could several others of the ten children in the family. He said when he was small he would roll a ball across the floor and Elizabeth would roll it back to him."

The family related an incident that happened when they were moving out. They had piled into a station wagon, and a moving man told Mrs. Fox that someone must have been left behind. She did a head count and said everyone was in the car. He replied, "But I just heard someone upstairs say, 'Please don't go.'"

Bonnie continues, "The woman told me she'd dust the mantel and then turn around to dust the table, and something she'd put on the mantel would now be on the table. And other little tricks that Elizabeth would play on them. I thought they were kooks at the time, till I had my first experience with Elizabeth. That was when a coffee cup came flying off a shelf and smashed against the wall between the heads of another waitress and myself. It flew a good six feet. It scared the hell out of us."

The ladies' room seems to be one of Elizabeth's favorite hangouts. A high point of the folklore of the place is the lady who had her hair lifted mysteriously. Bonnie Gamache was a prime witness.

"I was here when the lady was in the ladies' room," she says. "I heard an ungodly scream, and this woman came flying out the door, white as a ghost. She said she was standing in the bathroom in front of the mirror, brushing her hair. She had very long hair, down her back. She thought she saw something behind her and she turned around and looked, but there was no one there. All of a sudden the hair came up off her back and went up into the air, as though someone were holding it up there. That's when she screamed and came flying out. She was very angry; she thought we were playing some kind of a 'Candid Camera' trick on her and was threatening to sue us. But when I told her about Elizabeth she loved it. She went back into the bathroom and sat in there about half an hour waiting for Elizabeth to come back, but she never did."

I was so intrigued with preliminary reports on this restaurant that I brought along Jannika Hurwitt, a medium, to try to contact Elizabeth. Jannika brought two friends, one of them a psychotherapist. Several hours later, the therapist found she was missing a belt. She thought she might have lost it in the ladies' room and had gone back there three times to look, to no avail. As she was leaving, a waitress came running out to the parking lot, belt in hand. She had found it on top of the toilet paper rack. That, said the therapist, was the first place she had looked each of the three times.

Elizabeth is playful.

I had a fairly new car, but when I tried to start it after the séance was over, it would not catch. It had never done that before and never has since. A young man who professed to know something about cars checked it over but could find nothing wrong. Suddenly, mysteriously, it started. Jannika suspects it was Elizabeth playing games, that the séance may have upset her, that she may have been upset at the idea of leaving, which the medium had urged. "Or," Jannika says, "she could have wanted on the way out for one last time to get everybody's attention. Although those aren't her usual ways of getting attention, so my assumption is that she was a little upset."

Often in the course of writing these books on hauntings, I have found that recording tapes don't work right. Spirits seem to be able to affect them—but rarely with such wild abandon as when I was working on this story. Whether taping in the restaurant or by phone from my office to the restaurant or simply from my office to someone's home, when I was discussing Elizabeth I learned to be very happy when the tape worked right. Sometimes it would be blank. Sometimes the words would be sped up or slowed down. Sometimes the tape would jam for no apparent reason and suddenly start up again.

"When we first opened the restaurant," Meri Goyette Reid, one of the family that owns the restaurant, says, "we had an incident. There were four businessmen sitting at a table, and two of the plates that were in the middle of the table suddenly slid across the table and landed on the floor. Naturally, there was some consternation. The waitress went over and asked if there was a problem. They said yes, the plates had just slid across the table and onto the floor. The waitress said, 'Oh, that must be our ghost, Elizabeth.' And the four men stood up and walked out."

Meri goes on to say, "We have talked over and over about having a séance here. It would be interesting to get the story. In fact, a few years ago I arranged with a medium to do this, and then I kind of chickened out. If she *is* here, we weren't trying to drive her out of her own home. The medium said she could cause some problems. So we discontinued that."

Meri Reid asked me if I knew a good medium, and I said I did, so a couple of Sundays later I brought Jannika, a psychic who lives in Beverly, Massachusetts. A number of people, employees and regular customers of the restaurant, as well as friends of Jannika's and mine, gathered in the upstairs dining room, in the part of the building that was once the barn.

Jannika went off into a corner and meditated. She said she was in contact with the spirit of Elizabeth. "This woman," Jannika said, "was very much in love with the father of the child. What she's doing, she's like the mother animal constantly looking for her young. What we need to do is let her know that the child has passed on and that she can only unite with the child in spirit."

Jannika said that the husband had locked the woman in the attic of the house. He then took the baby and went to the barn and killed it. He then buried it under a tree near the house.

"Three days later," Jannika said, "he let the woman out. They had a tremendous fight. She was hysterical about her baby. She didn't know what had happened to it. I believe he stabbed her through the chest."

I told Jannika that local legend has it that he decapitated her, and she replied that he may have decapitated her too.

Jannika felt it would release Elizabeth if she were

Psychic Jannika Hurwitt lifts burning sage as part of her effort to contact Elizabeth, as a restaurant worker watches from the window. PHOTO BY TOM ELLIOTT

shown that the baby is no longer on the physical plane but in spirit, as she herself is. In fact, Jannika said, she felt that the baby has reincarnated more than once.

"But what Elizabeth must hear," Jannika said, "is that even though we can see you and feel you at times, you are not in your body."

Jannika explained her estimate of the situation to the group and asked Meri Reid if it would be permissible to urge Elizabeth to move to higher spiritual planes, to give up her earthly attachment. Many of the people involved with the restaurant are very fond of Elizabeth, and there was some reluctance. Jannika felt there had to be some agreement or Elizabeth would find it very difficult to leave the physical plane.

"It's difficult," the medium said, "for a spirit to make the transition of death initially, anyway—it's like a birth, it's difficult to get through the birth canal and scary—and that's what dying, or being a ghost and getting ready to leave, is like. So if everyone whom you're connecting with is putting out energy for you to stay, it makes it harder."

Meri reiterated her desire that Jannika proceed with

her efforts to persuade Elizabeth to give up her earth-bound, ghostly status.

Jannika went outside and dowsed several trees, and the information she came up with was that the baby was buried underneath a huge tree next to the house and that Elizabeth was buried under a tree farther out in back.

A number of witnesses say they have seen apparitions of Elizabeth looking out the window of what was once the barn toward the tree in back.

"When I dowsed that tree," Jannika said, "I found that Elizabeth had been buried there. But she thought the baby was there, and that's why she kept looking out toward that tree. Elizabeth assumed that her husband had buried them together, but in fact, out of his maliciousness and jealousy, he had buried them apart."

So Jannika, aided by a young man from the restaurant wielding a spade, did a token unearthing underneath both trees.

"What I wanted to show her," Jannika said, "was that she was still frozen in the moment when she was killed, that wherever the baby had been buried it had disintegrated and passed on, that there was no child for her to be hovering around looking for, as a ghost."

Here is testimony from some of the other people connected with the restaurant. Amy Turmel, a waitress, says, "I was vacuuming the upstairs dining room in what was originally the barn, when suddenly the vacuum went off. I saw something out of the corner of my eye and turned around and saw a woman standing, looking out the door to the back. She had all white on; it looked like a lingerie type of thing. She had long, white hair, which is not what I had pictured Elizabeth looking like. I expected brown hair. But her face was very, very young. She was about five feet, seven inches and slim. She was very good looking, in fact, beautiful. She looked at me for a second, and then she was gone." Amy says this is the only psychic experience she has ever had, before or since.

Brenda Porier, a manager, reports that she was splashed with Russian dressing. "I was walking through the kitchen one day about two years ago," she says. "Nobody was in there. I felt something on my head. Automatically, you look up at the ceiling, but there was nothing up there. I felt the top of my head with my hand, and there was salad dressing on it. I was just walking by the dressings at the time."

She tells of another incident that had happened to her: "I was finishing up my work in the dining room one night when I heard this smash in the next room. I went in there and there was a glass that had fallen off the table. But this glass was not next to the table, as a glass that had fallen would be. It was out about three feet, and it was really smashed. It looked like it had been pushed off the table. I went back into the dining room where I had been working and there was a glass on one of the tables. It had a setup in it—a napkin and silverware. I hadn't put it there. I asked the two other

Psychic Jannika Hurwitt attempts to contact Elizabeth.
PHOTO BY TOM ELLIOTT

girls who were working if they had put it there, and they said no, they hadn't been in the dining room.

"Little weird things like that were always happening. I'm going to miss Elizabeth if she's gone. It's those things you can kind of look forward to happening now and then, something to talk about."

Robbie Goyette, the kitchen manager and one of the owners, says "Mother's Day four years ago I came in about five in the morning—we were planning on opening up at noon. About seven I decided to take a little break. I felt like playing a video game. I was going to go outside to my car, which was parked by one of the fire doors, to get some quarters. It was a windy day, and as I went through the door the wind caught it, but I grabbed it before it closed. I decided to take my chances, but as I went to my car the wind blew the door and it slammed shut. I realized I had left my keys in there. I was getting ready to go to a store and call up one of the other owners to let me in, when all of a sudden the door just swung open. I said, 'Thank you, Elizabeth,' and walked in.

"Another time, my wife, Helen, and I were in here on a Sunday morning. We had a little husky puppy, about two months old. My wife went out to the front dining room to get herself a cup of coffee, and as she did she thought she saw a white image go by her, out of the corner of her eye. The dog was trotting along with her, and he suddenly stopped short and his ears perked up. Then he turned around and bolted back into the kitchen. The dog's name is Merlin, so he has magical powers."

Has Robbie ever seen anything?

"Sometimes early in the morning I'll see shimmerings out of the corner of my eye. I tell myself it's reflections from the street outside—but I know it's not."

Britta Peck, a waitress, says, "I've seen doors close when there's nobody there. I've heard footsteps upstairs, where there are offices, when there was nobody there. I saw eighteen glasses fall off a counter and smash when there was no reason for them to fall. They were not on the edge. I've had glasses break in my hand, but they have never cut my hand."

Bob Kennett, a customer of the restaurant, reports, "Late one night I was helping them clean up. I was carrying trays with dirty dishes, and I looked up as I came around the end of the bar. I had ducked under something, and as I stood up I realized I was seeing an arm. It was just a quick view, and then it disappeared. It was a woman's arm, a white arm. It was very solid appearing, not transparent or anything."

Bob tells of his friend Kathy MacPherson, who often has psychic experiences. Once she had visions concerning the restaurant in the office where they both worked and had to stop work for a short time. Kathy says, "When the restaurant first opened, my mother and I had dinner there and I felt something; I was very uncomfortable."

She avoided going back there, until she met Bob, who was a devotee of the place. Speaking of the vision she had, she says, "I got a vision of looking out of the barn window. I saw an oak tree and a well. It was as though I was looking out through someone else's eyes. I knew Elizabeth was buried out by the well. I told people and they said there was no well there, but later they found the cap of an old well."

History: The house was built in the mid-eighteenth century by a man named Ford, a sea captain and Elizabeth's husband. The house was a private residence until about fifteen years ago, when it was used as an office for a local politician and later as storage space for a ski shop. It became a restaurant—combined with the adjacent barn—about six years ago.

Identity of ghost: It would seem to be Elizabeth Ford.

Personality of ghost: Seemingly very sweet, lovable, and loving. Teasing and playful. Grieving over her lost baby.

Bonnie Gamache says, "I love Elizabeth. I've spent a lot of time with her, and I feel that she's my friend. She gives me comfort. I'm here by myself a lot, and I've never felt that I was alone. The morning after the séance, I went into the ladies' bathroom and told Elizabeth how much I was going to miss her."

Witnesses: The Fox family, Bonnie Gamache, Jannika Hurwitt, Meri Goyette Reid, Amy Turmel, Brenda Porier, Robbie Goyette, Britta Peck, Bob Kennett, Kathy MacPherson, many other employees and patrons of the restaurant.

Best time to witness: Elizabeth has seemed to be around at various times of the day or night.

Still haunted?: About six months after the séance I called the restaurant and spoke with Bonnie Gamache, who had seemed to be the closest to Elizabeth. "It's been real quiet," Bonnie said. "I don't think she's here anymore. I wish we had never held that séance." Bonnie had not been there the day we held it. I mentioned that Elizabeth was presumably now better off than in her long earthbound situation. "I know," Bonnie said, fighting back tears. "I didn't even get to say good-bye to her."

Investigations: A séance conducted by Jannika Hurwitt.

Data submitted by: Bonnie Gamache; Jannika Hurwitt; Meri Goyette Reid; Amy Turmel; Brenda Porier; Robbie Goyette; Britta Peck; Bob Kennett; Kathy MacPherson; Florence Shepard, a retired librarian in the nearby village of Amherst (until the town line was changed, the house and barn were in Amherst); Bob Smith of the Nashua Historical Society; Norm Gauthier, author of the book *Guide to New Hampshire "Haunted" Places You Can Visit!* Article by Joann Goslin in the July 24, 1988, issue of the *Nashua Telegraph.*

25
An Indiscreet Romance—Murder in the Bedroom

A Restaurant Haunted by a Mother and a Maid—or So the Story Goes

Location: The Double Eagle Restaurant is situated in the center of Mesilla, New Mexico, about forty miles north of the Mexican border, in the south-central part of the state. The town is about two hundred miles due south of Albuquerque, New Mexico, and about forty miles northwest of El Paso, Texas.

Description of place: Mesilla (the locals pronounce it MEH-*SEE*-YAH) is a colorful village, once part of Mexico, of about two thousand residents. The architecture is Hispanic, and the town's main industry is tourism. The Double Eagle, an elegant restaurant with several rooms, occupies a onetime aristocratic residence on the central plaza. It is a one-story building, with an exterior of brown adobe.

Ghostly manifestations: The restaurant certainly seems to be haunted; many employees, former employees, and patrons testify to parapsychological happenings. But how the ghosts got there might be a question. Regional records are sketchy. The favored story—the one they tell at the Double Eagle—involves a romantic tragedy. Some local history buffs say it is pure myth, and even those who tell the story are not sure who killed whom. But one thing seems fairly certain—the place is inhabited by at least a couple of ghosts, whomever they may be.

The standard Double Eagle story goes like this: A wealthy family named Maese, or a reasonable facsimile, lived in the house about one hundred years ago. They had a son named Armando and a maid named Inez. The young people became lovers. The mother, of violent temperament, found the two young people in a bedroom in a compromising position and, outraged at her son's democratic tastes, stabbed the girl to death with a pair of scissors. The son tore the scissors from his mother's hand and stabbed himself, dying a few days later. A variation is that he attempted to shield the girl and was stabbed accidentally by his mother.

The bedroom is today the Carlota Room of the Double Eagle, and manifestations seem to center there, although they also are reported elsewhere in the building. The current owner of the restaurant is C. W. ("Buddy") Ritter, who owns a number of other restaurants and hotels in the state. He tells a story about his first manager of the restaurant, Bill Bertsch, now deceased.

"Bill was very derisive of the idea of ghosts," Ritter says. "One night he was the last person there, and a late party in the Carlota Room had left part of a bottle of wine on the table. Bill took two glasses and poured them full. He offered to drink a toast with the ghost, drank his, and put it down, leaving the full one on the table. He locked the building and turned on the alarm, which is a motion detector system, and left. He came in the next morning, the first person to arrive, and found both glasses empty. He immediately left the restaurant and came over to the Holiday Inn [Ritter owns the Holiday Inn in nearby Las Cruces] and quit. Instead of letting him quit, we transferred him to the restaurant in the inn, but he never again set foot in the Double Eagle."

Another story Ritter tells is as follows: At one time, the front of the restaurant had a very heavy glass door, so difficult for children and old people to open that they eventually replaced it. One morning two maids were vacuuming in the area in front of the door and suddenly it swung open by itself. They left their vacuums going and ran to the office of the then-manager, Barbara Rosa. She went downstairs to look, and by this time the door had closed. The maids, Ritter says, would never again work in that particular area, and management people had to do the vacuuming there.

The facade of the Double Eagle Restaurant.

Barbara Rosa gives a convincing inventory of typical parapsychological manifestations in the restaurant. She reports cold spots in the Carlota Room, the scent of mysterious perfume, the clatter of pots falling in the kitchen when nothing was falling, photographs taken in the room—sometimes by professionals—that just don't come out, lights going on and off in an erratic manner in various parts of the restaurant, candles refusing to stay lit for no apparent reason, as though they were being blown out. Sometimes, she and others report, doors are found unlocked, even ajar, after they have been firmly locked and the alarm system set.

"When we remodeled the room when Mr. Ritter first took over," she says, "we rearranged things in the Carlota Room, and in the morning everything would be torn down, pictures would be moved. They had a hard time redoing that room."

The present manager, Yvonne Thomason, speaks of seeing an apparition and also suspects that a ghost has taken to imitating her voice. She says, "The Carlota Room is a small dining room that seats eight people. I had gone in to turn the lights off and was then going back to the kitchen. There was a knife on the floor, so I bent down to pick it up and I saw movement out of the corner of my eye. I turned around and there was a very tiny lady. She had on a long, black skirt and a white, long-sleeved blouse. She had her back toward me. She was going toward the Carlota Room. It was almost as if—you know when you're on skates and you glide?— that's the way she was moving. I saw it for about ten seconds.

"I closed the restaurant up, in shock, and never mentioned it. A week later, I was closing up and went into the Carlota Room to turn the lights off and heard a woman's laughter. It was happy laughter.

"About three days after that, early in the morning, I was in the office upstairs and our housekeeper, Herlinda Lujon, was in the ballroom cleaning. No one else was here. She came upstairs and asked me what I wanted. She said she heard me call her name three times, but I had not done this."

Herlinda corroborates Yvonne's account, saying that since then she has often heard a woman's voice calling her name.

"One morning about a week later," Yvonne continues, "Barbara Rosa—I was assistant manager then—was sitting in the bar doing inventory with the bartender. I was at home. She and the bartender thought they heard me talking to the cooks in the kitchen and then walk across the courtyard, laughing, but I never came into the bar. Barbara went into the kitchen and they said I hadn't been there, so she called me at home. Then I told her about the experiences I had recently had."

In the course of my inquiries, I ran into some hard-core doubtists who were certain that the Double Eagle was inventing spooks to help business. This seemed unlikely to me, although in preparing these books I have more than once scratched the mission on putative haunted restaurants and hotels that seemed to be phonies, whose owners I suspected were just trying to worm their way into my pages for the free advertising. I did not think that this was the case with the Double Eagle, but nevertheless I began to get a bit paranoid and began to look for independent witnesses.

Ritter had mentioned that a writer and singer named Pat Mendoza, of Denver, had written a ballad about the star-crossed lovers of Mesilla. I contacted Mendoza, and he had indeed. In fact, it had been choreographed by a Denver dance company and performed under the title "Amantes Cuiretos" ("The Beautiful Loved Ones"). In addition to being a writer, singer, and folklorist, Mendoza is a former cop, a combination of careers that you don't find every day. He is by no means sure of the authenticity of the story of the lovers, but he feels that the restaurant is definitely haunted by something. He has talked with various people at the restaurant who told him about their experiences.

"I'm an ex-cop," he says, "so I know about people trying to con you—body language, eye contact, that sort of thing. I was a homicide investigator; my specialty was forensic science. I'm used to interrogating people. And I felt at the Double Eagle that they were telling me the truth."

I myself am a veteran investigative reporter, and I like to feel I can tell if someone is conning me, but in the small of the night I am sometimes prey to misgivings, so it was comforting to hear Mendoza's corroboration. Nevertheless, I made a point of interviewing several people who are not connected with the restaurant.

One is Carol Henry, wife of a former manager of the restaurant, Allen Henry. They no longer live in Mesilla. Allen Henry reports, "A lot of little stuff happened. A guy took Polaroid photos in the Carlota Room, and they all came out blank. He'd go out of the room and take pictures in the hallway and they'd come out fine. We'd set up wine glasses every night before we'd leave, and the next morning the glasses in the Carlota Room would be broken."

Carol Henry says, "I had a real weird experience in the Carlota Room. It was late at night. There had been three parties, and the last party had left. The rumor was that the girl ghost did not like that many people in that room. I was coming in from the kitchen and I saw the image of a person in the mirror to my right. It was a girl in a maid's uniform, black and white. She had no face and sort of grayish hair. It wasn't even put up nicely; it looked as though she had had a hard night. My instinct was to turn and see who was being reflected in the mirror, and there was nobody there. When I looked back in the mirror, she was there. I'm not a believer in ghosts. I tell this story to people and they say, 'Oh, that didn't happen.' But it did happen to me—and it was weird."

Buddy Ritter tells of a photograph shown him by Dr. Thomas Gale, dean of arts and sciences at New Mexico State University. It seemed to show a figure that shouldn't be in the picture. Gale says, "We had these friends from California, the Stuart Fergusons, and we were eating in the Carlota Room. My son, Tom, who was then in his teens, took a picture of us, using Mrs.

This photograph was taken in the Carlota Room at the Double Eagle by Tom Gale, son of Dr. Thomas Gale of New Mexico State University. At the right is a figure that some believe is a ghost and others a double exposure.

Ferguson's camera. The camera jammed, so they couldn't take any more pictures. They went back to California and he developed the film himself (he's an amateur photographer) and they sent us the picture. It showed the group with sort of a figure standing in the background. It looks like someone with his arms folded."

When told of this photo, Pat Mendoza says he thinks the figure was wearing a twentieth-century suit. He suspects it's a mundane double exposure. At first glance, I too thought the figure looked like a man in a fairly modern suit. But on further inspection, I'm not so sure. It might even be a woman. The "ghost" seems to be looking directly at the camera, as if having its picture taken. And it's standing right next to the table, as if it were part of the party, or trying to be. Take a look at the photo and see what you think.

New Mexico State University did me proud in the case of retired English professor Lynn Moncus and a mysteriously upended salad tray. Another former manager, Berry Massey, tells about this incident. Moncus and a friend, Dr. Marian Hardman, also an English professor, often ate at the restaurant, Massey says. Hardman is now deceased, and a building on the university campus has been named after her. Moncus recently retired. Moncus corroborates Massey's account, saying, "We had heard about apparitions and breakage and all sorts of things. I hadn't paid much attention to the stories. We were there at a social gathering. I was standing about two feet away from the salad bar, and Dr. Hardman was seated not far away. I had my back to the salad bar, and there was a stack of trays on the table. One of the trays, as she described it, just upended itself. The description I had was that this tray went straight up and then fell over behind me face down, with a bit of a clatter. I heard the clatter, but I didn't see it doing what it did. There wasn't anybody else close by. It just came up and fell over behind me. It scared me. I almost staged a runaway. When something plops down right behind you and you didn't know anything was going to plop down right behind you, it gets your attention. Dr. Hardman wasn't the only one who saw it. The others seated at our table saw it. One of my friends came over and he wanted to know how I did that."

History: The house was built as a residence in 1849. It was used as a residence by various families over the years. It was converted to use as a restaurant by Robert O. Anderson, former chairman of the board of Atlantic-Richfield Oil Company, in the early 1970s. Anderson often renovated interesting old buildings for modern use as a contribution to the history of the region. The restaurant was bought by Buddy Ritter in the early 1980s.

Identities of ghosts: Anyone with romance in his soul would conclude they are Inez, the unfortunate maid, and Armando's volatile mother. Who the figure in Dr. Gale's photo is could be anybody's guess.

Personalities of ghosts: Playful, in need of attention.

Witnesses: Yvonne Thomason, Thomas Gale, Barbara Rosa, Herlinda Lujon, Bill Bertsch, Berry Massey, Allen Henry, Carol Henry, Lynn Moncus, Marian Hardman, many employees and patrons.

Best time to witness: Incidents seemed to have happened both day and night.

Still haunted?: It seems to be.

Investigations: Buddy Ritter says, "One time a group of parapsychologists were having a convention at Holiday Inn and went over to check out the Double Eagle. Other people have phoned asking permission to investigate there, and I always give it."

Data submitted by: Yvonne Thomason, Thomas Gale, Buddy Ritter, Barbara Rosa, Herlinda Lujon, Tom Mendoza, Berry Massey, Allen Henry, Carol Henry, Lynn Moncus, Rick Reece.

**26
A Thoroughly
Haunted
Restaurant in
Upstate New York**

Screams, Apparitions,
Flying Napkins—All on
the Menu

Location: Beardslee Manor is on Route 5, between
Little Falls and St. Johnsville, in the Mohawk Valley
Region of New York State, about seventy-five miles
west of Albany.

Description of place: The building is a replica of an
Irish castle, built with local stone about 130 years ago
by Guy Roosevelt Beardslee, a business leader who
brought electric power to the area. It *looks* like a
haunted house. It was the Beardslee family mansion
until 1941 and has been a restaurant under various
managements since the forties, owned for the last
dozen years by Joe and Lois Casillo. A two-story structure, both floors are used by the restaurant, which can
seat some four hundred people. A bar with eating facilities occupies the cellar.

Ghostly manifestations: There seem to be three reasonably recognizable ghosts haunting the place, although there are a number of added starters. Doug
Voorhees, until three years ago general manager—he
now owns his own restaurant—has had many experiences but is a bit reluctant to talk about them.

"Some of my experiences I really don't care to talk about because they were frightening," he says. "They were unbelievable. One time, for example, I was working a Ouija board there with another person, and we were both thrown across the room by a very heavy energy force.

"I'd see things there—figure outlines rather than actual apparitions. And there used to be balls of light that would go through the rooms. Other people have seen them. Some of the spirits took on lights of different colors. One was light blue and white, which is a sign of serenity. One was dark green and red; red is a very violent color. That could have been Dominie Jake, who was a rather vile man. I had a picture of him that was taken by a lady who was there at a party. She was taking pictures of friends, and he showed up in one of the pictures. He was a deacon of some sort.

"I remember there used to be a man sitting in a wing-back chair by the fireplace, where there wasn't a wing-back chair. Doors would open and close. We used to have heavy tables tipped upside down. Sometimes you'd go up to the top floor in the morning and it would be a shambles. And there hadn't been anybody in the building."

Some of the spooky ambience seems to come from before the mansion was built; it came with the territory. During the time of the French and Indian War, there was a small fort where the building now stands. There were tunnels under the fort, now sealed off, and the story goes that a band of daring Indians made a foray into the tunnels and tried to destroy the fort with explosives but in the process blew up themselves. "Right there alone," says Voorhees, "you have the basis for a very high level of activity, because Indians are very solemn protectors of their land and they have such strong spiritual beliefs."

A good overview of the ghostly activity at the manor is provided by Sherry Eckler, who was a waitress, hostess, and assistant manager there for twelve years. Sherry's name constantly comes up during interviews with employees of the restaurant. Many things have happened to her, and she is obviously very psychic, more open than the average person. The spirits seem to communicate, even play, with Sherry, and she has many corroborative witnesses among her coworkers.

"There are supposedly," Sherry says, "three people there who are spirits. One is Pop [Anton M.] Christensen, who bought the manor from Mrs. Beardslee and opened it as a restaurant. He hung himself upstairs. He's a little heller, the poltergeist type. One night a bartender went upstairs and in the corner where Pop supposedly hung himself, he saw a man hanging—he says to us.

"One time I had set all four settings at a table, with steak knives. I felt this sharp object hit the back of my leg. I looked down and there was a steak knife on the floor. But all the place settings were exactly how I had put them. I felt it had to be Pop. This sort of thing happened constantly. You'd put something down and look around, and it would be gone."

One story about Sherry was told to me by Lois Casillo, who owns the place with her husband, Joe. Joe had bought a new, wooden-handled screwdriver and was unwrapping it in the main dining room in front of the fireplace. He threw the wrapping into the fire but unfortunately also threw in his new screwdriver. Rather than reach into the fire, he walked away in disgust. A few minutes later, Sherry was walking by and felt something strike her leg. She looked down, and there was the screwdriver, its wooden handle unburned.

Lois at first denies having had any ghostly experiences herself, saying she had just heard about them from the employees, but with a little coaxing she cudgels her memory and comes up with a good one. "About six years ago," she says, "a man came in with his teenage daughter. It was her birthday. He had eaten upstairs at one time and wanted to go up there, but I told him that the room was now used as a banquet room. He said OK, but he and the girl went upstairs to the bathrooms. They came down and told me there were four people sitting in the corner having a candle-light dinner. I went up with them, and of course there was no one there."

One of the more ghastly features of the manor is the Big Scream. Sherry Eckler relates, "In the dead of winter a lot of things happened. It's quiet, the fireplaces are going, and I think the spirits like that. This was on a Monday night, and it was really, really dead, and we were getting ready to close the upstairs dining room. I did all my work upstairs, and I came downstairs and sat at the bar. We were waiting for twelve to roll around so we could close the bar. There was a big snowstorm outside, and we were watching TV. All of a sudden I heard what sounded like the bathroom door down the hall closing. I looked at Sheryl Ursi, who was bartending that night, and said I'd go check on it. There was nothing there. About twenty minutes go by and we hear what sounds like silverware, as though somebody had thrown a bunch of silverware on the floor. I went back again and nothing was there. Now we're getting cold chills. A friend of ours, Jeff Thomas, came to pick us up because neither of us had a car. He worked there. He was a college kid who was a dishwasher at the time. We started to go upstairs and this horrendous noise started that sounded like a mixture of a scream and a howl. It was like it was following us. We just ran so fast up those stairs. All three of us heard it."

When I interviewed Sheryl, I mentioned that Sherry had described the sound as a cross between a scream and a howl.

"Yeah, that's pretty close," Sheryl said.

Janet Tompson, a bank teller who does laundry at the manor on weekends, reports a similar experience: "I've never seen anything there, but one day I heard this terrible noise. I think they have heard it down in the bar, but I was upstairs, right by the kitchen, on the ground floor. It was a sound that was in the air, a strangling sound. It seemed to be everywhere. It was quite loud. It was around nine in the morning, and I was alone in the building."

Sheryl Ursi says she wasn't aware of much unusual while she worked at the manor, just little everyday things like blenders turning on and doors opening for no discernible reasons. But she does recall being a witness to a frightened Cathy Voorhees, wife of the aforementioned Doug.

"Cathy used to help around the place," Sheryl says. "One night she was upstairs late doing laundry. There's a walk-in freezer up there, which is locked from the outside. She heard a pounding from the inside. She came running down the stairs, screaming a little bit. So they went up and looked in the freezer, and there was nothing there."

The second prime ghost at the manor is believed to be that of a young woman named Abigail, who was a servant of the Beardslees. Abigail, tradition has it, choked to death on the premises. The more romantically inclined fancy a tale that she died at her wedding. The more prosaic lean toward the legend that she expired during an epileptic fit. Middle-of-the-roaders suggest that she had an epileptic fit while getting married. In any case, whenever anyone mentioned Abigail to me they referred me to Sherry Eckler, an unwilling expert on Abigail. Sherry says, "There was supposedly a woman there named Abigail. She died of some . . . she choked in some way. I used to hear her call my name, and other people did too. In a really soft whisper, she would say, 'Sherry' and there would be nobody there.

"One night I was at a bus station in the dining room and a waitress was in the kitchen, and she heard me screaming, 'Vicki, help! Vicki, help!' She came running out into the dining room, and I was just standing there.

She said she heard me screaming for her, but it wasn't me. I've always chalked it up to Abigail.

"When I was getting ready to stop work at the manor, I choked. I had a really bad experience. I started choking, and the cook had to do the Heimlich maneuver on me.

"Abigail didn't talk to anyone else; it was always me. One time Brad, who was the chef at the time, and I were unplugging the Christmas tree upstairs, and we both heard, in that really soft whisper, 'Sherry.' We went careening down those stairs so fast! I don't know why it was just me she picked on."

Experiences with the third most recognizable spirit, Dominie Jake, are described by several people. Sherry Eckler says she saw him once. She had been up on the top floor looking for a waitress, and no one was there. She started coming down the stairs and heard a bathroom door close. She went back up the stairs and says she saw a man dressed in black, walking. "And he just disappeared," she says.

Connie McAdams, a former waitress, tells of a possibly related frightening experience she had late at night, when the restaurant was getting ready to close. "I was in the bus station off the main lobby, getting supplies to reset a table. All of a sudden I felt really cold. I was afraid to look, but there at my right side was a hand. It was like looking at an x-ray; I could see the bones. I screamed, and it disappeared. The rest of the body could have been there, but I didn't see it. I'd say it was a man's hand; it was quite big."

Connie also tells of an experience a former waitress named Colleen Comara had, presumably with the dominie. "Colleen was sitting in the same archway where I saw the hand, and she saw a man standing there. He was very tall, in a black suit and a top hat. She saw him, and it was gone. Doug Voorhees used to tell us he was the violent one."

The dominie, according to annals of the manor, was

a clergyman who had molested children and had been disgraced. He reportedly hung himself in a tunnel under the building. Legends of an Abe Lincoln–type figure go far back in the history of the place. Another sighting of this apparition seems to have been experienced by a small child, Megen Conrad. Her father, Brian, at one time bar manager at the Manor, says, "I lived there for two years, in the carriage house next door. I didn't have any direct experiences at the manor, but my little girl did. She was three years old. Mary— her mother—Megen, and I were sitting at the bar. I was doing some laundry at the restaurant, and we were waiting for it to get dry.

"There was a thunderstorm outside. We went outside to look at the lightning and the bright red sky. Sherry Eckler, the hostess, had just brought her an ice cream. Megen and her mother were sitting at the bar. The rest of us had gone outside to look at the storm. Megen was looking toward the next room—a dining room—and she suddenly started screaming hysterically. She jumped on her mother's lap, scared to death. She said she had seen a man with black gloves and a black hat and that he was staring at her. Her mother didn't see a thing.

"We went over to the apartment to relax. After a while, I had to go back for my laundry, and Megen tried to stop me. We had never, ever discussed ghosts or monsters or anything like that in front of Megen."

Conrad says that although he has never seen anything himself, he has seen things happen to other people. "When I first started there," he says, "there was a balcony. I was setting tables upstairs and I could see downstairs. There was a girl there named Elisa McFarland. I remember her standing there scared to death, because the wine glasses that hung over her head in the bus station were all shaking. I could hear them. She went down on the floor in a ball, screaming."

Conrad was in college when he worked for the

manor, and he brought a group of film students to the building to spend the night there with a video camera and sound equipment. "There was no one else in the building, and we all stayed together," he says. "We didn't get anything on film, but one of the tape recorders upstairs recorded a woman's voice saying, 'Why?' very clearly."

It might be appropriate to touch here on some of the other manifestations that have been noticed at this rather offbeat, friendly neighborhood dining place.

I intermittently heard about a mysterious woman in white. Lois Casillo reports, "We had a waiter who was working at a bus station late one night, resetting tables, and he saw a woman in a white dressing gown carrying a bed tray up through the air. It was in a place where we knew there had been a stairway at one time. The waiter left and never came back."

Sherry Eckler says, "One night in the bar this lady got up to go to the ladies' room, and she followed in this woman with a long dress and long blond hair. And when she got into the ladies' room the lady was gone. A couple of other people have seen this woman too." Some observers suggest the woman in white might be Abigail.

Three employees, waitresses at the time, had an experience together and separately tell the identical story. They are Joanne Davis, Laurie Klawann, and Terry Sheely. To quote Laurie, "The three of us were upstairs setting up for a function. We would stuff things in glasses—forks, spoons, knives, and napkins. And on one table the napkin came flying out of the glass and landed on the floor. Nobody was near it. We just looked at each other and went on with our work. We were used to things like that."

Laurie also says, "You'll walk through the dining room and there will be nobody there, and you'll see a chair pulled out from a table. You'll push it in, come back, and the chair will be pulled out again. That has happened many times. Silverware will be rearranged, sometimes scattered."

A persistent manifestation is the sound of ghostly children playing. Leroy Looman, Laurie's father and a caretaker, declares he won't believe in ghosts till he meets one face to face. "But strange things happen at times," he admits. "I do hear children at play here. I think the Beardslees lost a child here. I hear it quite often, most generally in the morning, all over the building. I haven't seen anything."

Terry Sheely tells of an experience that seems typical of the sort of anecdotes the staff tells involving customers. "On a late Sunday night I was waiting on a couple. The woman kept holding her ear. She told me her earring kept falling out of her ear. She had pierced ears. They left, and about twenty minutes later the man came back in. He said she had walked out to their car holding onto her ear and that the earring kept falling out. But she kept hold of it. About ten minutes later, she touched her ear and the earring was gone. They could not find it anywhere in the car. So they turned around and came back. And the earring was on the table where they had been sitting."

Terry, who has just graduated from college, has another one for her grandchildren: "The freakiest thing that happened to me was when I was bartending one night. It was superslow. I had been given the keys to the restaurant by the manager, to lock the place up. I was so nervous about those keys that I put them on a chain and then put that chain on my own key chain. I locked the outside door of the barroom and set the keys on the bar. I went upstairs to tell the waitress, Liz Cibadoo, not to leave without me. Then I went back down to the bar and watched the news on TV. Liz came down, and we watched the news and then got ready to leave. We walked out the back door and I got my keys out to lock it, and all three keys to the restaurant were gone.

"I was going crazy. I couldn't find them anywhere. I

called up the bar manager to come down to the place and lock the door. All my keys were there; only the restaurant keys were gone, and it's impossible for them to fall off. He said he'd be right along. I went back into one of the main dining rooms and I stopped there and I screamed, 'I want my goddam keys, now!' I was so upset.

"I said, 'Liz, I'm going back down and look again.' I went down to the bar and looked and looked. Suddenly I heard her yell from upstairs, 'Teresa, I found them!'

"I ran upstairs and said, 'Where, where?'

"And she goes, 'It's the weirdest thing!' She had walked into the dining room where I had yelled. 'I stood right here,' she said, 'and I closed my eyes and tried to concentrate on your keys.' She said she heard the time clock click in the kitchen, and she got the weirdest feeling that they were by the time clock. So she went there. There were some trays there, and there was a tablecloth on top one of the trays. She picked it up, and there were my keys. And they were on the key chain I had put them on.

"I had another thing happen to me that night, after this whole ordeal. I always lock my car when I leave it in the restaurant parking lot. My passenger door is constantly locked anyway. I got in the car and started down the driveway and suddenly my passenger door swung open. And there was no way it could have been unlocked."

History: The earliest historical event for our purposes may date back to the 1700s and the small fort where the French fought the Indians. They then combined forces against the English. Somewhere along the line, a band of Indians inadvertently blew themselves up.

Around 1860 Guy Roosevelt Beardslee built the mansion, which became something of the social center in these parts. A son of the Beadslees is believed to have drowned near the house. Beardslee was a major stockholder in the New York Central Railroad and had his own personal railroad station at what was then called the Castle, complete with a private semaphore that stopped any train he wished to board. A fire in 1918 destroyed much of the building, and it was restored, although not to its former splendor.

Identities of ghosts: Possibly Pop Christensen; Dominie Jake; Abigail; the unfortunate Indians; members of the Beardslee family. And then there are such vague sojourners as the man in the winged-back chair, the lady in the white dressing gown, the blonde lady in the long dress, and the four people having the mysterious candlelight dinner. Also, the place, with its tunnels, was a part of the Underground Railroad, and perhaps some fleeing slaves remain behind.

Personalities of ghosts: No one seems to have been seriously harmed, unless you count the flinging of Doug Voorhees and his Ouija board partner. Abigail seems wistful, lonely, perhaps in pain; Pop Christensen, who hanged himself, may have gotten over his depression enough to play practical jokes; Dominie Jake is menacing but seems to go no further than scaring people; the generalized eerie roar might be Abigail in her death agony or more likely the suddenly departing Indians.

Witnesses: Laurie Klawann; Lois Casillo; Joanne Davis; Leroy Looman; Brian Conrad; Megen Conrad; Sheryl Ursi; Sherry Eckler; Connie McAdams; Janet Tompson; Terry Sheely; Doug Voorhees; Cathy Voorhees, many other staff and customers of the restaurant.

Best time to witness: As in most haunted restaurants, manifestations are most noticeable during off hours, when there are few people about.

Still haunted?: Seems to be, although Doug Voorhees says, "There was a time span when things were very active there, because they were doing a lot of renovations and that stirred up a lot of activity that would normally lie dormant."

Investigations: A number of psychics and groups interested in parapsychology have visited the place, some on a regular basis.

Data submitted by: Laurie Klawann, Lois Casillo, Joanne Davis, Leroy Looman, Brian Conrad, Sheryl Ursi, Sherry Eckler, Connie McAdams, Janet Tompson, Terry Sheely, Doug Voorhees, all current or former staff of the Beardslee Manor restaurant. Material furnished by Jean Sekel, Betty Bilowbraka, Bill Vanasse, the Margaret Reaney Library, in St. Johnsville. Tip from Martha Gates.

**27
Two Ladies in a
Haunted New York
Brownstone**

Confronted by a Variety
of Spirits, Complete
with Apparitions, Odors,
Ghostly Music, and
Situations That
Frightened the Animals

Location: A brownstone house on East Twenty-sixth Street in New York City.

Description of place: A three-story residential building, dating from 1859. Before Sandi Summer and Carole Boyd bought it in 1978, it had for five years housed a bordello. "It didn't need a lot of renovation," Sandi says, "but it did need some. For example, it had swinging doors with numbers on them."

Ghostly manifestations: Sandi and Carole are two very interesting and rather high-powered ladies. Sandi at one time was a college professor and for the past twenty years has been director of a private school in Manhattan. Carole has been a composer of popular songs and of music for films and TV commercials, a supper club singer, and an actress in numerous soap operas. She currently is an attorney, specializing in municipal, land use, and equine law. When she met Sandi, Carole was a tennis professional, and Sandi was her student. In 1984 they sold the brownstone and moved to New Jersey, where they breed race horses, of which they currently have eighteen.

"The first thing we noticed when we moved into the house," Sandi says, "was that unless your keys were in a zippered purse they were always missing. If you put them on a table and came back there would be no keys. Then we began missing rulers and tools such as hammers and pliers."

One of the early incidents happened while they were hanging a chandelier in a high-ceilinged room on the first floor. They had placed two ladders next to each other. Sandi had gone up one ladder holding the chandelier; Carole had gone up the other with tools— a hammer, pliers, a screwdriver, and an electrical connection. She put the tools on the platform of the ladder, then went down the ladder to plug in the cord. When she went back up the ladder, moments later, the tools were not there.

"The floor was wood," Sandi says. "If they had fallen we would have heard them. We looked all over the room. Then we heard a noise in the living room, sixty-eight feet away. On top of a china closet in that room was a very tall crystal vase. It was about seven or eight feet up in the air. I happened to look up, and there were all the tools sitting inside this vase. That was the first really major thing, and it was a very disquieting kind of event."

That night another incident occurred, which so frightened them that Carole called Duke University. They had heard of the ESP experiments of Dr. Joseph B. Rhine at Duke. Duke referred them to the American Society for Psychical Research, a New York–based, conservative, highly regarded organization that has been investigating psychic phenomena since 1885. The ASPR launched an extensive survey of the house, sending in many psychics at various times. The society eventually issued a twenty-nine-page report on the investigation, the gist being that this place sure was haunted.

The incident that spooked Carole and Sandi into taking action was as follows: A landing on the staircase between the second and third floors seemed to frighten the two dogs and cats. The cats would not step on the landing but would contrive to leap over it to an over-hang if they wanted to get up to the next floor. The dogs were not so agile and would just refuse to cross the landing. If Carole and Sandi wanted to get them up to the third floor they would have to carry them over the landing.

A very large Oriental carpet that had just been cleaned and rolled up in paper had been temporarily deposited on the landing. "We're talking about something that took two burly movers to get up the stairs," Sandi says.

About midnight she had gone up to the third floor and the carpet was on the landing. A few minutes later she came down and the carpet was not there. It was lying on the floor at the bottom of the staircase.

"This is an enclosed staircase," Sandi says. "At the base of the staircase I had piled every piece of crystal I own, on cafeteria trays. They were piled up to a height of five feet. If you went up the stairs, you had to turn sideways to get around the crystal, as there was only about a twelve-inch free space. There had not been one sound. Not one piece of crystal was disarranged.

"At this point we decided we needed to talk to experts. It became apparent that things we were passing off, saying we were just tired . . . well, there was more to it than that."

Shortly after this, Sandi had her first glimpse of one of the entities that might have been causing the pre-vailing discombobulation. "I was walking one of the dogs out on the street on a summer evening," she says, "and I looked up and saw a person in my bedroom. The windows are enormous. There was this little girl. She looked like Alice in Wonderland. She had long blonde hair with a pale blue ribbon holding it back, like a headband, and a white, frilly nightgown. She looked like she was about twelve years old. She was standing beside an old secretary I had, with a drop-leaf desk in it. I went into the house and there was nobody there, but my keys that had been gone the week before were on the secretary."

Incidents multiplied. "Some things became so usual that we just took them for granted," Sandi says. "For example, once we were having lunch with two friends after we'd been playing tennis. We could hear lovely music playing on the piano—Mozart. Our friends commented on the music and asked if it were a tape or a record. We said it was live music, of a sort. We took them into the living room where the piano was, and you could see the keys going up and down. There was nobody there playing. They thought it must be a player piano, but it wasn't; it was just an ordinary spinet piano. This happened routinely."

Another manifestation was a recurring smell of lavender. Many of Carole's friends were musicians. They would often bring their instruments, and the house would resound with music. "We noticed," Sandi says, "that on these occasions there would be a tremendously heavy smell of lavender, almost suffocating. People would be looking around, trying to figure out who smelled. This would also happen if Carole or I would play the piano. It was always when there was live music."

One incident involved a cat. The cat liked to sleep with Carole. He would sneak into her bedroom and drape himself on top of her. This annoyed her, since she was allergic to cats at such close quarters. So she always kept her bedroom door closed. One morning she woke up with the cat on top of her. She was furious and accused Sandi of letting him in.

"Well, I didn't put it there," Sandi deposes. "We thought there might have been a large mouse hole. We felt there had to be a logical explanation. That was a phrase we were using a lot at that time, just after we moved in. But we looked at every inch of the baseboard in the room, and there was no way for the cat to get in."

The most haunted part of the house, judging from a number of witnesses, including the psychics the ASPR sent in, was the back room on the third floor. Carole had taken over this room as a recording studio. "There seemed to be a lot of action in this room," Carole says. "In fact, at one time it was the room of one of the girls who had worked in the place, and she had seen quite a few things."

The house had an intercom system for Muzak that dated from its whorehouse period. (This reminds me of a news story I once saw about a Munich house of a similar nature that applied for such service, specifying it wanted the "light industrial" program.)

"The control was right outside of this room," Carole says. "I would keep hearing music and try to turn it off, but it was already off. But music came from that room quite a bit. I'd also hear people laughing and glasses clinking as though there were some kind of party. It took me a while to figure out that it was in the room. I'd go into the room and it would stop, but as soon as I was outside the room it would start again."

The music was 1920s jazz- and Charleston-type music. One workman in the house, Jim Gardner, was particularly aware of it. Early on the ladies had hired two painters. They worked for a day and a half, then left precipitously. Sandi says, "One man told me that all the day before he had been pushed around by unseen presences and that on the day they left somebody really shoved him on the landing and he almost fell. His partner went with him. They refused to take their pay."

The ladies then hired Gardner, who assured them that spirits wouldn't bother him. And indeed, he did not appear to mind the shoves. They were simply playful, he felt. What he *did* mind was interference with his rock and roll accompaniment to his labors. He brought his rock tapes along and played them over the house intercom. "But he could constantly hear jazz music, which he wasn't fond of," Sandi says, "and the sound of glasses and party laughter. The jazz would drown out his rock and roll. But he worked there about six months and completed the job."

In Carole's recording studio, she also became aware of an apparent animal ghost. "I always shut the door when I was recording because I didn't want the dogs or cats to come in," she says. "One day I felt the fur of an animal brushing against my legs. I was mad because I thought there must have been some cat hiding in there and it might ruin my recording, so I stopped everything and looked through the whole room, and there wasn't a cat. I couldn't believe it, so I went out and shut the door carefully behind me and looked through the rest of the house, and I found the cat downstairs in the front window, asleep in the sun. He had obviously been there a while, because he was real warm and totally asleep. That really unnerved me, so I called Sandi at school and told her what had happened, and she said, 'Oh, I've felt that, in the kitchen.'"

"Often when I worked in the kitchen," Sandi says, "I would feel long, silky hair rubbing against my leg, and I'd look down and there was no dog or cat there. When you went to the refrigerator and opened the door, you would get this caressing feeling on your leg."

Sandi notes that renovations to the premises seemed to step up ghostly activity, which is par for the course. But she also noticed that when the ASPR psychics began coming through it also seemed to stimulate the spirits. It was during this time that she met her favorite ghost.

"I was going up the stairs late at night and there on the landing was a man with long, white hair," she recalls. "He was tall, very slender, very delicately boned. He was wearing clothes of the 1700s, a brown, linen-type frock coat with knee breeches and black shoes with buckles. He was standing with his arms outstretched as though in benediction. Then he turned his hands so I could see the back of them, and I noticed an absolutely magnificent ring. It was an oval, gold signet ring, with a raven rampant holding a rose. There was a tremendous feeling of peace. I just kept walking up the stairs, and suddenly he wasn't there."

According to Sandi, several of the ASPR psychics saw this man and so did at least one of the girls who worked in the house when it was a bordello. Sandi continued to see this apparition intermittently, although she has not seen it since she moved from the house.

Carole told me of an incident that happened in her bedroom, the front room of the third floor: "One night I was getting ready for a performance. I was working at a club at the time. I had a bunch of plants—palm trees. There were huge windows and it was very light, so I could grow a lot of plants there. I had a phone on a desk near the windows. It had a very long phone cord. I walked in from the bathroom, and the plants were moving. I thought there probably was a cat over there. But there was nothing in the trees. But the phone cord, which was lying across the floor, started jumping around and waving and going crazy. It ran through some of the plants. I just stood there with my mouth open. I just watched. It looked like someone took the end of the cord and yanked it. It was rippling, the waves were like four feet high. This went on for about ten seconds, and then it just stopped and the phone cord settled back on the floor."

The ASPR report tells of a similar phenomenon experienced by Sandi, as follows: "On the morning of October 25th, 1978, while Sandi was in the kitchen preparing breakfast, she reports having seen the kitchen phone cord jump up and down rhythmically in two to three second intervals. There was no apparent explanation for this. Carole was upstairs getting dressed; the pets were in another room."

Investigations: When Carole and Sandi had been in

the house a short time, a friend, Ron Podesta, gave them a housewarming present, the services of a well-known professional psychic named Frank Andrews. Andrews declined to be the entertainment at a party but agreed to check out the place with only the owners and one or two other people present. He directed them to stay downstairs in the living room while he ranged the house.

Andrews told me: "When I walked in there, there was something sort of foreboding. I had brought with me a lot of Tibetan artifacts that I brought back from Nepal and India. Some of them were exorcist tools. One of these was a Tibetan bell; another was a four hundred-year-old phurpa, a ritual dagger with a three-sided blade. In one bedroom I felt something was leaving. Maybe I was a threat. I rang the bell three times, which usually summons any spirits that are there. It was as if things were swirling. I opened the door to a closet. There was a mirror on the door, and at the moment I did that the phurpa just jumped out of my hand and smashed into the mirror. Phurpas are used in Tibet when there are evil spirits. They are placed on altars, and they will move. At that moment everything released. I saw a figure in the mirror that looked like a woman. I can remember a mass of hair. It was very fast, and that was it. I felt that things had ended at that moment. I don't know if it was my presence or if it was because of what I had brought with me, because they are very powerful religious artifacts."

Andrews also says he sensed that violent things had happened in the house—suicide, murder, death by accident. He was aware of other presences, including a child. However, his memory of an engagement some ten years before is rather sketchy; Sandi remembered much more of what had happened that night.

"Downstairs, we heard what sounded like a little girl's voice, laughing," Sandi recalls. "We heard a loud crash and what sounded like glass breaking. Frank came down and said there was a young child who had told him her name was Anna Lisa but that she liked to be called Lisa and that she had died by falling over the bannister in her aunt's house. This was probably in the late 1800s or early 1900s. She had fallen onto the landing that the dogs and cats refused to walk on. After that night the dogs and cats walked very freely over the landing.

"Frank said he had attempted to perform an exorcism but that the child was unwilling to accept the fact that she was dead and was unwilling to go. She liked playing what she called tricks on people. Frank told us that Lisa would be responsive to us if we treated her like a live child. He suggested that we talk with her. We found that when things happened we could talk very directly to her and simply say, 'Lisa, we're very tired of this; we need those keys and we want them back,' and you would turn around and there would be the keys that you had been looking for, and you had just looked in that place. Actually, she could be helpful because if you misplaced something on your own you could say, 'I'm looking for X, Y, or Z,' and she would help you find it by placing it someplace very obvious. So she ended up being a help; she did not, however, leave the house."

A phenomenon possibly involving Lisa's helpfulness is detailed in the ASPR report. It tells of a missing hammer reappearing under special circumstances, as follows:

Since Sandi lives on the second floor and Carole on the third, they have arranged a system for returning each other's objects so that they would not have to walk up and down the stairs every time they wanted to give something back. The procedure is to leave the article on the second step of the stairway between the first and second floors, if it is Sandi's, and on the third step if it is Carole's. The last time it reappeared, the hammer, which is one

that had been given to Sandi by her father, was
found just after Sandi, Carole and their pets had
returned from a week's vacation—on a spot on
Sandi's stair. Another hammer, one that belonged to
Carole and had disappeared weeks before, also
turned up that day—on Carole's stair! The only
person who had come into the house during that
week-long interval was Frances, a physicist and
mutual friend of both women. Frances had been in
the house the morning of their return and had
noticed nothing on the stairs. When Carole and
Sandi came home to find their missing hammers
lying on their respective stairs, they both believed
Frances had found them while they were gone.
When they asked Frances about this, she denied
having anything to do with the discovery or return
of the tools.

Also concerning Andrews's visit, Sandi says, "Frank
saw the frightening woman in Carole's bedroom,
which apparently had been Anna Lisa's bedroom. That
was the bedroom the cat got into. I had seen another
woman in that room, standing over Carole's bed looking down at Carole sleeping. She was wearing black
and her hands were clasped. [Carole also reports wak-
ening and seeing this woman gazing down at her.]
There was also sometimes a smell of putrefaction,
which might have derived from the woman Frank saw
in the mirror on the closet door. We don't know anything about that woman. Lisa apparently led him to the
closet while he was attempting to persuade her to leave.

"Andrews also told us that the house had been lived
in by a man who made boats, that he used the garden
floor to make the boats and lived in the rest of the
house. Frank said he was the person who was taking
our tools. I mentioned this to a person who had grown
up in the neighborhood and he said yes, there was a
man who had lived there who built boats, and his name

was Fisher. When the tools went, we would ask Lisa to bring them back and they would appear."

Alex Murray, a prominent psychic who had been introduced to the house during the ASPR study, was engaged by Carole and Sandi to hold a séance. He remembered very little of the event, however. "It's been so long ago," he says, "a lot of water has gone under my psychic bridge since then. But I do remember that I felt presences in various rooms. I picked up a man and a woman and a child. I think the room in the back of the top floor was where the impressions were the strongest."

Sandi, however, remembers a great deal about the séance: "Alex said that the man in brown is my destiny. He said this man had been in the house waiting for me. He was my protector. Alex said the man was Austrian. I have an Austrian family background. The man was one of my ancestors. Someone had once given me an etching of my family crest. I had never paid much attention to it, but one day I took a close look at it and realized that the ring the elderly ghost was wearing—the raven grasping the rose—was my family crest."

During the séance an unexpected spirit appeared—Sandi's mother. "Alex described her," Sandi says, "including a couple of peculiarities that were true. She had different color eyes, and her name was the same spelled backward or forward—Eve. She would not leave, and she had very specific messages. So we never did contact any of the ghosts that lived in the house. My mother affirmed that there was a large, silky-haired dog that lived in the kitchen, although it also moved around the house. She said it would follow me because I was the provider of the animals' food. My mother dismissed Lisa as a naughty little child, totally undisciplined, although very charming. She said the man in brown—who sometimes also wore gray—would be around all the time."

History: In 1835 the land was deeded by Charles

Ruggles, who created Gramercy Park, to his son, Samuel, as a wedding gift. Samuel built six attached brownstones on the property, this particular house in 1859. The first owner was Alanda Hanna Barker, who lived there for more than fifty years with two sisters and a maid. In 1920 someone named Zimmerman purchased the house. The next owner was the aforementioned carpenter and boat builder, whose name is reputed to have been Fisher. He is believed to have died in the house. His widow lived there for another five years. In 1973 the house was acquired by a real estate investor who leased the house to a man of many pseudonyms, among them Hal Green, who established the bordello there. He was also known as Mr. Big. Sandi says he was very large.

According to Sandi and to ASPR research, the neighbors became restless when the house was included in a magazine article describing the ten most interesting whorehouses in New York—this one being noted for the intellect of its inmates—and Mr. Big moved his operation elsewhere. Sandi and Carole dealt with Richard Milk, a real estate broker, but met Mr. Big and his wife, who had been one of his employees in the house. She had used the very active third-floor back room, which became Carole's studio, and reported a number of interesting experiences. She was the only girl, she said, who was willing to use that room.

Mr. Big proved to be benevolent toward the new owners. For a time after Sandi and Carole bought the house, they had constant male visitors who were not aware the house had changed hands. "The bell kept ringing," Sandi says, "very attractive men. We could have bought that house fifteen times over if we had been so inclined. We did find a book with the names of clients and their interests and sexual preferences, and I must say it was very interesting reading."

But there were other, less innocuous visitors. Street prostitutes (who still haunt the block) were accus-

tomed to lounging on the steps of the house, perhaps
hoping to waylay the gentlemen callers. They continued
to use the steps as a rallying point, and Sandi and
Carole continually shooed them off. One time Sandi
and Carole found that someone had thrown a gallon of
green enamel over the steps. They contacted Mr. Big,
and he said he would give them a present. "The present," Sandi says, "was two guards around the clock for
a month. They would sit in a car nearby, and nobody
touched the house from that point on. It was as though
the Godfather had given his message."

Identities of ghosts: The man in the eighteenth-century clothing; the little girl; the boat builder; the
mourning woman in black; the silky-furred dog; the
wild woman encountered by Frank Andrews.

Personalities of ghosts: The man in the two hundred-year-old clothing seemed benevolent; the little girl
was mischievous; the woman in black seemed to be
grieving; the boat builder is suspected of being the
thief of tools; the dog seemed hungry, either for affection or food, or both; the wild woman seemed dangerous.

Sandi says the elderly ghost told her he had frequented the Austrian court and had known and supported the career of Mozart, so he may have been the
one playing the piano.

Witnesses: Sandi and Carole are the prime witnesses
in this account, but there are many others. Mr. Big's
wife told of constantly seeing the elderly ghost and
coming to look upon him as a benevolent, protective
presence. Another employee of the house when it was
one of ill fame was the manager, who was given the
pseudonym of Sal by the ASPR researchers. Sal said
there were areas in the house where he became physically ill, one of them being the landing subsequently
shunned by the animals. He spoke of bringing his sister
to the house without telling her what he had experienced, and she felt the same way in the same locations.

Sal also smelled an odor he described as decaying food. Others also smelled this unpleasant odor. Sal mentioned a "whitish ghost," presumably the eighteenth-century man. He told the ASPR that at least two of the girls spoke to him of seeing this apparition. One woman was frightened, the other was not. The latter woman first thought it was a client. She saw him going into a bathroom and followed him in, to find nobody there. Many people, he said, heard the party-type sounds later described by Sandi, Carole, and others.

Some of the men who patronized the house also saw apparitions, it was reported. There was no extra charge for this service.

At one point, Sandi and Carole duplexed the house and sold the upper floors to a Swedish film actress named Guje Kanter. Kanter, who had been apprised by Sandi and Carole of the house's ghostly tendencies, later told them that a child once materialized to her, but from then on she would only hear its voice singing. Her daughter, a woman in her thirties, visited her and said that a child came to her and sang her to sleep every night she was there.

I interviewed two people who disclaim having any unusual experiences in the house but corroborate being told of such things. One is Frances Riccobono, who played tennis with Sandi and Carole. (She is mentioned previously in a passage from the ASPR report.) She tells about the rug that was so mysteriously transported down a flight of stairs. "It had been on a landing propped in a corner," Riccobono reports, "and they found it down in the foyer. They called me to come and see it. I had known it was on the landing. It could never have gotten down that way on its own."

The other person is Richard Milk, who sold the building to Sandi and Carole. Milk tells of their telling him about the manifestations, and said he believed them. He says Hal Green also told him about strange things that had been encountered by his girls.

Best time to witness: Things seemed to happen around the clock.

Still haunted?: The house was acquired in the mid-1980s by a writer of reggae music named Kate Pierson. Sandi says she saw Pierson about a year following the sale, and Pierson denied having any unusual experiences. It seems likely, however, that the new owner was just not open to psychic phenomena. It seems most unlikely that the house's otherworldly tenants suddenly moved out.

Investigations: The research done by the ASPR. A talk on the case was given at a convention of parapsychologists in San Francisco by the ASPR director, Donna McCormick. The séance by Alex Murray. The apparent exorcism performed by Frank Andrews.

Data submitted by: Sandi Summer and Carole Boyd; Frank Andrews; Alex Murray; Frances Riccobono; Richard Milk; Donna McCormick. Thanks for the assistance of Marlene Harding and for the tip on the case from Nancy Regalmuto.

28
Who's Holding Those Wild Parties Upstairs?

Nobody—It's Just a Little Old Time Warp, or Something

Location: An apartment house in the Chelsea area of New York City.

Description of place: A six-story apartment house in the west twenties built in 1939. It is the only residential building on a light industrial block that is pockmarked by abandoned buildings. However, this building is filled, with probably around a hundred residents.

Ghostly manifestations: Tips on haunted places come in a variety of ways, but this was a new one. I wanted a chapter in Manhattan, but I had been having a hard time getting a good one. Lead after lead soured—an obvious phony or an unlikely, unverifiable legend or some other sort of wrong number. Suddenly a good story came in the mail.

I teach in a correspondence school for people who think they want to be writers. The first ten lessons involve newspaper writing. I had recently been assigned a new student, one who continued to amaze me. She never did anything wrong; she was better than most professional journalists I've known. She was one of those rare people who can do things right, and she was the best student I had ever had, out of several hundred.

Anne Lombardo had an interesting background. She had been the producer of the "Long John Nebel Show," a famous New York radio talk show. She had also been assistant to a producer for Jackie Gleason. This was with only a high school degree; she did it on pure competence. She had also once been an assistant to a magician. She was married to a man named Guy Victor Lombardo, a nephew of the other Guy Lombardo.

One fateful day, Anne sent me a story about a haunted apartment house she had lived in from 1952 to 1964. I immediately called her. "Is this all true?" I asked. She said it was and sent me a tape recording of a report she had made to a parapsychologist, Stewart Robb, back in 1965. She and Robb, whom I happen to know, had been planning an investigation, but she moved before they did it. I was impressed by the meticulous, apartment-by-apartment report Anne had made.

Where shall we start in this house of many mysteries? Let's start with Penny Hatt, who was the wife of the building superintendent, Don. Don also drove a cab. They were former newspaper people down on their luck; they had come to New York to make it in the music publishing business but instead had lost it. Tough karma.

Don has now relocated to the next dimension, but Penny is still alive and kicking. Yeah, she says, that place sure was strange. In fact, she wrote an article about it that was published in *Fate* magazine. She has a gratifying array of anecdotes.

"We had an actress," she says, "who lived on the second floor, and her neighbors were always complaining that she practiced her lines too loudly during the night. She was a young girl, Vera. She came crying to me, saying it wasn't true. She said the people next door were always fighting with each other all night. I knew them, and I knew they weren't fighting all night.

"There was this one person who kept complaining that the people upstairs were dancing in the middle of the night. She tried to give them a rug so they wouldn't make so much noise, but they wouldn't accept it because they weren't making noise in the first place.

"There was this woman who was accused of shaking her dust mop against the fire escape at four o'clock every morning. Nobody ever saw her, but they said they could hear her. Of course she said she never shook her dust mop at four in the morning.

"There were these two young girls who lived there, and underneath them was an old lady named Mrs. Katz. Mrs. Katz was always down complaining that the girls were prostitutes, that she could hear men's shoes dropping on the floor every night. Just to be sure, Don and I watched for a while. The girls weren't bringing in any men. But they heard about Mrs. Katz's accusations and were so upset that they moved out. The apartment became empty. But Mrs. Katz still came to us complaining about hearing men's shoes dropping on the floor over her head."

The only people who seem to have seen an apparition were the Hatt family, Penny and Don and their small children, Donald and Kathleen. Kathleen, now twenty-eight, says, "There was one particular being that occupied the basement apartment. It was a woman. I saw it many times. I was very small, and it's hazy, but I remember it well; you don't forget something like that."

Kathleen says she is psychic. "I've had so much experience with beings that it's incredible," she says. "The building I live in now, I've had experiences with two beings."

Penny herself is clairvoyant. Throughout her life she has had experiences with the apparition of an old lady. The entire Hatt family saw an old lady, but Penny thinks this one is different from what she calls her "personal old lady."

"This woman used to come into our apartment," she reports. "We saw her many times. She looked like an old peasant woman, with a bandanna on her head. Once our son Donald came to us in the middle of the night and said an old woman was playing with his toys. We had never discussed this in front of him."

In her report to Stewart Robb, Anne Lombardo— then Anne Pacurar—said: "One morning, Penny and Don's two-year-old son, Donald, came to them and asked if they had had a party. They got up and found that in the living room the furniture was all turned over. A chair was slashed to pieces. The entrance door was still bolted from the inside, and the windows were not jimmied. They had a trained watchdog that did not make a sound all night."

Another story on Anne's tape is as follows: "One night Penny was alone. Her husband comes in late. Penny felt someone sit on the bed and thought it was Don, but the light did not go on. She got up and felt the pressure go, as though a person had gotten up. Down the hall, she saw a figure. There was an impression on the bed as though someone had sat there. Penny has never seen the full face, but Don has."

Anne said she could often hear a sound overhead, as though someone were rolling children's blocks across the floor. But the apartment over her was empty. She was greatly relieved when an ad man from the Gleason show was visiting and asked what that was he heard upstairs. She sometimes would hear a man and a woman talking in her apartment. She finally went to a psychiatrist, who told her she was as neurotic as the next New Yorker but she didn't have anything that would make her hear voices. Other people also complained of voices. One young woman became so frightened that she moved out, and then she no longer heard them.

Anne reported that a young man across the hall sometimes found drinking glasses broken when he re-

turned home. One time, he told her, he was getting
dressed, laid his trousers out on a chair, and when he
turned to get them they had disappeared. They reappeared a few days later.

Noisy parties were a staple of the reports in those
days, but people rarely seemed to be having parties.
Loud music was another constant complaint, but on
inspection no one seemed to be playing it. Another
complaint was that someone was playing a piano, although the piano or the pianist were never found.

In one series of apartments, Anne reported, the tenants seemed to become terribly depressed for no apparent reason.

History: Bernard Eisenberg, head of the firm that
had owned the building in those days, says all this was
news to him. His father, Jacob, built the building, he
says, but they had never heard reports of hauntings.

For her *Fate* magazine article, Penny Hatt had done
some research and had come up with some useful information.

"I found out," she says, "that there used to be kind of
a rooming house and bar right on that spot before the
building was built. It was run by an old Irish lady who
would become pretty violent herself when her patrons
got drunk and violent. She'd fire off guns and clear
them out. I thought that was very interesting, because
it would fit in with all these voices people heard and
the piano playing.

"That street, as a matter of fact that whole neighborhood of Chelsea, was filled with sailor hangouts. It was
a port area. Sailors would come in off the ships,
straight up Twenty-third Street into the old bars."

Identities of ghosts: Could it be some sort of time
warp situation, a hangover from the days when the
space contained a wild sailors' bar? Was the piano
playing and general tumult a nostalgic vibration from
another time?

However, the Hatts' little old lady doesn't seem to be

a place-memory sort of apparition; she seems a real ghost.

Personalities of ghosts: Mostly wild.

Witnesses: Anne Lombardo; Penny, Don, Kathleen, and Donald Hatt; apparently many tenants of and visitors to the building. Willie, the window washer in the Hatts' time, had known the old bar. In fact, Penny thinks he owned it for a time.

Best time to witness: Most of the manifestations were reported after dark, but that might be because fewer people were in the building during the day or perhaps because the old bar lit up after dark.

Still haunted?: I contacted a number of present tenants of the building, and none had anything unusual to report.

Investigations: Anne and Stewart Robb tentatively planned one, but she moved out before they did it. Penny says that she and her husband didn't need to bring in a psychic, because they were psychic themselves. She reports they had a few séances with friends, but nothing occurred other than a few raps. Could the Hatts, with their psychic proclivities, possibly have inadvertently set off the manifestations? "Who knows? I have no idea," Penny says.

One longtime occupant of the building mentioned a young actress who lived in the building back then who had been practicing black magic and who eventually leapt to her death from her apartment window. Could that be a clue as to why the manifestations suddenly surfaced and then as mysteriously seemed to stop?

Data submitted by: Anne Lombardo, Penny Hatt, Kathleen Hatt, Bernard Eisenberg, various current occupants of the building. Thanks for the assistance of Marlene Harding. Penny's article appeared in the March 1974 issue of *Fate* magazine.

**29
The Haunting of
Engine Company
Eighteen**

Strange Footsteps and
Rumors of Apparitions
in a Firehouse in
Syracuse, New York

Location: The firehouse is in a residential section of Syracuse, at 176 West Seneca Turnpike.

Description of place: An old-style firehouse, a brick building with two bays, two floors, and a tower that rises about fifty feet from the ground above the building proper. The tower was once used to dry hose. Four shifts of five fire fighters each work out of the station.

Ghostly manifestations: The sound of footsteps when nobody from this world seems to be up and around are commonplace at Engine Company 18, say the fire fighters who are stationed there. Chuck Ward has worked there off and on for thirty years. His deposition is typical.

"I was up late one night," Ward says. "It was about one in the morning. I was alone, watching television. I was on the main floor. All of a sudden I heard a door open behind me. I could hear the latch turn and the door open. I called out, 'Who's coming in?' and nobody answered. I looked around and nobody was there. The inside door was open, but the outside door was locked. Another fireman was asleep in a room on the main floor; I could hear him snoring. Two other firemen were asleep up in the dormitory on the second floor. This was about a year ago.

"Other people have told me about this sort of thing. One time I was on watch, the only one downstairs, and I could hear people walking around upstairs. I could hear this for about half an hour. I wondered if it might be one of the firemen upstairs, but the next morning they swore that nobody was up, and they weren't kidding me."

Fire fighter John Larison says, "Some people say they have seen a person at night at the end of the dormitory. All I've done is hear things. I've heard people go up and down the stairs and walk across the dormitory floor, and there's nobody there. Everybody here has heard that. They'll start sleeping facing the wall, and before the night's over they'll roll over facing the door because they'll hear people going up and down the stairs.

"I was in the bathroom one time, and I heard somebody in the dormitory. I wondered who it could be, because the company was out and hadn't come back yet. I looked out in the dormitory and nobody was there. I went back to the bathroom, and I heard it again. So I got up and looked again, and the dormitory was completely empty.

"Sometimes I'll be upstairs writing at the desk, and everybody will be downstairs. And all of a sudden you'll hear somebody walking toward you. You lean out and look, and there's nobody there.

"I don't know anybody who's been stationed here for any length of time who hasn't heard something or other."

Fire fighter James Vossler also tells of hearing the downstairs, inner door open and close by itself. He also says he knows of two fire fighters who say they have seen apparitions at the end of the dormitory.

I checked with both. One denied he had seen anything. I didn't talk to the other, but I did talk with his wife at home—he was fixing the roof—and she said he denied having seen anything. However, the apparition in the dormitory seems to be a solid part of the Engine Company 18 lore; maybe it's just that nobody wants to rush into print admitting he's seen it.

History: The building was put up in 1927. West Seneca Turnpike is a main thoroughfare in Syracuse. "The Seneca Turnpike," Vossler says, "has historical significance. In the early 1700s it was a stagecoach trail. Across the street was a drill grounds for the Revolutionary War militia. Before the white man, the turnpike was an important Indian trail."

Identities of ghosts: Some fire fighters wonder if the manifestations could have something to do with some Indian burial ground nearby. Most, however, suspect the mysterious happenings have to do with now-dead fire fighters who once were stationed there.

They have jokingly named the ghost Tyler Green, after a dead fire fighter who was stationed there.

"We'll all be sitting there watching TV," Larison says, "and you'll hear somebody across the dormitory, and everybody will look at everybody and go, 'There goes Tyler Green.' It's got to be kind of a joke."

"The only thing I can think of," says Chuck Ward, "is that there are so many who have passed on. This is an older firehouse, and a lot of the men who worked here are gone. The furniture is all like it was. There's a big, round table on the main floor, and they played cards at that table for years."

Personalities of ghosts: John Larison puts it this way: "All I know is that they don't seem to be bothering anything."

Witnesses: James Vossler, John Larison, Chuck Ward.

Best time to witness: "It happens both day and night," says Ward, "especially if you're alone there, if the company has gone out."

Still haunted?: It seems to be.

Data submitted by: Fire fighters Chuck Ward, James Vossler, John Larison, and John Whitney. Tip from Richard Sparrow of Marlboro, Massachusetts.

30
The Ghost Who Mourned Her Child

An Experience in an Old Country House in Ohio

Location: A house in the country near Twinsburg, in eastern Ohio.

Description of place: The place is a stone farmhouse, some two hundred years old. About 1970 it was purchased and renovated for use as a dwelling by the parents of Nancy Kendall. It is now owned by her brother.

Ghostly manifestations: Nancy Kendall lives in Taos, New Mexico. She is an artist, with a graduate degree from the Cleveland Institute of Art. She is also a librarian, with an undergraduate degree from Hiram College and graduate work at Kent State University.

Nancy says she has been psychic as far back in her life as she can remember, but she suppressed it during her childhood. "It was not accepted in my family," she says, "so I hid it. When I was very young, I would see faces around me, and I would communicate with them, I'd talk with them. But by the time I hit college, I denied all this. I was very cold and practical."

But some years after this, she began to change. She

began to rediscover the abilities she had carefully tucked into the closet.

"Something else happened to me during this period," she relates. "I had a couple of falls in which I hit my head. I had a horrible concussion in one of them. I think this had an effect of opening me up again psychically. Also, I was going to art school around this time, and I was becoming more aware of my imagination, of that side of life."

About this time Nancy's parents bought the house near Twinsburg. Nancy often visited them. She found there was something about the upstairs of the old house that disturbed her.

"The bathroom upstairs was small," she says, "like it could have been a child's nursery. Between the bathroom and the bedroom there was a corner where I sensed a presence. I didn't like to go upstairs at night. I'd only go up for a very short time, like if I had to take something up there or close a window. I was always very, very uneasy up there.

"Then I began to hear, like in my head, my name being called by a young woman. I'd hear, 'Nancy . . . Nancy.' I would say, 'No, don't bother me.' I would be very tense.

"At the time, I was taking a course in photography at the Art Institute. One night there was a terrible storm, and I wanted to take photos of the trees in the wind. I went outside to take some. Later on, back at school, I developed the negatives, but I didn't make prints until a long time afterward. When I did, there was the face of a woman. The features seemed young, but the tone of the complexion seemed drained, washed out, gray. The features were small, delicate. The face was rounded. There was no makeup. I had the impression that the hair was pulled back and that it was white, but the face had an expression that was almost childlike."

Some time after taking the photos, Nancy was alone in the house. Her parents were out, and she was in the

Nancy Kendall.
PHOTO BY ARTHUR MYERS

kitchen preparing a meal for their return. "I heard footsteps coming down the stairs," she relates, "a definite sound of someone walking. I heard my name called, first quietly, in my head, 'Nancy,' then audibly, 'Naaancy.' I was very frightened. I turned the stove off and went outside till my parents came home.

"Later, that evening, I was upstairs in my mother's bedroom and suddenly again I sensed a presence. For some reason, this time I was not frightened. Perhaps the energy came more gently. I sensed a weeping young woman, not more than in her early twenties. It flashed through my mind, the whole story. I sensed the loss of a child, a little girl about seven, due to a virus. It was like the loss had just happened.

"I spoke to the young mother. I told her that I had just read a book that said that death comes at a set time. I said, 'You could not help it. It was meant to be this way. You loved your child very, very much. Your child knows this and returns your love. You did everything you could, but this was the time for your child to leave.'

"Almost immediately, I sensed a gentling. From that day on, there was like a gentle feeling in the room, there was peace. Never again was I aware of any restlessness there.

"I went downstairs and told my mother what had happened, and she was very upset. She said, 'Don't tell me any more, Nancy, I can't handle this!'

"I didn't print my storm photos until about a year later. I showed them to people, and some people could see the face. But I began to feel that if I talked about it I would hold her back, so I got rid of the pictures."

History: According to Nancy, the house, built in the eighteenth century, was a working farm until the early part of the nineteenth century, but she knows nothing else of its history or the people who lived there. She says she got an impression that the woman in the photograph might have been Amish.

Identity of ghost: Presumably a woman who had lived in the house and lost her child there.

Personality of ghost: Depressed, guilty about the loss of her child.

Witnesses: As far as Nancy knows, only herself.

Best time to witness: Nancy was aware of the spirit at various times of the day and night.

Still haunted?: Nancy feels that the spirit of the woman released its attachment to the physical plane when Nancy reassured her.

Investigations: Nancy is unaware of any contacts with the woman aside from her own.

Data submitted by: Nancy Kendall.

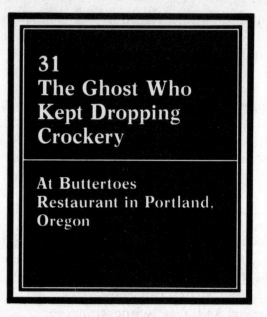

31
The Ghost Who Kept Dropping Crockery

At Buttertoes Restaurant in Portland, Oregon

Location: The restaurant was at 1244 Southeast Belmont Street, an older, residential area of Portland.

Description of place: A Victorian house dating from the 1890s. The restaurant occupied the first floor and used the basement for storage. A stairway leading to the second floor had been walled off, and the upper floor was used—and still is—as an apartment. One of the former occupants describes the place as follows: "The house was like a San Franciscan–style house. The apartment had a dome room that had a steeple in it and a balcony going off of it."

Originally a residence, the house has more recently been used for commercial purposes, with the apartment upstairs. Three daughters of a Portland clergyman, Carolyn Hulbert, Sharmen Newsom, and Charis Newsom-Palmer, leased the place to use as a restaurant in 1979 and operated it for nine years. They closed the restaurant in March 1989. "It was a great deal of work," says Carolyn, "and we were terribly burnt out."

The owners of the house had died not long before,

and it is being administered by the Historic Preservation League of Oregon. Cathy Galbraith of the League says the downstairs will probably be rented for commercial use and the apartment will be maintained upstairs.

The name Buttertoes came about in the following way: When Carolyn, the eldest sister, was in high school she played the part of Buttercup in the Gilbert and Sullivan operetta *HMS Pinafore*. Her sister Sharmen, then a little girl, saw the show and, possibly confused by the dancing, proudly called her sister Buttertoes, and the family nickname stuck.

Ghostly manifestations: This is the sort of case that is dear to the hearts of parapsychology journalists such as myself. Witnesses abound and are very believable. The fact that the restaurant is now defunct suppresses suspicion that this could be some sort of publicity ploy. In fact, some witnesses were not connected with the restaurant. One witness is a fundamentalist Christian who doesn't like to talk about this sort of thing—but did. The witnesses are mostly smart and full of fun.

The ghost seems to be female. "I myself have never seen her," says Carolyn, "and really was very skeptical. I went along with it because it was good publicity. But my friend Barbara Bliss, who was working as a waitress, actually saw the ghost in the middle of the lunch rush. I've known Barbara since fourth grade, and when she actually saw it and was shaken by it I believed it, because I trust her."

Carolyn mentions a number of witnesses, including:

- Janilyn Heger, a cook, who kept seeing the ghost and being touched by her.
- Heidi Pflum, a waitress. "Heidi quit," says Carolyn, "I think because it spooked her. She's sort of a fundamentalist Christian type and she didn't know how to take it all, how to

explain it. She was the first one who told me
about it."

- A young woman who rented the upstairs
  apartment and whose live-in boyfriend had
  dreams of a lady in an old-fashioned dress
  and hair piled up on her head. He had not
  known the place was reputed to be haunted.
  Later, he saw the lady while he was awake.
- Carolyn's sister Sharmen, who lived in the
  apartment for three years and had many
  experiences, including a rocking chair that
  rocked without anyone visible in it.
- Another sister, Charis, who early in the
  morning used to play catch with the ghost,
  constantly lunged for crockery that would
  drop mysteriously from kitchen shelves.
- Mitch Martin, who currently lives in the
  apartment upstairs, who would continually
  find semiprecious stones missing, which
  would reappear a few days later. His
  girlfriend once saw the ghost.
- Tracy Maitland, a waitress who tried to make
  a joke of the ghost stories—but the ghost
  wouldn't let her.

Let's let the witnesses tell their own stories.

Barbara Bliss recalls, "There were three of us in the
restaurant one morning, and I knew where the other
two were. I was in the kitchen. I felt something go by
me. I turned to the cook, Janilyn, and she said she felt
something too. So I looked in a little storage room at
the back of the kitchen, and as I looked around the
corner I saw a long, white dress. I did not see her head
or her face; I just saw from the shoulders down. She
had on old, dark-colored shoes. The very instant I saw
her she vanished.

"I was aware of other strange happenings. Once a
menu was turned around the first thing in the morn-

ing, after I had set things up. Once there was a banging sound on the outside of the building; we looked outside and there was no one. Sometimes the bells on the front door would jingle when no one was there. I once came in early in the morning to cook and found a bread-board in the middle of the floor, for no reason."

The Buttertoes Restaurant.

Charis Newsom-Palmer, one of Carolyn Hulbert's sisters, reports, "The experiences I had always happened early in the morning. Typically for about six years I was the person who would come in and get the food started. It was usually still dark outside. I never saw the ghost. The type of thing that would happen to me is that I would walk by a shelf and something would start to fall off and I would have to catch it. That would not happen every morning, but it would happen one thing after another on the same morning. It would destroy my routine, put me behind schedule; it would frustrate me. I didn't feel afraid of it; I would feel annoyed. Things would fall from high places that I would have to catch. Nothing ever fell without my catching it. It was like someone had timed it perfectly so I could catch it before it would hit. It was like mischievous."

Sharmen Newsom, Carolyn's other sister, says, "I had several experiences when I lived in the apartment upstairs. The house would be completely locked up at night, and I would hear noises out in my living room. The rocking chair would be rocking completely on its own. One time I woke up and from my bedroom I could look out into my kitchen, and I saw a lady spirit form pass by in the kitchen. She was tall and thin, with long, flowing hair. She loved to go through my books and papers in the front room. Probably every other night I would hear motion in that room. She'd be going through papers and books. There was always something askew from the way I had had it."

Heidi Pflum says, "The first experience I had, and this was before I knew there was supposed to be any kind of a haunt there, I was making coffee at the coffee machine out in the restaurant. I was standing in front of what used to be a staircase; it's now blocked off. I felt someone standing behind me. I got the impression it was a woman and that she might be middle-aged. It was almost like I could see somebody. I turned around, and she wasn't there. This happened several times over a period of one evening.

"Another time I was sitting in the dining room. It was between lunch and dinner, and the restaurant was empty. There were only two of us in the building, myself and the cook. I was reading a novel. I began hearing noises in the kitchen. The cook was outside watering the plants, and I assumed she had come back in. I heard several noises. A little while later the cook walked in; she hadn't been in the building. When I went out to the kitchen the only thing I saw out of place was a large, heavy lid that had been on a big pot on the counter, and it was in the center of the floor.

"There's a real spooky basement. I'd get things out of refrigerators down there. I'd be down there, and I'd think I heard the front door open and footsteps go across the floor over my head.

"I'm a Christian, and after I started having these experiences I started really getting uncomfortable. At one point, I started praying that I wouldn't have these experiences anymore, and they stopped for me. I stopped working there not long after that; I was just too uncomfortable."

Mitch Martin says, "I never experienced anything too dramatic in my apartment upstairs, like they did down in the restaurant, with things dropping all over the place. However, I would have small things, like stones, disappear for a few days and then be back there again. I had a piece of turquoise and a piece of amber and a little Egyptian scarab all sitting together, and the amber stone would be gone. Then three days later it would be right back in place.

"Also, I never felt alone in the place; it was a feeling thing. It was pretty subtle; it seems that the ghost spent most of her time in the downstairs part of the house. But I had a housemate, a girl, for a short time who had visual contact once. She saw your classic vaporous image, a ghostlike image. It was feminine, in a dress or something like that."

Janilyn Heger reports, "I worked there earlier than anyone in the morning. Oftentimes someone would touch my shoulder or brush by me. I felt strongly that there was a presence, but I never felt that she was something that would hurt me.

"When I very first started working there I had a big bowl of salad in my hands. You know how someone plays a joke on you and hits something from the bottom and makes it fly up? I felt that someone hit it, and this bowl of salad flew out of my hands and ended up upside down on the floor.

"She had a way of playing peekaboo with you. There was a pass-through window for the waitresses, and she'd play peekaboo through it. You'd see dark hair that was up and like the white part of her skin—either her neck or a collar. It was like a bobbing. You'd turn your head and you'd catch this, sort of a shadowish effect. She really seemed to like to do that.

"And she would do things like turn off the water—or turn it on. That was pretty unsettling.

"Sometimes when I'd come in, before anyone had been there, I'd find things that had been on top of the refrigerator dumped off into the middle of the room.

"One of the waitresses, Tracy Maitland, kept insisting it really wasn't anything, but finally she came to admit that it really must be. It seemed almost as though the ghost picked on her, not in a vicious way, but in a I'm-going-to-prove-to-you way. Tracy had no time for it; she didn't want to see her—but she did finally see her."

Tracy Maitland recalls, "Yeah, well I made a lot of jokes, because they talked about it all the time. Weird things happened to everybody, but nothing had really ever happened to me. I guess she just wanted me to know she really was there, because I did have one experience

"My sister and I were working together; it was closing time. She was cleaning in front, and I was doing dishes. I sensed someone over my shoulder who I thought was my sister, and as I turned I saw the upper body of a woman and her back going away from me. She had blond hair done up and a high-collar dress. She went around the corner. That was about it. She never showed to me again."

History: The house was built as a residence, in the 1890s. In the mid-1960s, there was a mysterious fire there. The place was purchased and restored by the next-door neighbors, Ben Milligan and Jerry Bosco, who were experts in restoring architectural antiques. Before the sisters leased the place, Milligan and Bosco had a business there called Victorian Facades.

Identity of ghost: They call her Lydia. Once two women came into the restaurant and said their Aunt Lydia had lived upstairs for a long time. She never married; she had a series of personal tragedies, including the death of a sister.

Barbara Bliss spoke of a psychic named Madelon, a friend of her haircutter, who came in several times. Madelon's reading of the situation was that a woman who lived in the house had had an affair with a married man, who killed her and bricked her up in a wall. Madelon maintained that her spirit was trying to get out. There is a fireplace upstairs that could be a candidate for the burial crypt in this scenario.

Personality of ghost: She seems gentle and playful, more like the description of Aunt Lydia than like a murdered mistress.

Witnesses: Carolyn Hulbert, Sharmen Newsom, Charis Newsom-Palmer, Barbara Bliss, Heidi Pflum, Mitch Martin, Janilyn Heger, Tracy Maitland.

Best time to witness: The ghost seems to walk at various times of the day and night.

Still haunted?: Presumably.

Investigations: Visits by Madelon, the psychic who opts for the slain-mistress theory, as well as other psychic people.

Carolyn Hulbert says, "I'm not aware of customers seeing ghosts, but we have had people come in who are psychic who have sensed there's energy here. And people have come in who have lived in the house in the past and who would ask us if we've encountered the ghost yet.

"I was waiting on a woman one day who was asking me questions and who said her eyes kept going up to the ceiling. If there was a body there it would have been right above her. I told her the story, and she said, 'That feels right to me. I just can't keep my eyes off the ceiling. There's something up there that's pulling my eyes up.'"

Suzanne Jauchius, a psychic from Portland, had an

experience at Buttertoes. She says, "I just went to have lunch there one day before I realized it was psychic, before the article came out in the paper. I asked a waitress if the house had a ghost, it's such a fine old house, and the waitress acted as though I had thrown hot water on her. So I didn't pursue it with her any further. Maybe it was against her religion to talk about stuff like that. I didn't really feel anything; I wasn't in that space when I went in there, I was just having lunch with friends."

Data submitted by: Carolyn Hulbert; Sharmen Newsom; Charis Newsom-Palmer; Suzanne Jauchius; Barbara Bliss; Heidi Pflum; Cathy Galbraith; Mitch Martin; Janilyn Heger; Tracy Maitland. Article in the October 31, 1986, issue of the *Oregonian* newspaper.

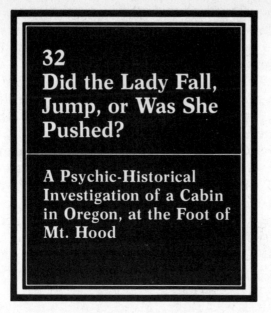

**32
Did the Lady Fall,
Jump, or Was She
Pushed?**

A Psychic-Historical
Investigation of a Cabin
in Oregon, at the Foot of
Mt. Hood

Location: The cabin is on Roberts Avenue in the town of Welches, Oregon, on Highway 26 about forty-five miles from Portland.

Description of place: Built at the turn of the century, the two-story structure is of hand-hewn cedar, set in a wooded area, with a magnificent view of snowcapped Mt. Hood. It now has three bedrooms upstairs, which can be reached by either of two staircases that lead in opposite directions onto an indoor balcony. At both ends of the balcony are doors that open onto empty air, about nine feet above the ground. It is believed the doors were placed that way because in earlier days snow drifts would pile up to that height.

The house was once called Welches Roadhouse and was used as a stop for stagecoach passengers. It has since been used as a ski lodge, weekend retreat, and year-round home.

Ghostly manifestations: Apparitions and other parapsychological happenings in this house have been a local tradition for many years. There are, in fact, a number of haunted places in these parts. Michael Jones, a local historian, says the area has seen much violence, which is typical of places that seem inhabited by restless spirits.

"You have an area here," he says, "that was heavily used by the Indians, and they were forced out by the whites. There were bounties put on them. This is an area where many people escaped to, people wanted by the law and so on. There were highwaymen, and there still are haunted roads up here." Jones is currently working on a book he has titled *History of the Haunting of Welches Roadhouse.*

The house was bought in 1979 by Donna Kinlan of Vancouver, Washington, and her husband, Truman Rew, as a rental property and possible retirement home. They have had various tenants, all of whom have had ghostly experiences.

The first was Roger Mead, a Mennonite who was separating from his wife. He was then a traveling salesman and is now a chef. His three children would visit him on weekends. The two older boys did not report any experiences, but his daughter, Michelle, eight, did. She was sleeping in the bedroom where the lady believed to be the predominant spirit in the house is

A view of Mt. Hood.

thought to have slept. Twice, Mead says, his daughter felt as though she was being pulled out of bed, and she landed on the floor. She has never fallen out of bed before or since, he says.

Mead reports that there frequently would be power outages, apparently normal. But the candles that he lit did not burn normally. They would be hard to light and hard to keep lit. They would take on odd shapes, as though a heavy draft were blowing on them. Earlier tenants also have reported this difficulty with candles.

Mead says that he once inexplicably broke his finger while trying to change a candle in a wrought-iron holder on the wall. "I don't know what happened," he says. "The candle wouldn't stay lit, so I reached up to pull it out and the next thing I knew my finger was broken, my ring finger." A psychic told him she felt the mishap was caused by a spirit.

Mead also reports that he had trouble taking photographs in the house. "I never could get decent pictures in there," he says. "They always turned out dark, almost black. You could barely distinguish anything."

Another tenant of the building also had ghostly experiences. "The man was using cocaine," Donna says, "and he told me the ghost—a woman—would appear and tell him she didn't want anything negative happening in the house and if he continued with drugs she would make his life very difficult. One time the neighbors saw him hanging out the window yelling for help at 6:30 in the morning. Apparently she appeared and scared him."

Michael Jones says the young man once called and said the house was frightening him. Jones visited him and was aware of psychic occurrences.

The present tenants are Gary and Debbie Anderson and their son, Aaron, now fourteen, and daughter, Clarissa, eleven. All have been aware of footsteps, lights being turned off, objects being moved or disappearing altogether. Sometimes a music box is heard playing. Sometimes people hear what sounds like a woman's humming. A number of visitors have seen an apparition of a woman and have described her to the Andersons.

"She's usually up by the second floor window, looking out at the river," Debbie says. "She wears a heavy dress with a low yoke, floor length with puff sleeves. Her hair is done up in a bun. Two of my friends who saw her at different times discussed what they had seen and came up with the exact same thing."

The boy, Aaron, is apparently very sensitive and has had the most vivid experiences in the family. In fact, a psychic, Suzanne Jauchius, who visited the place while I was researching this chapter, suspects he is a medium. He believes he saw the ghost in his bedroom one night.

Suzy Black (left) and *Suzanne Jauchius.*

"It was around twelve o'clock," he recalls. "My friend Jake was spending the night, and he was sleeping on the floor. I woke up, and the chair was rocking back and forth and there was a shadow in it. At first I thought it was Jake. He always wears black clothes and he's an Indian, so he might be hard to see in the dark. But I looked around and Jake was on the floor, asleep.

"It looked like a person sitting there. It looked like it had a bonnet, like its hair was tied up. I looked at it for about fifty seconds."

Aaron also says that the ghost sometimes turns off the stereo when he and Jake play it too loud for her taste. One morning, he says, he made his bed and went outside. Later he came back and found that the bottom blanket, which was orange, had disappeared.

Sometimes Aaron, an adolescent and perhaps reluctant to be different, is rather secretive about his experiences. They come out in a roundabout way. When Suzanne Jauchius was interviewing Debbie, she said, "Jake told me that Aaron woke up one night and screamed and told him the lady was looking down at him with a murderous look in her eye; she was just transformed, because other people have described her as gentle and wistful. That's the only time I've heard of her acting like that."

Suzanne suspects it was another entity in the house, a violent, negative one, who is drawn to Aaron and who was impersonating the woman.

Debbie said she sometimes hears a deep voice in Aaron's room. She said that Aaron has had connections with spirits in other places they have lived.

History: The house was built by Samuel Welch, an Oregon Trail pioneer, who homesteaded the valley and put up many buildings. One was a hotel, which opened in 1890. Welches Roadhouse was used as an overflow for this hotel. The woman believed to be haunting the house was the caretaker. She died violently, but there are a number of scenarios as to how this happened. Jones offers this one: "The house originally had a hidden room. It was above the front door and occupied the front portion of the house. Two prisoners escaped from a nearby jail, in striped prison garb, and she hid them in the secret room. One may have been her lover.

"They became restive there and wanted to get away, and the lady became upset, because she loved one of them and there are reports that she was pregnant. His partner was extremely dangerous, very violent. He made advances toward her. The lady's lover may have decided that they should leave to get him out of there. The woman threatened that if her lover left, she would commit suicide. This went on for several days. One story is that she got very upset, ran down the hall, threw herself out the north door, hit a tree, and broke her neck. Another story is that she was killed by her lover's partner."

Jones says he was told by a woman who once lived in the house that a landlord had found two old prison uniforms while digging under the house.

A standard tale in the area is that the woman committed suicide by jumping off the balcony, but Debbie Anderson says she doesn't believe that. "Nobody jumps from a nine-foot ledge to commit suicide. I believe she was pushed."

Investigations: Suzanne Jauchius visited the house after I had done considerable research. Afterward, we pooled information I had received from Michael Jones and from another informant, and she felt it cleared up some questions she had.

She went to the house with a friend, Suzy Black, who is a sensitive, and a friend of Suzy's, Carol Crisler, who operated a video camera. For starters, Suzanne told me there were eleven minutes missing on the tape, although there had been no indication that the camera wasn't working.

"I have a sense," Suzanne told me, "that the woman didn't commit suicide, that it was an accidental death, that she was fleeing, she was backing up from her pursuer and she fell out the doorway and hit her head on a rock." Later in their investigations, the women noticed that there was a large boulder just beneath the door.

"I felt it was a love triangle," Suzanne went on. "When I had my hand on the stairway—the stairway was the only remnant of the old house that was really clear psychically—I could actually see an argument that started at the foot of the stairs, and as she ran up

I could feel her dress brush across my face. The man she was arguing with was an older man."

I told her that Jones had said these men were escaped convicts and one was her lover, and Suzanne said, in a tone of sudden understanding, "Aah, aah, OK." I mentioned that Jones thought the older man might have killed the woman's lover, and Suzanne replied, "Yep, that's what happened. She didn't commit suicide. She always stands at the window, and from the window you can see the river. I believe she saw him kill her lover. When he came in she went at him; they had a violent fight." (Jones told me that the young man who had drug difficulties told him he had seen a male apparition with a knife.)

The mountain cabin.

Suzanne went on: "She dashed up the stairs, and he went after her. She turned around and started backing up from him and backed right out the door. I don't know what happened to him. He might have gone on about his life, but I really have a sense he might have died here too, because his presence is very strong in the house. There are definitely two presences."

One person who asks to remain anonymous tells of

sitting in the living room and suddenly "flipping out."

"I was gone," he says, "like I had left my body. I saw the lady. I saw the argument she had had the day she died. She told me they come back and go through the whole routine, and her death is reenacted."

This man also told me that there is the spirit of a child in the house and that the woman ghost told him that it is the spirit of the fetus she was carrying when she died.

Identities of ghosts: "There are two feelings here," Debbie Anderson says. "She's real mellow, and there's another feeling that's not so mellow."

There are also indications of the spirit of a child. While Suzanne Jauchius and her associates were investigating the house, Suzy Black mentioned that she had a feeling of nausea. Debbie Anderson replied that she often wakes up with the same feeling, as though she were pregnant and had morning sickness. This usually happens, she said, when she sleeps in the bedroom the spirit supposedly used when she was alive.

Suzanne told Debbie that she was tuning in. "When we tune into spirits," Suzanne said, "it's like their feelings were our own. We'll feel sad and won't know why. We take it on as if it were our own. It could be her way of communicating. I definitely feel a pregnancy and anger."

Personalities of ghosts: "This is her house," Debbie says. "She doesn't make people uncomfortable. She's not a scary person; she's part of the house. We accept her for what she is. She's not mean—she's sad, very melancholy. She's very wistful looking; she has no happiness. I think a man hurt her."

Debbie also reports feeling a dangerous, hostile presence. "It's very oppressive," she says, "like whatever it is was not a good person."

Witnesses: The Anderson family; Aaron's friend Jake; Roger Mead and his daughter, Michelle; Michael Jones,

Suzanne Jauchius, Suzy Black, and Carol Crisler; many neighbors, visitors, and former residents.

Best time to witness: The manifestations seem to occur at any time.

Still haunted?: Yes.

Data submitted by: Debbie Anderson, Aaron Anderson, Donna Kinlan, Roger Mead, Michael Jones, Suzanne Jauchius, Suzy Black, Carol Crisler.

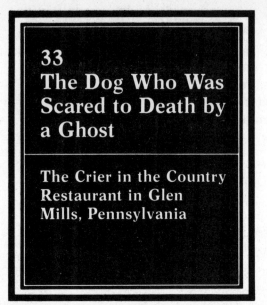

33
The Dog Who Was Scared to Death by a Ghost

The Crier in the Country Restaurant in Glen Mills, Pennsylvania

Location: The restaurant is on U.S. Route 1, the original freeway that runs from Maine to Florida. Glen Mills is seventeen miles south of Philadelphia and ten miles north of Wilmington, Delaware. About three miles away is Brandywine Battlefield Park, a national public park on the site of the Battle of Brandywine, a Revolutionary War conflict.

Description of place: The restaurant is housed in an L-shaped building. The back part of the building, originally a Pennsylvania farmhouse, dates from 1740. The front part, the major portion, was added in 1861. The place is constructed of local field stone. A residence for more than two centuries, the building was first used as a restaurant in 1968. The first two floors contain dining rooms. The third floor is used by the current owners as occasional living quarters. Part of this third floor area—the part that is in the original, eighteenth-century building—is called the loft and is the scene of the dog's sudden departure from the building and from this plane of existence.

Ghostly manifestations: Spooky happenings abound in this building and are of many varieties. However, the incident of the ill-fated dog seems the most unusual, so let's start with that.

Ciro J. ("Jerry") Iannucci, paterfamilias of the family that owns the restaurant, first told me of the dog's flying lunge. He had acquired the dog, a German shepherd, from the Upper Darby, Pennsylvania, police department. It was a trained attack dog, but apparently it tended to overdo things. It was so vicious, according to Iannucci, that the police were going to "terminate" it. This was in the early 1980s, when the Iannuccis had just acquired the empty building, which had been derelict for a few years, and were renovating it. One of the Iannucci sons, Rick, was living on the third floor. Jerry got the dog as added protection for the building.

"But within one week," Jerry says, "living up on the third floor, that dog jumped out of a window and killed himself. He turned into a wimp as soon as he got here. There was something here that would cause him to creep around and cower in the corners."

Another son, Rob, actually saw the dog's fatal leap. "That dog was always freaked out here, from the day we got him," Rob says. "He would shy away from certain areas of the building, and he especially stayed away from the third floor."

At one point Rick was away, and the dog was alone in the building all night. Rob arrived in the morning, and the dog followed him around, staying as close to him as possible.

"He was really palling around with me," Rick said. "After a while I had to go up to the loft, and I could see he didn't want to go up the stairs, but he finally followed along after me. When we got up to the loft, I started working on some things. The dog was acting strange. He would freeze. You would think that somebody else was in the room. It was as though something was doing something to the dog. He kept flinching. You would think that something was standing next to him, trying to hit him with a stick or poking him. The dog was looking around wildly. He saw daylight and just dove out that window, three stories up."

"And this," says Jerry Iannucci, "was a dog that was so aggressive and vicious that the police were going to shoot it."

(I like to think that when the dog hit the ground, and possibly the spirit world, he raced back into the building, up the stairs, and gave the ghost an enthusiastic bite where it would do the most good.)

One of the chief ghostly features of the Crier in the Country seems to be a spirit who likes to mess up preparations for festive occasions. It doesn't appear to be done destructively but rather, it would seem, playfully. "It's like she wants to be part of it," says Cissie Iannucci, wife of Jerry. Cissie is referring to Lydia Pal, onetime matriarch of the house. Almost any informant at the restaurant has some version of this sort of mussing-things-up caper to tell, but let's go with Cissie, who experienced one directly.

"My son Rob and I were setting up for a wedding one night," Cissie relates, "which was scheduled for the next morning. It was about 11:30 P.M. There wasn't anyone else in the building; everybody had left. We have tables that can be pulled apart to accept a center leaf, but they were closed and covered with lace table cloths. There were eight tables. Two of them we had shoved next to the wall, on either side of the fireplace. In the center of each table we had put a centerpiece consisting of a bone-china teacup and saucer, with dried flowers in the cup. After we'd finished setting up, my son went out to the kitchen to check the refrigeration, and I was in the front hall getting ready to leave."

She had been out of the dining room only a minute or two when she happened to glance through the doorway. The two tables against the wall had been pulled apart, so that the lace tablecloths and the teacups with the flowers hung down, as Cissie puts it, in a "gully of lace."

"Sometimes," Cissie says, "in various rooms we'll walk in and all the napkins are lying on the floor. It's usually when there are preparations for a big, festive affair."

Rob has seen other mysterious discombobulations of the furniture. "I've seen chairs turned around," he says. "You'll have set up for an affair, and you'll leave the room and go back about forty seconds later and the chairs and tables will be moved. Sometimes there'll be salt all over the tables. We'll set up flower arrangements late at night, and the next morning all the petals will be off them, lying on the table."

Perhaps the star witness of Crier in the Country weirdness is Kathy, Rob's wife. She is an obviously psychic young woman, aware of happenings that waft by most of us like a light breeze—unseen, unnoticed. Kathy has been involved with Rob for the past eight years. They lived in the loft for about a year. Occasionally she helps out at the restaurant as a hostess or in the check room. She is a main actor in a story Jerry tells.

"Just before we opened in December 1983," Jerry says, "my two sons went down the street to a huge disco that was just starting up. There were a lot of dance girls there, and my sons decided to invite them over to our place for a Christmas holiday because they were away from home. Kathy was up in the loft, and she heard frolicking downstairs—glasses clinking and laughter and singing. And she thought it was these people coming back to party. So she goes downstairs, and there's no one there. She went back upstairs, and the laughter and what-have-you started all over again. She went down, and again there was nobody there. Later they did arrive."

This seems to be a fairly regular occurrence, one that a number of people have reported. Kathy tells of having dinner with Rob and one of his brothers and a friend of the brother. They all stayed in the building overnight, and the next morning, as Kathy puts it, "They said, 'You guys must have had quite a party. First a picture fell off the wall, and then we heard all this laughing and glasses clinking and people talking downstairs.' I told them we were sleeping all night."

Pictures falling off the walls in the middle of the night seems a common occurrence in the place. The nail will be still in the wall and the wire supporting the picture will be intact.

A few years ago the Iannuccis built a guest house next to the main building, and although no manifestations have been reported in the new facility, the construction, as is often the case, seemed to activate the spirits.

Kathy says, "The night before they broke ground, I heard music playing downstairs. I walked down there, and there was a perfume smell all over the place. It seemed like it roused them up. Actually, when the main house was being remodeled is when most of the stuff happened."

Kathy says that in dealing with the spirits she has taken a leaf from Cissie's book. "Rob's mother," she says, "is a very forceful person; everybody listens to her. This stuff used to happen when she was there, and one day she screamed out, 'This is MY house! Get the hell out; you're not allowed in here anymore!' And now nothing ever happens when she's there.

"One night I was in the loft, and I was really being frightened. I heard all these footsteps walking around and doors slamming. So remembering Cissie's approach, I called out, 'You can go anywhere else in the house; just don't come up here!' Right after I said that, I heard footsteps on the second floor, coming right to the bottom of the stairs. They approached the door to the stairs that come up to the third floor. I heard the door shaking and the doorknob turning. I get shivers just talking about it. But they didn't come up.

"Sometimes I'd be giving people a tour of the house, and as soon as I would mention the ghosts a light would flicker, a chandelier would sway. It was so weird. It would happen in front of people, sometimes a whole roomful of people.

"My sister is into this sort of thing a little, and she told me that salt will bring out positive energy if you sprinkle it in the corner of a room. I was with a cleaning girl one day, and she was wiping off the tables in one of the rooms. We both left the room for about thirty seconds, and when we went back in every table, twelve of them, was just covered with salt. There was no salt on the tables originally. The salt cellars were kept in a hutch in a corner of the room, and as far as we could tell it was all still there."

The ladies' room on the first floor seems a focal point for various sorts of hauntings. There's a small statue of a Victorian woman on a table in the room, and in the morning it is often found turned facing the wall. Sometimes it is dumped in an adjacent trash can or shut up in a closet. This after the building has been locked up all night. Many people have reported this, but Kathy, as usual, has had the most vivid experience.

"I was in the bathroom early one morning. Nobody was in the building except Rob, who was upstairs. I was in one of the stalls. Suddenly I heard the door to the bathroom slam, and about four different voices started screaming."

When she emerged warily from the stall, there was no one there.

Apparitional appearances do not seem to be the style of the spirits that may be haunting Crier in the Country. I heard of only one such incident during the interviews I conducted. Jerry says, "My son Rick thinks he saw a grayish form hover over his bed on the third floor. It was a sort of presence that he felt was trying to encompass him. He fought it off, and it went away."

History: The original house was built in 1740, the homestead of a farming family named Pennell. In 1861 Thomas Pal, who married Lydia Pennell, added on the larger, more imposing structure. In 1873 Lydia, by then widowed, lost the place by auction. The house became the home of a family named Saulnier for many years. After World War II, it was briefly used as an old-age home. The first restaurant use was in 1968. Two owners operated restaurants unsuccessfully in the 1970s, and the house became derelict for a few years until the Iannuccis bought it. During this time, Jerry Iannucci says, derelicts and motorcycle gangs hung out in the place.

Identities of ghosts: Jerry and Cissie Iannucci think much of the phenomena are being caused by the spirit of Lydia Pal. One of the dining rooms is, in fact, called the Lydia Room, where many manifestations occur. Jerry thinks Lydia's spirit is uneasy because she lost the building. "It was a distress sale," he says. Cissie says, "Lydia buried three grandchildren on the grounds. Their bodies were exhumed about one hundred years ago and put in a cemetery down the street, but they're only about a block away. I think maybe she has stayed to protect the kids."

Jerry suspects it is Lydia who is turning the little statue in the ladies' room to the wall or sometimes disposing of it in a trash can or closet. The statue has an "exposed decolletage," he says, and Lydia, reportedly a prim lady, possibly is shocked.

Kathy thinks there is a lot more to many of the disturbances than the spirit of Lydia. "I don't really know what it is," she says. "It's usually not anything evil, but I have, one or two times, felt something evil and I've really been scared."

She recalls instances that occurred when she and Rob were living in the loft. "Sometimes," she says, "we'd be upstairs and the doorbell would ring, and he'd go down and there would be nobody there. As soon as he'd start up the stairs there would be scratching on the windows. It seemed like they were just playing with you, trying to scare you."

Kathy says while sleeping at the place she sometimes has nightmares involving soldiers dressed in blue with white ribbons crisscrossing their chests. This seems to approximate the dress of some Colonial troops during the Revolutionary War. "These soldiers would be hung from trees and mutilated," Kathy says.

During the Revolution, at the time of the Battle of Brandywine, British soldiers were encamped on the grounds now occupied by the restaurant. A guide at Brandywine Battlefield Park told me that there was a local history of two Colonial soldiers being hanged in the vicinity for misbehavior, although by the American military rather than the British. I don't believe that Kathy was aware of this legend, for when we talked she did not know—nor did I—whether the Battle of Brandywine was fought during the Revolutionary or the Civil War.

Personalities of ghosts: The elder Iannuccis seem to lean largely toward Lydia and fun and games. Jerry says he feels the happenings are playful. "They just want to let you know they are there," he says. The younger Iannuccis don't seem to completely buy that concept of innocence.

Witnesses: Jerry, Cissie, Rob, and Kathy Iannucci. Linda Kaat, formerly a hostess at the restaurant, says she was told of disturbances by other employees, although she denies she experienced any herself. Marianne Redding, sister of Kathy Iannucci.

Best time to witness: Phenomena seem to have occurred around the clock but with the large majority at night.

Still haunted?: Manifestations seem to have quieted down a bit, but they still happen.

Investigations: Jerry says a group of aficionados of the occult wanted to investigate the place, but he turned them down, feeling they might stir things up.

One time, he says, a Catholic priest who had taught him in high school, visited, and he told the priest of some of the weird happenings. The priest, Jerry recalls, "smiled patronizingly." But Jerry asked him to bless the place, which he did, and Jerry says, "I think since then fewer things have been happening."

A professor of folklore at a nearby college also visited the place and told Jerry that the behavior of animals seemed to indicate a haunting. He was referring to the unfortunate police dog and also a local cat who, when his mistress would visit the former owners, would refuse to stay on the third floor.

And it would seem that in their daughter-in-law, Kathy, the Iannuccis have a resident psychic, along with her sister, Marianne. "Marianne had experiences there with me," Kathy says. "She wouldn't even walk in the door the first time we got there, it freaked her out so much. Another time we were sitting there talking, and a little vase of dried flowers flew off the table while we were talking about ghosts. And the lights flickered."

Data submitted by: Jerry, Cissie, Rob, and Kathy Iannucci; Linda Kaat; a guide at Brandywine Battlefield Park.

**34
A Wedding
Portrait and the
Scent of Lavender**

The Logan Inn, in New
Hope, Pennsylvania

Location: The inn is located at what Gwen Davis, the innkeeper, calls "the focal point of New Hope," across the street from the well-known Bucks County Playhouse. The town, long a magnet for successful writers and artists, is about an hour from Philadelphia and an hour and a half from New York City. It lies on the border of Pennsylvania and New Jersey, on U.S. 202, about a half hour from I-95.

Description of place: It's a three-story building, built, Davis says, circa 1722. The facade is pointed field stone. The inn has sixteen rooms and extensive restaurant facilities. It changed hands in 1987 and was extensively renovated. One longtime New Hope resident described it as now being "all gussied up in Revolutionary splendor."

New Hope, and Bucks County in general, is proudly considered by its currently living residents to be one spooky place. They have ghost tours there, conducted Saturday evenings from June through November by Adele Gamble. In fact, the tours start in front of the

257

Logan Inn. "New Hope is one of your basically haunted places," says Adele. "It's an old place; it has a lot of Revolutionary War history. A lot of sensitive people live here—artists, writers. People will talk about these things here."

The Logan Inn.

Ghostly manifestations: The outstanding eerie feature of the inn seems to revolve around a huge portrait of the grandparents of the previous co-owner of the inn, Carl Lutz. "It goes from floor to ceiling, that's how big it is," says Susan Causton, an assistant manager. The portrait depicts a fashionably dressed lady and gentleman and gives the impression of being a wedding picture. Carl Lutz says he believes his grandfather had it painted around 1904 as a twenty-fifth-anniversary present to his bride. "It was probably done from a photograph," Lutz says. The elder Lutz had come to this country from Austria and had founded a successful restaurant–beer garden in Brooklyn. The painter of the portrait had done a number of murals for that restaurant. The man is wearing a lavender boutonniere, and the woman is wearing lavender in her hair. Lutz says he always associated lavender sachet with his grandmother.

When Lutz took over the inn, about twenty years ago, he hung the portrait in the main dining room. Since then it has been moved to a landing between the first and second floors. "People would notice the smell of lavender in the dining room," Lutz says, and his testimony is corroborated by a number of longtime New Hope residents.

But the scent of lavender also seems to pervade room 6, on the second floor. Davis says, "People in that room will mention the lavender and ask what kind of soaps and aerosols we use, and I'll think, here we go again. Actually, our amenities are from England, and they're not lavender-scented."

The room is strange in more ways than its scent. The television set keeps turning off for no apparent reason. "We had our television sets all delivered at the same time," Davis says, "and we don't have any trouble with any of the others."

And the door to the room, says Susan Causton, is constantly open. "We'll close it behind us; it locks. We'll go up there again and it's open, and nobody's been there."

Another housekeeping oddity of the room, says Davis, is that the mirror in the bathroom is constantly spattered, "either with water or toothpaste or something." And the room has been empty and locked.

The new co-owner of the inn is Steve Kates, who was on an extended vacation on a Caribbean isle when I did this investigation and was not available for interview. However, Mike Moore, the bar manager, says that Kates had a frightening experience in room 6. "He was working late one night," Moore says, "and he went up to room 6 to lie down for a while. He woke up and the room was very bright. He glanced in the mirror and saw a glowing apparition. At this point, he got up and left the room, and he hasn't been back in it since."

Another intriguing aspect of room 6 is that photographs taken in the room usually come out blank.

What is this thing about room 6?

Lutz thinks it derives from the big brass bed that was in the room until he sold the place. The bed was originally his grandmother's.

Lutz's grandmother seems to be only one of the spirit residents of the place. Another is the Revolutionary War soldier. Gwen Davis says, "The story is that there is a Revolutionary War soldier who haunts the inn and is seen stalking through the hallways and downstairs in the basement. The story is that he probably stayed here before one of the battles and was killed in battle and came back to haunt the inn. People on the housekeeping staff have twice this year seen an apparition walking from the dining room into the bar. It's of a tall person."

Carl Lutz says that during his time at the inn he several times saw "shadows passing" and that others have too. The music director of the Bucks County Playhouse saw a more definite figure, according to Lutz. "He was on his way from the bar to the men's room, which is downstairs," Lutz says, "and halfway down the stairs he saw the figure of a man in knee breeches. The man bowed and disappeared."

This sort of thing is still going on, according to Anthony Gazillo, who works on the housekeeping staff. He had his experiences in the basement, where he would gather materials to clean the restaurant in the early morning.

"I saw something," he says, "that made my hair stand up. It made me so afraid that I won't go down in the basement by myself anymore, and I'm not one to be afraid of anything like that, ever! I just saw something . . . it was so weird . . . it was like a shadow going across the back of the basement. I saw something going back and forth. It was freaky, so scary! Both my roommate, Ron Durroch, who works with me, and I have seen the

The wedding portrait on the stairs.

thing several times in the basement. It was like something flying in the air, like a shadow."

Spirit lore involving the inn and its environs further abound—for example, there is the reported apparition of a little girl in the parking lot who, according to legend, had drowned in the adjacent canal. And then there's the flying paperweight.

My first interviewee at the inn, Susan Causton, told me of three times seeing a paperweight by the cash register of the bar fly off and away and hit an adjacent wall. Later in this investigation, while I was interviewing Mike Moore, he brought up the paperweight without any prompting, which impressed me.

"There's this paperweight," he says, "that we used to keep next to the register in the bar. I had heard that it used to take off by itself. One evening I finally saw it. I was sitting at the bar; the place was closed, it was after midnight. I just happened to glance over toward the register, and the paperweight shot off and hit the speed racks on the bar, places where we store liquor. You can reach them real easily and pour liquor from them."

History: According to Ann Niessen, a local historian, the inn was built in the early eighteenth century by John Wells, a carpenter from Philadelphia. He also operated a ferry, and the town at that time was called Wells Ferry. The inn became known as the Logan Inn sometime in the late eighteenth century, Niessen says. It's now on the National Register of Historic Places.

Gwen Davis, who in addition to her duties as innkeeper is also executive director of the Solebury Township Historical Society, says the place is one of the five oldest taverns in the United States. It was built as an inn, a stagecoach stop. Stories of its haunting go back into history, she says, but it is hardly exclusive in the area on that score. "You'll find that most inns along the [Delaware] river are haunted," she says. "The stories usually revolve around the building of the [Delaware] canal or the Revolutionary War."

Identities of ghosts: Where shall we begin? In order of prominence, perhaps. Surely, Carl Lutz's grandparents and their lavender scent deserve first billing, even if it's not his grandmother who is turning off the TV and spattering the bathroom mirror in room 6. Then there is the Revolutionary War soldier who seems to appear in various guises and the little girl in the parking lot. Who is flinging the paperweight in the bar is anybody's guess.

Personalities of ghosts: None of them seem to be causing anyone any trouble, except for an occasional fright.

Witnesses: Carl Lutz, Susan Causton, Adele Gamble, Mike Moore, Anthony Gazillo, the music director of the Bucks County Playhouse.

Best time to witness: Seem to be around-the-clock performances.

Still haunted?: Seems to be.

Investigations: Various psychics have visited the place. A recent one probably came because she knew Joseph Fiorelli, the food and beverage manager. He had met her at a food fair. "She is very reputable," he says. "She works a lot with police departments. She came up to me and started to tell me about myself. She's pretty accurate, based on what she told me was going to happen and what has happened to me." He preferred not to reveal her name.

"She came in for lunch one day with her son," Fiorelli says, "and walked the site. She said the spirit in room 6 is friendly, but that there is one on the third floor, in room 16, that she gets some hostility from." Various guests who have stayed in the latter room have told of mysterious knockings on the door; when the door is opened nobody is there.

Data submitted by: Carl Lutz, Gwen Davis, Susan Causton, Ann Niessen, Adele Gamble, Elma Herman, Mike Moore, Anthony Gazillo, Joseph Fiorelli. Tip on the inn from Gladys Ivy, a local psychic.

**35
The Ghost Who
Haunts a
Newspaper**

Mysterious Footsteps
and a Few Other
Irregularities at the
Sullivan County News,
in Blountsville,
Tennessee

Location: Blountsville is a farm town of about four thousand in eastern Tennessee. The newspaper is on the main street in the middle of town.

Description of place: A brick building of one story, with a basement. The business offices and news room of the weekly newspaper are located on the street floor; the basement is occupied by the print shop. The front door of the building is on the street level; a back door gives access to the basement.

Ghostly manifestations: Among witnesses are Glen and Melvin Boyd, brothers who worked as printers at the *News* about twenty years ago. Both tell of constantly hearing footsteps at night on the upper floor while they were working down in the print shop. They would go upstairs, but no one would be there and the front door would be locked. Many other people had the same experience, according to the Boyds.

"I must have gone up a hundred times," Melvin says, "and there was nobody there. Usually we didn't bother to go upstairs. In fact, if somebody actually had come in, the people downstairs would be very startled."

The place is full of legends built around the "ghost," who has been given the nickname of George. Glen Boyd says, "One editor—he's dead now—had quite an experience there one night. He was in his office at the back. He could hear someone working downstairs; he could hear a Linotype machine going. He thought it was me, and he came down to talk to me. But I was out covering a story. [The employees of this little paper wear different hats.] When he got downstairs nobody was there. But now he could hear something upstairs, someone walking around. He went upstairs, but there was no one there and he went back to his office. Then he heard the front door open. It got to a point where it shook him up. He had a pistol in his desk drawer, and he got it out and went out into the main room. He didn't see anybody, but the newspaper files were moving, as though somebody were flipping through them. He had a little .25 automatic gun and he had his finger on the trigger, and it went off twice, putting two bullet holes in the ceiling. The marks are still there."

Thelma Harrington, another former editor of the *News*, confirms there are definitely two holes in the ceiling, although she wouldn't vouch for their being bullet holes. "I'm no expert on things like that," she says.

But she has had a few experiences herself. "The most dramatic experience," she says, "was when I was working in the darkroom alone on a Saturday and I heard someone whistling. I thought it was another employee, and I opened the door and called his name and he didn't respond. I looked out in the parking lot and his car wasn't there. So I went into the dark room, and the whistling started again. I went all through the building, but there was nobody there."

What was he whistling?

"I couldn't identify it," she replies. "Just a happy tune."

Occasionally people have seen what appear to be apparitions. Glen Boyd tells of an account given many years ago by Jim Gose, "who owned the job printing part of the paper." Gose told of working alone one night and seeing a tall, slender man dressed in a gray suit come in the back door, walk ten feet to the stairs, and go up the stairs. Gose immediately followed him but could find no one up there.

Another sighting is related by Thelma Harrington. "One time," she says, "I saw a person in the office across the hall from my office. It appeared to be a young man with blond hair and a crew cut, which was not usual for that time—crew cuts were long past. He was wearing a white oxford shirt and blue pants with pleats in front. All of that stuff was completely out of style at that time. This was about four in the afternoon, about seven years ago."

She immediately went over to the other office, but there was nobody there. The building was completely locked up, she says.

The most widely reported phenomena seems to be the front door opening and closing with no discernible assistance. June Eaton, the advertising supervisor, says, "We'll all be working and the front door will come open. That door will sometimes open and shut several times a week.

"And we're all the time missing things. They'll be there, and all of a sudden you won't see them—scissors, flowers, pencils, anything."

Eaton says she had her first experience soon after she was hired. "Two other people and myself were standing in the hall," she says, "getting ready to go home. Nobody was near the coat rack, but it just started trembling all over. We made a real quick exit."

History: The building seems to be a nondescript structure, too old for the memories of people who are now alive but not old enough to interest the local historians. The *Sullivan County News* began using the building in 1944, and a paper called the *Blountsville News* occupied it before then. George the ghost seems to be notorious to generations of employees, but no one seems to be sure how he got there.

Identity of ghost: A persistent legend is that at some time in its murky past the building housed a pool hall, and someone was killed in that ungentlemanly environment and still haunts the place.

Then there is the man neatly dressed in the gray suit, sighted by the printer.

Or Thelma Harrington's meticulously described young man in the crew cut and white oxford shirt.

Not that a pool player couldn't be neatly dressed.

Personality of ghost: He doesn't seem to be bothering anybody, except scaring them a little maybe.

Witnesses: Melvin and Glen Boyd, June Eaton, Thelma Harrington.

Best time to witness: The opening and closing front door seems to happen often during usual working hours. The footsteps are more discernible during the evening or on weekends, when only one or two people are in the building.

Still haunted?: The footsteps and merrily swinging front door are still constantly reported.

Data submitted by: Melvin and Glen Boyd; June Eaton; Thelma Harrington; David McGee, present editor; Betty Ashmore, print shop employee.

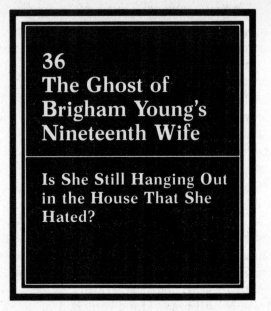

**36
The Ghost of
Brigham Young's
Nineteenth Wife**

**Is She Still Hanging Out
in the House That She
Hated?**

Location: The chief haunted house in this chapter, known as the Brigham Young Forest Farm House, is part of a Utah state park called the Pioneer State Trail Park, which is on Sunnyside Avenue in Salt Lake City.

Description of place: The Forest Farm House is one of a group of nineteenth-century Mormon homes that were moved to the park in the 1970s from other locations in the city. All are originals except two, which are re-creations.

The display, called Old Deseret, is similar to Williamsburg in Virginia and Sturbridge in Massachusetts, which bring to life historical buildings and lifestyles, with attendants dressed in the modes of former days and demonstrating various old crafts. Old Deseret is open to the public from Memorial Day to Labor Day.

The Forest Farm House was one of the houses of Brigham Young, who became leader of the Mormon Church after its founder, Joseph Smith, was killed by a mob in Illinois in 1844. Young took the devotees of the new religion west to what has become the state of Utah.

One of the tenets of the early church was polygamy, and Young was an ardent supporter. However, in his nineteenth wife, Ann Eliza Webb, he came something of a cropper. She was a strong-minded woman, an early feminist, who divorced him and toured the country denouncing Mormonism in general and Young in particular. She published a book titled *Wife No. 19: The Story of a Life in Bondage.*

She hated the Forest Farm House, to which she had been rotated by Young. She particularly detested that the stairs to the second floor started in the living room and often complained to Young. He built her a town house and promised not to start the stairs in the living room. But he did, apparently figuring no wife was going to tell him where to put stairs. That seems to have terminally blown Ann Eliza's gasket. She had been getting pretty restive about the whole marital arrangement, anyway. The church, incidentally, outlawed polygamy in 1890.

The farmhouse was originally a few miles from its present location in the park. It was the center of the colony's experimental farm. It is a wooden house of two stories, gabled, with a porch that wraps all the way around. The building has a stucco coating. It contains two living rooms downstairs as well as other rooms. Upstairs there is a ballroom, plus bedrooms and a sitting room.

Ghostly manifestations: Many guides at Old Deseret report parapsychological phenomena, to such an extent that there seems little doubt that ghosts walk, run, dance, laugh, and generally fool around there, particularly in the farmhouse. One of the most ardent witnesses is Clara Seaton, a guide. She reports sighting a female ghost while two other guides were giving her a little birthday party in the kitchen of the house. One of the other guides, Marilyn Bergstrom, also saw the apparition, but the third, Verlyn Kimball, had her back turned at the time. "Verlyn has been mad at us ever since for not saying anything," Clara chuckles. She says, "We both looked up and saw the figure of a woman in the dining room, standing at the window and looking out. We didn't say anything to each other at the time. We just went on about our business and then gave a tour to some people who had come up. Later that evening, one of us mentioned to the other, 'Well, Ann Eliza came to the birthday party,' and that's when we began comparing notes. We had both seen a figure dressed in black. Her hair was up on her head. Neither of us could see her face, but she was a small woman. Instantly, we knew it was Ann Eliza."

I asked Clara why she was so sure it was Ann Eliza. "Because she's our hero!" she exclaimed.

As well as being a guide at the farmhouse, Clara is in charge of the Jewkes-Draper Home, where spinning and weaving are demonstrated. She says that one evening her husband, Don, was sitting in that house when the front door began shaking and rattling as though someone had hold of the doorknob. "There was no one outside, and the wind wasn't blowing," Clara says. "I had worked in the house for three years and nothing had ever happened, but the very next day the same thing happened to me. I went to the door and said, 'If you want out, all you have to do is ask.' I held the door open for a little while and then closed it, and we haven't had anything happen since."

Many people tell of hearing footsteps and the sounds of children cavorting in the houses. Duane Ashby, a retired computer technician who is now a full-time guide, says, "I definitely have heard children in the farmhouse. The story is that Brigham Young was a smart guy and he had his lovely home in town, and he had the intelligence to know that the best place for a teenage party is in your neighbor's house. So when he built this farmhouse, which was four miles southeast of town, that's where he built the ballroom for the kids; that's where the kids would have their parties. And every once in a while their noise has been reported;

that's what I heard last March, these kids having a party.

"I had been alone in the house all morning, and I heard these kids playing and singing and dancing and banging and bouncing around. I walked all the way around the house, and there was nobody even in the park that I could see. The park was closed. So I went back in the house, and in a matter of a few minutes it was back again—music, singing and dancing, and kids running around. These could have been kids anywhere from twelve on up. But they sounded more like the littler kids. I looked all over the house, and it was empty."

Marilyn Bergstrom has a theory why the sound of children has been reported so much recently. The first she heard the phenomenon was early in 1989, while cleaning up the house after it had been flooded. She reports, "We heard children downstairs playing. Up until that time we hadn't had any Young family pictures in the house. But during the flood all the pictures that were in there were ruined, and they brought in family pictures. And since the family pictures have been there, there have been children in the house. I've heard them twice, once playing in the parlor and once upstairs. It sounded like small children. There are three individual pictures of Brigham Young's children and three groupings.

"We've also smelled chicken soup cooking. One day a maintenance guy was downstairs, and he called up to us, 'Are you guys cooking lunch, because I can smell chicken soup down here.' We weren't cooking anything, but you could smell it in the kitchen. Another time, you could smell potatoes frying. And you can't cook anything in there; there's a stove, but it's not hooked up."

I wasn't able to find anyone who professed seeing an apparition of Mary Fielding Smith standing in the doorway of her house, but that's one of the standard tales of Old Deseret.

"She had owned the house," Marilyn says. "When

they brought the house up to the village, and it was originally facing the town. Maybe if they turn it around, she'll leave us alone. She was married to Hiram Smith, who was Joseph Smith's brother. Several people have seen her. They say she shakes her finger, probably angry because they've put her house in the wrong direction."

Until recently, the park was reluctant to reveal this rather offbeat aspect of its attractions. "This is a very conservative religious area," Mike Johnson, until recently curator of education at Pioneer State Park, says. He mentions that some people formerly in charge have had parapsychological experiences there but kept it under their hats. However, under his stewardship the lid was loosened, and employees were no longer wary of talking publicly about their adventures.

"I never experienced any ghostly phenomena over there," he says, "but when I first came to work there I found a logbook that had a recording of an interesting incident, the one with the hair wreath. A guide was giving a tour at the farmhouse. I think this was around 1986. They were in the parlor, and she was pointing out a wreath on the wall that was made out of human hair, a common decorative art form in Victorian America. According to this recording in the log, as she was pointing it out it lifted off the wall about four inches and just hung there and then went back to its place. She looked at her tour and asked, 'Did you see that?' They all nodded yes. And they went upstairs fast."

History: I came across a fascinating chapter in the history of the Brigham Young Forest Farm House while perusing a story by Paula Huff in the *Salt Lake Tribune*. It related many of the above incidents and also referred to Gwen Wilcox, who with her husband had owned the house for fifteen years. Antiques dealers, they had renovated it in authentic period style and had given it to the Mormon Church, which traded it to the state, which moved it to the park. Paula sent

me two earlier articles in the *Tribune* about Gwen
Wilcox's prowess as a psychic, which seemed to be
considerable and well attested. Various police officials
had used her powers in investigations and were not at
all reluctant to give her full credit.

Gwen told me she and her husband bought the house
without knowing it had once belonged to Brigham
Young but were soon informed about the house's history by a neighboring church official. She told me she
had been in the house six weeks when she saw a man
sitting in the front room. She asked him who he was,
and the "impression" came that he was Brigham
Young.

"He had his foot up on a stool," she recounts, "and
had a cane in his hand. He seemed about seventy-five
years old. I often saw him. I did the restorations on the
information he gave me. Brigham Young was my best
friend for fifteen years."

Gwen says there were five spirits in the house:
Brigham Young; Ann Eliza; Sarah Decker, his second
wife; John A. Young, Brigham's "favorite son"; and a
"frightening spirit." The last, she says, was a man who
had killed a man in a robbery nearby and had hid in
the house, then a church. This, she says, was around
the turn of the century.

They all appeared to her as apparitions, she says, and
she talked to them. "When we gave away the house,"
she reports, "there was an open house for the LDS
[Mormon] hierarchy, and both my husband and I were
there. This very good-looking man came up to us and
talked to us at length about the house. He was wearing
beautiful clothes that dated from about 1880. We
didn't know he was a ghost until a newspaper photographer took pictures of my husband and me. We were
conversing with the ghost, but he wasn't in the picture."

Identities of ghosts: A rundown of nominees: Ann
Eliza, Brigham Young, Sarah Decker, Mary Fielding

Smith, Joseph A. Young, the fleeing killer, children of Brigham Young and their guests. Various others perhaps—who lifted the hair wreath and who rattled the door of the spinning room?

Personalities of ghosts: "Docile and friendly," says Clara Seaton. Gwen Wilcox is nervous about the thief and murderer. Mary Fielding Smith, the lady whose house was put down backward, seems a bit irritated.

Witnesses: Clara Seaton, Marilyn Bergstrom, Verlyn Kimball, Duane Ashby, Roy Hansen, Gwen Wilcox, Mike Johnson, Paula Huff. Many visitors to Old Deseret.

Best time to witness: Phenomena have been reported around the clock.

Still haunted?: So they say.

Investigations: Gwen Wilcox seems to have carried on a fifteen-year investigation. No formal psychic inquiries are reported, but phenomena have been reported by many staff members, and some visitors.

Data submitted by: Clara Seaton, Marilyn Bergstrom, Verlyn Kimball, Duane Ashby, Roy Hansen, Gwen Wilcox, Mike Johnson, Paula Huff. *The Twenty-seventh Wife*, book by Irving Wallace. *Wife No. 19: The Story of a Life in Bondage*, book by Ann Eliza Webb. Articles in the *Salt Lake Tribune* February 6, 1989; August 29, 1977; and September 23, 1974. Tip from Nancy Osborn.

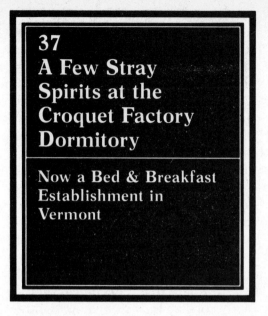

37
A Few Stray
Spirits at the
Croquet Factory
Dormitory

Now a Bed & Breakfast
Establishment in
Vermont

Location: Inwood Manor is located near East Barnet, Vermont, a tiny village well up toward Canada, near the New Hampshire state line.

Description of place: A large, attractive, wooden building, vaguely in the Greek Revival style. The inn has thirty-two rooms and is decorated, says one of its two proprietors, Peter Embarrato, in "early attic." Actually, it is most engagingly and tastefully furnished. The place is a favorite with bikers, hikers, dowsers, and skiers. The grounds include twenty wooded acres and a pond with a beach area. There is an adjacent river. The place is near Danville, Vermont, which every September is site of the national convention of the American Society of Dowsers.

Ghostly manifestations: Often a house comes to be known as haunted because the people living there are open to such phenomena; they're psychic and are aware of what is going on in the space around them. About ten years ago, two young men moved in to run the then-dilapidated building as an inn. Both seem to be aware of other dimensions than the one most of us are tuned in to. One is Ron Kaczor, who was a Marist brother for four years and spent much time in meditation. He had always wanted to become an innkeeper, and when he saw the old house in the woods he bought it and moved in the same day.

Soon after, a friend, Peter Embarrato, moved in. Embarrato, a New York packaging designer, had been psychic all his life. As a child, he did a lot of astral projection. When he told his parents, they laughed at him, so he suppressed his psychic abilities. But they were always there, and they came to the surface when he moved into the old building in Vermont.

The previous owner was William Ayres, a scion of a prominent Baltimore family, who had been a member of an Anglican order called the Graymoor monks. He had lived there for many years with another onetime member of the order, Larry Stearns, who had died a few years before. "They were together for thirty-five years," Peter says.

Peter says he immediately became aware of a presence. "I would feel a cold pressure, accompanied by a door closing or opening," he says. "You just felt that something was there, watching. I was not put off by it. I felt that somebody was looking to see what I was doing, to see whether he should approve or not."

He felt that it was Larry Stearns, who had himself been eager to turn the place into an inn but whose dream had never materialized. And here were two young men toiling away to do just that!

"I felt that Larry was looking to see if it were genuine, to see if we were sincere in our efforts to restore the building," Peter says. "I don't think the dream was as strong for Bill as it was for Larry. Larry really wanted this place to be productive.

"Bill lived here for a while while we were here, and whenever a light would flicker he'd say, 'Oh, cut it out, Larry.' And the light would stay on. He would speak to

Larry while we were around. It kind of kept him going, I think. He's now seventy-five and living in New Hampshire."

Incidentally, at meals Bill would always set a place for Larry, which may seem a teensy bit flaky, but let's give him the benefit of the doubt.

Some years ago a psychic came to stay at the inn for a few days and scheduled appointments. During a quiet time one evening, he offered to hold a séance with Ron and Peter. They sat down at a heavy, oak, five-legged table in the dining room. Very quickly, the table began to vibrate violently. "The psychic felt it was the spirit of Larry," Peter says.

Nancy Kendall, a psychic person who stayed in the inn while attending the dowsers' convention, told me that she was aware of spirits there and suggested I check the place out. She said she did not believe Larry was there any longer, that he had stayed only as long as he was unsure what Ron and Peter were doing with the house, and when he was satisfied he left.

There have been, however, a number of other manifestations there. When Peter first moved in, he says, he was on the phone with a friend in New York. Suddenly he heard sounds from an old grand piano downstairs, a series of tuneless notes. "Hold it," he said to his friend, "either the cats are playing on the piano or something strange is happening."

He left his bedroom and started to go downstairs. "All of a sudden," he says, "a woman in a striped uniform, with a light-blue aura about her, was kind of floating up the stairs. It really set me back, but I said, either I give in to this and pack up and go back to New York or I live with it. It was startling but not frightening to me. The woman floated up the stairs, turned to me, smiled, turned back, continued on up, and disappeared. I've never seen her since."

They later found that Peter may have seen a figure from local history. A mother had drowned in the nearby river while trying to rescue her daughter. "We also found out," Peter says, "that the mother was a hospital candy striper. The piano, incidentally, was covered when I went down to look, and the door to that room was closed."

Peter tells of an incident that might be attributed to the daughter. He was sitting at a table in the kitchen with a group of people when they heard steps coming down a stairway. The only other person in the house at the time was a boarder who at last report had been asleep upstairs in his room, and they thought it must be him.

"At that moment," Peter says, "the door to the cellar, which was just below the staircase, swung open. I saw a small hand, a child's hand, about a third of the way up from the bottom of the door. The door closed, and we heard steps going down to the cellar. The people at the table freaked out. Everyone there saw it, but they didn't believe what they had seen. They insisted that the footsteps on the stairs must have been those of the

Inwood Manor. PHOTO BY ARTHUR MYERS

boarder. So I went upstairs, and he was still in his room, asleep. I went back to the kitchen and suggested that we all go down into the cellar, but none of them would."

Ron and Peter also tell of small objects vanishing. Over a period of several weeks, a few years ago, these items had disappeared from various parts of the house. They were either gold or had the appearance of gold. One was Ron's grandfather's ring. Also missing were gold-colored safety pins, a card of brass objects, and a box of gold paper stars, the sort teachers give out in elementary school. "They all," Peter relates, "disappeared from where they were usually kept and reappeared in the same place at the same time." He and Ron were renovating the kitchen and were taking out a cupboard. "They were behind the cupboard," Ron says, "all together."

History: Although it is not apparent to the casual observer, the house came in two parts. The original part was put up in the 1820s and served variously as a farmhouse and a stagecoach stop. A century later, in 1925, the Roy Brothers Company, referred to proudly by locals as the largest croquet factory in the world, built on an addition as a boarding house for male employees. East Barnet lost its claim to sporting fame when the factory burned down in 1936.

Identities of ghosts: They would seem to be Larry Stearns and the mother and daughter who drowned.

Personalities of ghosts: They seem like nice people.

Witnesses: Ron Kaczor, Peter Embarrato, Bill Ayres, and numerous people who have stayed at the inn. In recent years, Ron and Peter say, various guests have mentioned being aware of the mother and daughter.

About his own experiences, Ron says, "I never had anything as intensive as what Peter has had. I'd hear people walking around, but when I'd go to investigate I wouldn't see anything. Sometimes I'd see sort of mists or auras but nothing definite. After a while, I got to

Peter Embarrato (left) and Ron Kaczor. PHOTO BY ARTHUR MYERS

know the footsteps of the ghosts, because each was different from anybody else's. It's similar with our live guests; after a while you get to know their footsteps."

An unusual thing happened several months after I visited Inwood Manor and interviewed Ron and Peter. I was researching a chapter on a purportedly haunted covered bridge near Stowe, Vermont, and was talking with Ed Rhodes, a prime modern-day witness of spooky doings at the old bridge. Ed mentioned a couple of other supposed ghostly doings about town and then mentioned a place he had visited a few years before— Inwood Manor, in the eastern part of the state, about an hour and a half drive from Stowe. He had seen an elderly man looking in the window, he told me.

"I was sitting in the living room, and I saw this guy walk right by the window. He looked in at me. These are friends of mine who run the inn. I said, 'There's somebody out in the yard.' We looked out and there was nobody there. I sat back down on the couch and looked up at a portrait on the wall, and I said, 'That's who it was, right there.'"

I (the author) called Inwood Manor and spoke with

Ron. "I remember that night," Ron says. "I remember going outside and looking, and there wasn't anyone there. I remember standing over by the stove and seeing Ed's reaction. I think there were other people in the room that night who saw something."

The portrait mentioned is of an elderly man, whom Ron identifies as Bill Ayres's grandfather, a tool-and-die magnate in Baltimore. Ron says he believes the man's name was Francis Ayres. He didn't have anything to do with the inn, Ron says, except that Bill Ayres had had the portrait, and he and Peter had kept it up on the living room wall. Perhaps it was this portrait that drew the spirit.

Best time to witness: Manifestations have been reported at various times of the day and night.

Still haunted?: Indications are that Larry Stearns has left, but the mother and daughter are still there and possibly Francis Ayres.

Ron and Peter think things have quieted down lately, but they recall a strange incident at the beginning of the summer of 1988. A group was supposed to arrive at 11:30 P.M. They didn't show, so the hosts went to bed. "About 1:30," Peter relates, "I heard all kinds of banging around, and I figured it must be the guests. They were getting kind of noisy. Are they having a party down there or what? I wondered. I didn't want them to wake up the other guests, so I went downstairs. When I came back upstairs, Ron asked what was going on. I said, 'I'm glad you heard those noises too, because there's no one down there.' Incidentally, those people never did show up."

Investigations: The only person in this account who comes officially billed as a psychic may be the man who gave readings at the house several years ago. However, both Ron and Peter seem to be psychic, as does the previous owner, Bill Ayres. Also, many of the guests are empathetic to this sort of thing, since for a week in September the place is filled with conventioneering dowsers, who are people who tend to open themselves psychically.

Ron says, "As a monk, someone who was interested in spirits all my life, when I came into a place like this and found that it was haunted, instead of feeding my ego by saying, 'Oh, we have a haunted house; let's bring everybody in,' my desire was mainly to put the spirits at peace and to allow their souls to develop and go wherever they're supposed to go."

Although Ron and Peter are willing to talk about their hauntings, they show no eagerness to publicize their inn as being haunted or in fact to publicize it at all. I appeared unheralded on a Saturday afternoon while they were preparing for an influx of twenty new guests, and I had to do a lot of fast talking to get them to submit to an interview, although once they got rolling, they got into the spirit of the thing.

Data submitted by: Peter Embarrato, Ron Kaczor, Nancy Kendall, Ed Rhodes.

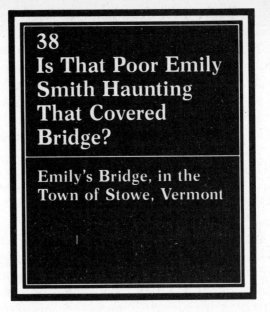

**38
Is That Poor Emily
Smith Haunting
That Covered
Bridge?**

Emily's Bridge, in the
Town of Stowe, Vermont

Location: The bridge, usually called Emily's Bridge, spans Gold Brook in Stowe Hollow. In fact, sometimes the bridge is called Gold Brook Bridge and sometimes Stowe Hollow Bridge. Whatever the name, a lot of locals think it's haunted. It's on Gold Brook Road, which makes a loop off Route 100, a couple of miles north of the center of the town. The town is in the north-central part of the state.

Description of place: Stowe residents proudly describe their town, perched under Mt. Mansfield, as the largest ski resort in the East, but they are quick to add that the place is active year-round, with crafts shows, dog shows, horse shows, and other activities. The picture-postcard New England village has under a thousand permanent residents but is constantly crammed with summer and winter visitors.

Emily's Bridge is the oldest in the county, built around 1844 by John Smith of Moscow, Vermont, an active covered-bridge builder in those days. Emily's Bridge is described in *Covered Bridges of Lamoille*

County as being fifty feet long, with an unpainted board siding and a metal roof. A sign at the south end reads: SPEED LIMIT—HORSES AT A WALK/MOTOR VEHICLES, 10 MILES PER HR.

Ghostly manifestations: *Covered Bridges of Lamoille County* wasn't much help as far as the haunting is concerned; it tends to concentrate on jokes teenagers were wont to play on each other at the bridge. However, Ed Rhodes, a lifelong Stowe resident and descendant of original settlers, turned out to be something of a goldmine of Emily ghost lore. Ed is vice president of the Stowe Historical Society.

One night about fifteen years ago, Ed says, he and a friend, Jim Holden, were in a car chasing a thunderstorm. Ed, who was driving, pulled into Emily's Bridge to escape the pelting rain. "Suddenly," Rhodes says, "Jim heard voices. He didn't say at the moment that he had heard anything, he just said, 'Let's get out of here!' We drove up the road a ways and I asked him what had happened, and he said he had heard a female voice hollering 'Help!' So I said, 'Let's go back and check it out.' We turned around and went back in, and this time I was sitting where he had been before because we'd turned the car around. And right where he had heard the voices I saw a flashing white light on the side of the bridge, like a strobe light. It flashed six or seven times. We got out of there fast."

Ed says people have told of warm spots on the bridge in January and cold spots in July. Hats have been blown off when there is no wind. "Many of the older people had experiences," Ed says, "but they're no longer here. If you could contact Ruth Pike—she had a farm near the bridge—she could tell you some things, but she's been gone quite a few years now. She told me about the breezes and things like that."

Ed did have a more or less direct experience a few years ago when he was leading local tours. "One little girl, about seven, was on a tour I was doing," he relates. "When we started out she began talking to me and told me about a dream she had had the night before. She said she had dreamt about a woman in a flowered white dress and with long brown hair. She told me this before we got to the bridge. When we got to the bridge, she said, 'That's where my dream was, that's where I saw her, right there.' "

And Ed told me about a photographer for a fashion magazine who came to Stowe to pose models against the colorful New England background. "When he got the pictures developed," Ed says, "everything was in focus but the model. The model, who was standing at the end of the bridge, was just a blur. Everything else, the bridge, the trees, and the leaves, was in focus."

History: Emily Smith is believed to have lived during the latter part of the 1800s. "People have done research," Ed Rhodes says, "but records of deaths at that time weren't so good. People died and were buried on farms, and no record was ever made. Especially if it was a suicide or something like that, something they didn't want to make public."

Stories about Emily's death abound; all involve suddenness and thwarted romance. According to one story, on the day before her marriage she was trampled to death by a team of runaway horses. In another she was on her way to her wedding when her horse bolted at the bridge, and Emily was thrown out and killed on the jagged rocks below. A more complicated variation has the groom failing to show up at the wedding and Emily's grabbing a wagon, rushing off and being killed when the wagon overturned at the bridge.

A high school student named Susan Twombly carried out some concentrated research in 1969, interviewing elderly people who were conversant with the stories of Emily.

"A popular story," Miss Twombly wrote, "is that Emily was supposed to meet her fiancé at midnight in the bridge. They had planned to elope but he never came. Finally, Emily hung herself in the bridge."

My favorite story is as follows: "One of my sources," Miss Twombly wrote, "says that Emily was fat, 36, and not very pretty, but she was very much in love with a young man named Donald who, unfortunately, didn't like her at all. He did, however, get her pregnant. Emily's father was furious and was going to force the couple to get married. In desperation, Donald jumped off the Gold Brook Bridge and died. A month later, Emily gave birth to twins, who died shortly after birth. In despair, Emily jumped off the bridge in her bright red wedding dress."

I would not be doing justice to Miss Twombly's research if I did not record that she thinks it really happened to a different couple, who were traveling by wagon at some distance from the bridge when their rig hit a culvert and the woman was thrown out and hurt. The couple then sued the town for damages and the town officials settled out of court. This has a very American ring to it.

Identity of ghost: According to local tradition, Emily Smith. "Well," says Ed Rhodes, "I'm forty years old, and it's been Emily's Bridge for as long as I can remember."

Personality of ghost: "I'd say disturbed," says Ed, "not deranged, but disturbed."

Witnesses: Ed Rhodes, Jim Holden, the little girl, the fashion photographer, neighbors and users of the bridge.

Best time to witness: "It was a dark and stormy night," says Ed of his experience. The little girl had had her dream at night, but her experience of seeing Emily at the bridge during the day. The photographer was operating during the day. Almost any time will do, it would seem.

Still haunted?: Why not?

Investigations: "I'm not sure any psychics have done anything," Rhodes says, "but we're open to investigation."

Data submitted by: Ed Rhodes. The Stowe Free Library. *Covered Bridges of Lamoille County,* by Robert L. Hagerman. Article by Ken Castle in the November 1987 issue of *Ski* magazine.

39

The Mad Lady Who Got Shot in the Head

Does She Wander Foxcroft School in Middleburg, Virginia, and Frighten the Girls into Enjoyable Hysterics?

Location: The school is in the small village of Middleburg, on Route 50, about twenty-five miles west of Washington.

Description of place: A posh girls' school that has catered since early in this century to families who can afford to send their daughters to posh girls' schools. The scene of the murder and possibly the chief haunting site is Brick House, the original building of the school. It was built in the 1700s, a big plantation house with four stories and an attic. At one time, the whole school, founded in 1914, was in this building. Now the old building houses school offices and a dining room. There are a number of other buildings on the campus, and sightings have been reported in some of them.

Ghostly manifestations: In my book *The Ghostly Register*, I had a chapter on a ghost who seemed to constantly take baths on the otherwise unused third floor of a house in Merion Station, Pennsylvania. The house had once been a bordello, and the bather was suspected to be a deceased prostitute who had developed a Lady MacBeth complex.

I was given the story by Meridith Smith, who had lived in the house and who now, coincidentally, lives in Bath, Maine. Some time later, I received a letter from her daughter, Vivi Stevenson, with a personal addenda to the bathtub story plus a ghost story of her own— concerning her alma mater, Foxcroft School. She now works in an ad agency in Nashville, Tennessee.

Vivi said that when she was a baby in Merion Station her cradle would be found rocking mysteriously, with her in it. When she was about four, she would hear a lady calling and would wander around looking for her. The voice seemed to come from the third floor, but she was afraid to go up there; one night a guest found her crying at the foot of the stairs that led to that floor and put her to bed.

I recount Vivi's early psychic adventures because they indicate she is a sensitive, who might well be aware of manifestations that would pass by most of us. I hope that is the explanation of her observations at Foxcroft School, since she is the only person I could find who had actually seen, heard, or felt anything unusual at the school.

Nevertheless, the ghost of the murdered lady is a firm tradition at the school, fostered by the founder, Miss Charlotte Haxell Noland, and kept alive by hundreds of girls over the years. So who are we to sneer? In cautioning against a cavalier rejection of this tale, I might mention another chapter from *The Ghostly Register*, which recounts the witnessing by many reliable people of the ghost of the writer Edith Wharton in a mansion she built in Lenox, Massachusetts. Some years ago, the house, now occupied by an acting troupe called Shakespeare and Company, was a dormitory for a now defunct girls' school of similar name and tone to the Virginia school, called Foxhollow School. A Foxhollow graduate told me that when she was a student she had heard the legend of the Wharton ghost. "Of course," she says, "girls' boarding schools will be girls' boarding schools." She didn't give it much credence.

But some years later, when she was in her twenties, she spent a summer in the old building repairing the ceiling of the ballroom and, she says, one afternoon she indeed saw an apparition of Edith Wharton walking up and down the patio.

Vivi Stevenson had her ghostly experiences not in the original Brick House, where the murder occurred, but in Court Dormitory in the late 1970s. The ghost ranges the campus, according to student wisdom.

"Once my roommate and I heard sobbing," she says, "when everybody else was out at a dance." Could it have been a live girl passing up the dance for some melancholy reason? "There was nobody else in the dorm," Vivi insists. "We looked around and couldn't find anybody."

Lights tended to go off and on when there was nobody flipping any switches, Vivi says. "Doors slammed a lot, and it's not a drafty building. One of my roommates said she saw a white apparition going through a door to the attic of the dormitory. No one had the key to that attic, but sometimes we would see a light on up there."

Perhaps if I had interviewed more graduates of the school I could have gotten some additional buttressing of this account. The only Foxcroft alumna I was able to run down, however, was Andrea Adams, living in New York City and gearing up for law school. Although enthusiastic, she wasn't much help.

"Yes, I remember Vivi telling me her experiences," she said.

But did *she* have any?

"No, I never did, but I'd like to."

The faculty and staff of the school were friendly but not much help, either.

Jane Lockhart is assistant dean and has been at the school for twenty-four years, twenty of which she has worked in Brick House. "They say you can hear the ghost walking," she says, "but the building's so old you hear all kinds of squeaks."

Mrs. Chal Hemmenway, an art history teacher, has been there for thirty-seven years. She says, "I'm not a believer or a nonbeliever; I'm an agnostic. Brick House is a very old, eighteenth-century house. Some of the fourteen-year-olds think they've seen Mrs. Kyle [the presumed ghost] on the sleeping porches at night, but I do not credit that. Fourteen-year-old girls can get into wonderful hysterics, which they enjoy thoroughly. A curtain blowing can be seen by a fourteen-year-old as Mrs. Kyle in person. I've talked to a lot of kids about being terrified by the ghost they've seen on the dormitory porches. It's contagious."

History: Brick House, the first brick house in that part of Virginia, was built by a lawyer named Kyle. He and his wife, née Jane Ball, called it Locust Lawn. Mrs. Kyle, according to historical material provided by the school, became mentally ill, violent, and was chained in the attic. One account has it: "Soon afterwards Mr. Kyle was called to Philadelphia on business. Upon his return he heard a tragic tale. Mrs. Kyle had escaped down the stairs, tripping, falling, breaking her neck. It was July and very hot and she had been buried immediately in the orchard."

A century or two later, Miss Charlotte had bought the land and started her school. The material provided me goes on: "From the beginning Foxcroft had a ghost—Mrs. Kyle, the mad wife of the builder of Brick House. Her spirit haunted the old house, roamed the orchard and became especially active on Halloween. It was evident she was unhappy. Rumors persisted that instead of dying from the fall down the stairs, she had been shot by her frightened keeper as she tried to escape."

By Vivi's time, the girls had created some alternative, even more colorful, theories. In her letter, she wrote there was some suspicion that a groundsman had been making advances upon Mrs. Kyle. Another theory had it that the attraction was mutual. Perhaps the girls had been reading *Lady Chatterly's Lover.*

"I also heard," Vivi wrote, "that Mr. Kyle came back to find the groundsman and Mrs. Kyle together and pushed her down the stairs."

Miss Charlotte seems to have been convinced the place was haunted, and she leaned toward the shooting version of Mrs. Kyle's demise. She had quite an exotic sense of fun, apparently. One day she rewarded six honor students by taking them out of class and digging for Mrs. Kyle. According to Vivi, the Court Dormitory was being built at the time, over Mrs. Kyle's grave, so it was apparently then or never. To quote Miss Charlotte:

> I decided to dig up Mrs. Kyle and find the trouble. Of course, the girls were thrilled with the idea of such excitement so I let the six high honor girls from the school be there for the digging. We got two gravediggers and we began digging. We made three holes and found nothing and the sun was going down. By the next day each girl had invited a friend to come. Finally the gravediggers struck a bone—a great big man's femur. We got the bone out and several more rib bones in good shape, but they were a man's bones.
>
> By this time the excitement was great and we knew that Mrs. Kyle must be buried on his left side as wives always were. We stopped for that day and the next day we let everybody come. Sam Scroggins fixed a great long table of tea by the fence in the orchard so it was a real party. The girls kept leaning over the grave and finally one leaned over so far she fell in. We pulled her up, and had a rope put around the digging.
>
> We finally hit some bones and some nice lady-like ribs, some small leg bones and, at last, the skull. The minute that got there, the secret was out—she had not broken her neck at all, she had been shot. Right through the middle of her head was a bullet hole. That's what she had been trying to tell us in

wandering around for one hundred seventy-seven years.

I wrapped the skull up and two days later took it to the Smithsonian in Washington where they had a ballistic department. My only dishonesty was that I told them that I had found it in a plowed field, for no one is allowed to dig up graves in Virginia. They gave it a thorough examination and told me it was a pre-Revolutionary bullet.

We then collected Mrs. Kyle's bones, and I found a huge stone pickle jar about three feet high and two across, and put them all in it and buried them up at the end of the orchard. It is marked with a nice brass marker and I hope will stay there forever.

Identity of ghost: If it isn't Jane Ball Kyle, Miss Charlotte—now in spirit herself—must be extremely vexed.

Personality of ghost: According to Vivi Stevenson, prior to the famous digging picnic the ghost had been quite violent, possibly angered that it was not known she had died by gunshot. If she is still around, she seems to be much more passive.

Witnesses: Vivi Stevenson and various anonymous students over the years.

Best time to witness: Vivi's experiences seem to have taken place after dark.

Still haunted?: The author declines to speculate on this one.

Investigations: No formal psychic inquiries were reported.

Data submitted by: Vivi Stevenson; Andrea Adams; Jane Lockhart; Chal Hemmenway; Sharon Deal, dormitory supervisor; Betty Livingston, former teacher; Johnny Smith, butler at the school for fifty-seven years; Dick Wheeler, former headmaster. Published material provided by the school.

**40
Building a Library
over a Graveyard
Can Really Liven
Up the Place**

Strange Goings-On at
the Library in Green
River, Wyoming

Location: The Sweetwater County Library is situated in Green River, Wyoming, a town on Interstate 80 in the southwestern part of the state, about 180 miles northeast of Salt Lake City, Utah.

Description of place: The library is a modern, brick and glass building, constructed in 1980. The land around the structure and directly beneath it was once part of a cemetery, and there are still probably unmarked graves in the area. Whenever mass exhumations are done, as they have been continually over the years for one reason or another, additional incognito corpses come to light.

Green River is the county seat, a town of twelve thousand. The main industry is the mining of trona. The area is virtually the sole U.S. source of this rather offbeat mineral. Trona is used in the making of glass and as an ingredient for soap powders.

Ghostly manifestations: The library personnel have observed parapsychological events that are so frequent and so standard that there seems little question that the place is being visited by inhabitants of a different dimension than the one we're used to. So far, there have been no apparitions sighted, but the library staff is poised in expectation—some hopefully, some fearfully.

Whenever rattles, creaks, and quavers afflict a building, left-brain types hasten to insist the building is merely settling. It turned out that this building *was* settling. The subsurface was not compacted properly, and the structure began settling so rapidly that the County Library Association sued the builders and collected. But there's more to the saga of the Sweetwater County Library than that.

Helen Higby came to Green River as chief librarian about two years ago. At the first staff meeting the librarians began to tell her about some of the peculiarities of the place. She thought they must be kidding. "She thought it was an initiation rite," says librarian Judy McPhie, who has worked there since the building was erected. "She thought we were putting her on." But although Helen has yet to see anything exotic with her own eyes, she's a sport about it. "The previous librarian," she says, "tried to pooh-pooh it so that the staff didn't get too excited. My attitude is that it's foolish to try to deny what people are seeing. I don't say they're ghosts—let's just say unexplained phenomena." Her response was a policy under which no one would work alone in the building after the place was closed. "I felt if someone were frightened they might be injured," she says.

Someone who says she has had a number of outre experiences is Judy McPhie. One of her choicest memories is standing behind the circulation desk with another librarian and both seeing the metal bar just inside the entrance to the library begin to swing violently. It was just as the library was closing, and no one was there except the two librarians. This happened about a year ago, and it looms large in the ghostly annals of the library.

"And," Judy relates, "not too long ago we were closing on a Friday, at five o'clock. There were several of us there. We heard a noise like someone was hammering on a door, trying to get out. It seemed to come from the back part of the building, where there are offices and an all-purpose room, but we couldn't find anyone."

On another occasion, Judy was closing up the library at nine P.M. with a high school girl who worked there. "There were only the two of us in the building," she says. "And there was a noise like someone was shutting up a briefcase. It sounded like someone slamming books into a case and the case being closed. The little girl said kind of nervously, 'That must be the guy who was studying in the back.' And I said, 'No, there's nobody here but us.'"

The Sweetwater County Library.

Maintenance people are often reservoirs of information in cases like these, since they tend to work alone and at odd hours. One longtime woman custodian constantly heard things but was careful not to look. She no longer works there. Another woman custodian was working early one evening in the multipurpose room. There is a stage at one end of the room, and a program was to be held, so the curtains, usually drawn, were open. The woman noticed this, since she had never seen them open before. She went about vacuuming, and next time she looked up the curtains were closed. A bit perturbed, she went out to the front desk and accused the people there of playing a trick on her, of pushing a button that closed the curtains. However, there was no such control at the front desk; the button that electrically closed the curtains was on the stage, in full view of the cleaning woman.

Marlin Dillard, a young janitor who left about a year and a half ago, tells of constant light games. "You could walk in a room and the lights would be off, and you'd check later and they'd be on. And I'd be the only person in the building."

One night he was going up to some rooms on the second floor. He turned on the light at the foot of the steps and started up. When he got to the top, the lights went out. "I went down to look and the switch was still turned on," he says. "I couldn't figure that out at all."

Don Leasor, the chief maintenance man, is a storehouse of peculiar memories. Lights would go on and off routinely, he states. Once he heard voices, a man's and a woman's, arguing in the all-purpose room. They were speaking in English, he believes, but he could catch only an occasional word. A man of some valor, he went to the door of the room and opened it. The voices stopped immediately; no one was visible. Door latches often click, he says, when no one is around. Once while vacuuming, he heard a jingling of keys. They sounded like his own keys, but he checked, understandably startled, and they were still on his belt. And *they* weren't jingling.

Perhaps his outstanding auditory experience is his hearing the four opening notes of Beethoven's Fifth plunked out on the piano in the redoubtable all-purpose room, late one night while he was alone.

History: The history of the library is short, but that

of the cemetery is long, at least for those parts. According to Henry Chadey, director of the Sweetwater County Historical Museum, the cemetery goes back to the early 1860s. It soon began to fill up with pioneer folk, to which might occasionally be added, other informants told me, the odd Chinese railroad worker or Ute or Shoshone Indian.

By the mid-1920s the cemetery had grown to such an extent that it was swallowing up prime real estate, and the marked graves were moved to a new place. But a number of unrecorded interred had been left behind, and this came to light in the late 1940s when veterans' housing—now torn down—was built. Marna Grubb, a lifelong resident of Green River, told me of naughty boys in the 1940s, her contemporaries, leaping into newly opened graves and stealing rings from the fingers of the deceased. She remembers seeing a red-headed corpse with a long red beard.

The next chapter in this necrological account comes in 1980, when the library was built. But that isn't the end. About four years later it was decided to put in a retaining wall for a flower bed. Back to the shovels again. Sure enough, more unrecorded bodies were turned up. Kathy Maldonado, a librarian who lives across from the library, remembers seeing a redheaded corpse unearthed at this time, possibly a relative of the one Marna Grubb saw forty years before. Kathy also tells of hearing about an Indian corpse wrapped in buffalo skins.

Identities of ghosts: It would be nice to think that someone really exotic is wandering the halls and stacks of the library, such as a Ute or Shoshone on the warpath at being ripped from his resting place. Or perhaps a Chinese pick-and-shovel man, wandering far from his native shores. Or maybe one of those redheaded Caucasians of times gone by. But could it be a more contemporary businessperson or student doing a little research? The click of an attaché case has a modern

ring to it. And who were the man and woman screaming at each other in the multipurpose room? Who was
pounding on the doors? Who plunked out Beethoven's
majestic opening? Keep tuned for the next installment.

Personalities of ghosts: They don't seem to be really
bothering anybody. In fact, they do keep the staff en-
tertained.

Witnesses: Judy McPhie, Don Leasor, Marlin Dillard,
other staff members.

Best time to witness: The occurrences often seem to
be noted just as the library is closing, either at 5 P.M. or
9 P.M. Before Helen Higby's advent, many things were
reported after the library had closed, when an employee was working in the building alone.

Still haunted?: Seems to be.

Investigations: No formal psychic inquiries are reported.

Data submitted by: Judy McPhie, Don Leasor, Marlin Dillard, Helen Higby, Marna Grubb, Kathy Maldonado, Henry Chadey.

Index